Rethinking Race, Class, Language, and Gender

Rethinking Race, Class, Language, and Gender

A Dialogue with Noam Chomsky and Other Leading Scholars

Pierre W. Orelus

ROWMAN & LITTLEFIELD PUBLISHERS, INC.
Lanham • Boulder • New York • Toronto • Plymouth, UK

Published by Rowman & Littlefield Publishers, Inc.
A wholly owned subsidiary of The Rowman & Littlefield Publishing Group, Inc.
4501 Forbes Boulevard, Suite 200, Lanham, Maryland 20706
http://www.rowmanlittlefield.com

Estover Road, Plymouth PL6 7PY, United Kingdom

British Library Cataloguing in Publication Information Available

Library of Congress Cataloging-in-Publication Data
Rethinking race, class, language, and gender : a dialogue with Noam Chomsky and other leading scholars / Pierre W. Orelus.
p. cm.
Includes bibliographical references and index.
ISBN 978-1-4422-0455-3 (hardcover : alk. paper) — ISBN 978-1-4422-0457-7 (ebook)
1. Critical pedagogy—United States. 2. Discrimination in education—United States. 3. Equality—United States. I. Orelus, Pierre W. II. Chomsky, Noam.
LC196.5.U6R485 2011
379.2'60973—dc22 2011007288

™ The paper used in this publication meets the minimum requirements of American National Standard for Information Sciences—Permanence of Paper for Printed Library Materials, ANSI/NISO Z39.48-1992.

Printed in the United States of America

To Joe Kincheloe

This book is dedicated to the late public intellectual, professor, and mentor, Joe Kincheloe, to whom I am most grateful for helping me publish my first book while I was a doctoral student and for mentoring me and many more emerging scholars and students. Joe was the humblest and kindest person that I have ever met.

Contents

Foreword

REVOLUTIONARY CRITICAL PEDAGOGY AGAINST THE RESURGENCE OF CONFEDERATE IDEOLOGY

Peter McLaren

Rethinking Race, Class, Language, and Gender comes at a portentous time. Following in the wake of the collapse of free market fundamentalism, the ever-turbulent topic of race is at the forefront of discussion, even when it is discernibly absent from view. The ever-present tendency to view race as a code word for "special interests" has never been more prevalent, even though Blacks, Latino/as, and other oppressed minority groups still lack the social power to transform in any serious way the complex system of social relations that oppresses them. With the first African American president now at the helm of the country, a powerful White backlash has been unleashed against people of color. The mere mention of race in the public square is now considered by many White people (who consider themselves to be the new, unacknowledged, oppressed) to be a declaration of war against them.

While capitalism is seen as "naturally" producing the conditions for democracy, it has become increasingly clear that capitalism has, in truth, betrayed a long history of calculated insouciance toward democracy, necessarily subordinating it to the requirements of capitalist production. While the United States beckons enticingly to the world as the greatest living democracy, behind its multiparty elections and its claims to be representing the people it has revealed itself to be little more than a caricature of democracy, spawning a cruel and demeaning racialized hierarchy that has worked to transform living people into alienated people on a magisterial template bloodied by the crimes of history that clearly reproduces White privilege and legitimates White violence. But the problem of creating a democracy of equal opportunity and outcomes goes well beyond the

United States. Indeed, one of the greatest challenges of the twenty-first century that we are now facing is what Manning Marable (2006a) has coined as "the problem of global apartheid." Marable describes this condition as "the racialized division and stratification of resources, wealth, and power that separates Europe, North America, and Japan from the billions of mostly black, brown, indigenous, undocumented immigrant and poor people across the planet." The poison of global apartheid percolating through the veins of America is made possible and protected by what Marable refers to as the *new racial domain*. This new domain of exploitation and suffering is different from the old racial domain of slavery, Jim Crow segregation, ghettoization, and strict residential segregation that were grounded in the political economy of U.S. capitalism, where antiracism was linked to the realities of domestic markets and the policies of the United States. Whereas the struggles involving the old racial domain were debated "within the context of America's expanding, domestic economy, and influenced by Keynesian, welfare state public policies," the new racial domain, by contrast, "is driven and largely determined by the forces of transnational capitalism and the public policies of state neoliberalism." Marable describes these forces as "an unholy trinity," or "deadly triad," which he enumerated as unemployment, mass incarceration, and mass disenfranchisement.

Echoing Marable's sentiments, E. San Juan (2009b) writes,

> No doubt, racial thinking still pervades the consensual procedures of our society—from the categories of the Census to the neoconservative attack on Affirmative Action and the gains of the Civil Rights struggles. It has acquired new life in the sphere of public, especially foreign, policy whenever officials rearticulate the binary opposition between us (citizens of Western civilization) and them (the barbaric fundamentalists, rogue states, terrorists of all kinds). The common life or national identity rises from the rubble of differences vanquished, ostracized, and erased. The twentieth century that ended with wars in the Middle East, Africa and the Balkans, thus began with the entry of the United States as competitor in the game of colonial plunder.

Marable ties the processes of the new racial domain to the advent of neoliberal capitalism and to the emergence of the transnational capitalist class. The social consequences of these policies has witnessed the creation of

> an unequal, two-tiered, uncivil society, characterized by a governing hierarchy of middle- to upper-class "citizens" who own nearly all private property and financial assets, and a vast subaltern of quasi- or sub-citizens encumbered beneath the cruel weight of permanent unemployment, discriminatory courts and sentenc-

> ing procedures, dehumanized prisons, voting disenfranchisement, residential segregation, and the elimination of most public services for the poor.

Here, Marable echoes the view of Ahme Shawki (2006), who writes,

> Both the ideas and institutions of capitalist society have been permeated by racism, influencing all aspects of society. But racism is not simply the result of the dominance of ruling class ideology in the government, media, and schools. There is a material basis for racism built into capitalist competition. (p. 245)

The material basis of racism in the United States, born of the colonial plantocracy of Virginia, and made manifest in today's transnational capitalist relations, is showing no signs of cracking. And while this material basis of racism remains largely hidden except to those with eyes discerning enough to see it, the epistemological roots of racism have been glaringly laid bare, although those committing the most egregious acts of epistemic violence (such as the Tea Party advocates and the Republican leadership that supports them) are loath to recognize it as such. Since the election of Barack Obama, right-wing pundits have unchained a racist fury across the U.S. mediascape, accusing the president of being "demonstrably a racist," of pandering to people of color, of being a race-baiter, of being the "most racial president," of having appointed a "racist administration," of using a "Black accent" when he addresses groups of African Americans, of preying on "White guilt" and using "racial anxiety" to get himself elected, of "defending racism," and of supporting civil rights groups that are nothing more than "race-baiting poverty pimps."

Critics complain about feeling pressured not to criticize the president because he is of "mixed race." First Lady Michele Obama was accused by right-wingers of not attending the funeral of White senator Robert Byrd because she has "authentic slave blood," whereas President Obama does not possess such blood. Some media pundits argued that private businesses "ought to get to discriminate" and that "it should be their right to be racist." These are not isolated comments from fringe Internet wing nuts but kenspeckle actions from popular radio and television personalities who not only echo pre–civil rights era racism but have spawned a new species of racism that suggests that anyone belonging to ethnic minority groups can be labeled racist if they happen to draw attention to the problems within their own communities and blame it on the wider White society. While African American and Latino/a politicians are decried by Whites as being in favor of their own ethnic constituencies, Whites, on the other hand, blinded by the pervasive ideology of the Anglosphere, fail to see how the entire legal system and educational system in the United States is structurally advantageous to White people.

However, in the eyes of many conservative Whites, to point out this structural inequality is tantamount to a racist act, to manipulating the wider White society by promoting special interests on behalf of one group against another. In this view, the only acceptable response to racism is complete silence on the matter.

Newt Gingrich, a likely contender for the presidency of the United States in the near future, has astonishingly claimed that President Obama is allied to a "Kenyan, anticolonial" worldview. He agrees with D'inesh D'Souza, who claims the Obama is being ruled by the political ideology of his father, "a Luo tribesman of the 1950s . . . [a] philandering, inebriated African socialist, who raged against the world for denying him the realization of his anticolonial ambitions" (2010). D'Souza goes on to argue,

> Colonialism today is a dead issue. No one cares about it except the man in the White House. He is the last anticolonial. Emerging market economies such as China, India, Chile and Indonesia have solved the problem of backwardness; they are exploiting their labor advantage and growing much faster than the U.S. If America is going to remain on top, we have to compete in an increasingly tough environment.

Here, D'Souza is actually claiming that the solution to backwardness is "exploiting labor advantage" (completely ignoring the idea that what is important is not economic growth but economic development). But how can you exploit labor advantage without exploiting the labor power of the poor and powerless? In his enfeebled defense of the United States, D'Souza astonishingly makes a case for the exploitation of human labor as a way for "backward" nations to join the ranks of the "civilized" nations. Those that he claims still live in the "backward" nations (i.e., Africa) are those that have allowed themselves to be exploited by economic powerhouses like the United States. The implicit solution to colonialism offered by D'Souza is to join the ranks of the exploiters and beat them at their own game. What is worse, he hides his own ideological agenda under the banner of free enterprise democracy.

Nowhere does D'Souza refute the fact that the United States is or was a colonial power; all that he manages to say is that now there are other, formerly backward countries that are doing the job of exploitation almost as well as the United States, and supposedly this is enough of a reason to claim that colonialism is now a "dead issue." In fact, this lame assertion is a perfect example of the logic of neoliberal capitalism in one of its most pernicious forms. It also reflects to a large extent the racism that operates under the cover of race-neutral, color-blind language, one that is accompanied by an ideological attack on the ramparts of human decency. It is a language that calls for a dismantling of unions, and it embodies a xenophobia and ethnic and religious intolerance against Muslims and Arab Americans that fires a new American hyperpatriotism in a way that could "potentially reinforce traditional White racism against all people of color" (Marable, 2006a).

While I agree with Marable, I would like to take his argument even further by arguing that White people have been won over to a new transnational Southern Strategy grounded in a larger neo-Confederate Zeitgeist, a newly furbished and retrofitted retreat into the ideological imperatives of the Confederacy whose roots can be traced to the apartheid caste system sanctioned by the 1896 *Plessy v. Ferguson* judgment, the persistence of racism in the United States, and the racist pathologies left in the wake of slavery and segregation. Here we are witness to new forms of racism that are accompanying neoliberal transformations driven by privatization, financialization, the management and manipulation of crises, and state redistributions.

Here we need to pause to ask the question: Why do White workers accept racist ideas? Keeanga-Yamahtta Taylor (2011) gives a very effective Marxist response to this question:

> This leads to the question: If it isn't in the interest of white workers to be racist, then why do they accept racist ideas? But the same question could be asked of any group of workers. Why do men accept sexist ideas? Why do Black workers accept racist anti-immigrant ideas? Why do many Black Caribbean and African immigrant workers think that Black Americans are lazy? Why do American workers of all races accept many racist ideas about Arabs and Muslims? If most people agree that it would be in the interest of any group of workers to be more united than divided, then why do workers accept reactionary ideas? There are two primary reasons. The first is competition. Capitalism operates under the laws of false scarcity, which simply means that we are all told there isn't enough to go around, so we must compete with each other for housing, education, jobs and anything else valued in society. While the scarcity is false, the competition is real, and workers fighting over these items to better themselves or their families are often willing to believe the worst about other workers to justify why they should have something and others should not. The other reason is, as Marx wrote in the *German Ideology*, that the ruling ideas of any society are the ideas of the ruling class. We live in a racist society, and therefore people hold racist ideas.

Steve Martinot (2010) expands on the historical reasons why White workers accept racist ideas by persuasively arguing that there is a duality of class systems in the United States—a White class system composed of capital and White workers, and a racialized class system in which White society as a whole, with its White class system embedded in it, has created a ruling elite, first over a Black bond-laborer working class on plantations and then over a continental Black and Brown workforce, and finally, with the rise of twentieth-century U.S. colonialism and imperialism, an international third world working class. Theodore Allen (1997) has demonstrated that racism first manifested itself in the "New World" when the European colonial settlers based on private property in land and resources subdued the indigenous population. White supremacy was constructed at a particular time by the plantocracy when survival (as it usually does) demanded class warfare, and after the defeat of Bacon's Rebellion, the result was, in San Juan's (2009) words, "a flexible and adjustable system that can adjust its racial dynamics in order to divide the subordinates, resist any critique of its ideological legitimacy, and prevent any counter-hegemonic bloc of forces from overthrowing class rule."

If, as many socialists argue, racism is an instrumentality of class rule and is not in the material interests of White workers, why then does this racism persist? Martinot (2010) provides an interesting, if not partial, explanation for why the White working class has preferred the social cohesion of White identity over the struggle for economic equality, which I expanded on in the preface to Abul Pitre's *Freedom Fighters: African American Students and the Struggle for Black History in School.* According to Martinot, this attitude can be traced to the country's colonial origins and the persistence of slavery until the Civil War. Martinot borrows Oliver Cox's distinction between a social class and a political class. A social class is aware of itself conceptually, it constitutes part of an established system, it is conditioned to accept more or less the stability of its social contract with the ruling class, and it reflects the social order of which it is a part, without necessarily generating a consciousness of having a common goal or interest—such as the class of wage earners.

A political class does not constitute an organically integrated component of society but instead constitutes a group that is actively and protagonistically struggling for power and change under the guidance of a common vision. A political class need not be limited to members of a single social class. The United States grew out of a colonial society founded on the genocidal massacre of its indigenous population and preserving slavery as its fundamental economic form. What was unique about this colonial society was that it possessed a corporate structure, requiring a stratified organization whose template was sacrosanct and whose members were expected to behave as a social class (social class here refers to a more-or-less stable contract with the ruling class and an organic integration into the dominant society).

Allegiance to the corporate organization took priority over the social class unity found in the common vision adopted within one's political class (such as the struggle for a better wage). After Bacon's Rebellion, English bond laborers were made into a "control stratum" whose task was, as White people, to police the African slaves. This broke the solidarity between the English bond laborers and the African slaves that had been part of Bacon's Rebellion and precipitated gratuitous violence on the part of the English bond laborers against the slaves. Such violence was rewarded by the colonial elite. White identity was therefore tied to the location of Whites as part of a "control stratum" established by the colonial corporate entity of the state, a stratum that resulted in making social cohesion and unification part of White racialized identity. A dual class consciousness or dual identity among working-class Whites can be seen historically in the conflicting way that they maintain their identity as members of a social class of laborers, and as members of a political class that operated as a control stratum of the corporate/colonial plantocracy in policing African slaves.

Racist violence on the part of Whites, for instance, through the rejection of Black workers in White-dominated unions, damaged their power as a social class but enhanced their cultural power as members of White society within the larger corporate/colonial plantocracy. When faced with a choice of class struggle or social cohesion as Whites within their political class, White workers chose to maintain the cohesion of their political class. In other words, they refused to abandon their historical role as a control stratum and attempted to define a class difference between themselves and Black workers by taking advantage of the fact that White workers had direct access to capital through their wage labor, while Black workers were forced to rely on the White control stratum for work. This enabled the consolidation and unification of White workers as a political class.

Racialized violence marked the entrance of working-class Whites into a political class in which their primary allegiance was to White society rather than to working-class solidarity. As a political class, their primary function was to establish social cohesion through a dominant White consensus. Their consciousness as a social class was not overtly racist, but their existence as a political class was grounded in White supremacy and membership in the White socius. This could account, at least in some significant way, for the reason White racism has historically been so successful as a divide-and-rule tactic against working-class organizations. Martinot concedes that there have been some noted historical exceptions when White people have supported the antiracist and prodemocracy struggle—during, for instance, the slavery era, the Jim Crow era, and the present era. But in each of these eras, when White people stood in opposition to the antidemocracy of White exclusionism—embodied in the Declaration of Independence of 1776, the Emancipation Proclamation of 1863, and *Brown v. Board of Education* of 1954—they were defeated by forms of White populism that emerged from the White socius as various manifestations of control stratum activity. The abolitionists, for instance, were attacked as communists, anarchists, or socialists, and White supremacist culture took control of the country.

The same attitude today is reflected in the ratcheting up of the racialization of the country, which we have witnessed in the attack on ethnic studies, the rollback of civil rights victories and the repeal of affirmative action standards, racial profiling, and the expansion of the prison industrial complex used to warehouse "unruly" people of color. The official ideology of color blindness now makes it a cultural offense to speak out about racial prejudice against any specific group—except that now aggrieved Whites are often wearing the mantle of the oppressed and are using the Tea Party and Republican platforms to air their grievances in the court of mainstream public opinion (fostered by the corporate media). Liberals are now derided as socialists and Nazis, and new public programs sponsored by the federal government are seen as part of a communist takeover of the country.

Clearly, White workers would need to abandon their role in the control stratum (Martinot, 2010) in order to further the goals of class equality. But to do that would mean that Whites would lose their social identity as White people, as they would necessarily have to join forces with workers of color who represent a different political class. White people, in other words, would need to abandon their role in generating White racialized identity and reconstituting White supremacy. But given the ways in which the dialectics of race/class has unfolded in the context of U.S. colonial history, with the system of apartheid having been given its imprimatur in the court of neoliberal capital, surely White workers must find a way of joining forces with constituencies of color in the struggle for a socialist alternative to capitalism. That is the wager of revolutionary critical pedagogy and the promise of *Rethinking Race, Class, Language, and Gender*.

One of the challenges of this book is to create the theory that can help us understand our lives in their totality so that we can change the circumstances that surround us, and change ourselves in the process. We do this, as *Rethinking Race, Class, Language, and Gender* attests, through political-practical struggle, by reading the word and the world simultaneously, as Paulo Freire would put it. The scholars taking part in this magisterial volume all recognize that our classrooms are not only in schools; they are in factories, in libraries, in church basements, in community centers, in all those spaces where people are in the process of becoming human, or are in the process of dehumanization due to the conditions of neoliberal globalization not of their own making. We need to recognize that the making of theory is very much historically connected to the making of human history and the direction in which we choose to take history. If we believe that theory is universally fixed, then we will not be making history; rather, history will be making us.

It is important that progressive-left educators create a project of decolonization that will be sufficient to contest the coloniality of power of modern imperial nation-states, and that in the process we do not lose sight of the struggle for a socialist alternative to capitalism. Manning Marable (2009a) sees hope for the future in a broad, united front that includes the valiant struggles of those who fight on a daily basis against everyday oppression and domination by the state.

Working to build this united front are Pierre Orelus and the group of scholars he has brought together in this dynamic and pathbreaking book. *Rethinking Race, Class, Language, and Gender* reveals a singularly perspicacious discourse made possible by the inclusion of seasoned scholar-activists, many of whom have been at the forefront of the struggle for social justice for the last several decades and more. Their arguments are richly layered, critical, and heuristic, and such a project of theoretical understanding and political praxis could only be made possible by the keen perception of Orelus, who not only has exhibited the courage to pose the most difficult questions related to the exploitation of humanity, but whose nuanced elaborations on vital issues affecting education today were able to elicit provocative and profound commentaries by his many interlocutors.

This book is as much an astute exercise in critical analysis as it is a polemical attack on the ideological and material foundations of racism, classism, sexism, and the many other antagonisms experienced in and made possible by neoliberal capitalist relations of exploitation now commanding the entire planet. It is a book that offers a wide range of explanations and analysis, not all of them socialist or Marxist, but where each of the scholars is joined together in the common quest for racial, economic, and social justice. We cannot wage our struggle as if these arenas are discrete and unconnected. Only by fighting at the material, epistemological, and political levels simultaneously can we achieve our goal. That is one of the most important lessons of *Rethinking Race, Class, Language, and Gender*, and it needs to be engaged by educators worldwide.

Acknowledgments

Perhaps unlike other writers, I sometimes find it hard to write the acknowledgment section of my books, though arguably it is the easiest part in many ways. My reason for saying this is the following: it is challenging to list the names of all the people who have directly or indirectly contributed to the materialization of my books, especially this book. With that said, I hope I do not leave out the names of loved ones, colleagues, and good friends who have supported me while I was finishing the manuscript of this book. First, I want to begin by thanking my wife Romina Arisbel Pacheco for her incredible support.

Second, I want to sincerely thank all the scholars, educators, and cross-border intellectuals and activists who contributed to the materialization of this book. Without their generous and invaluable contributions, this book would not have been possible. I am deeply indebted to Professors Peter McLaren and Christine Sleeter for taking time out of their busy schedules to write the foreword and the afterword of this book, respectively. Their incredible support for this book is greatly appreciated. Third, I particularly feel deeply indebted to Richard Delgado, David Gillborn, and Zeus Leonardo, who provided me with a lot of guidance and vital advice while I was working on the manuscript. Many thanks, Richard, David, and Zeus!

Fourth, I am immensely grateful to Professor Kevin Kumashiro, who was the first scholar who agreed to write a blurb endorsing this book. Thanks a million, Kevin! Likewise, I am deeply indebted to Professor Jean Stefancic for giving me constructive feedback on the first draft of the manuscript and for graciously endorsing it. Fifth, I want to sincerely thank Professors Manning Marable, Maxine Greene, Richard Wolff, and Ricky Allen for their generous endorsements of this book. Each endorsement of these highly respected scholars means a lot to me. Sixth, I wish to thank the staff at Rowman & Littlefield, particularly Patti Belcher, for their hard work. Patti was excellent from the beginning to the end of the production of this book, providing me with constructive feedback on the manuscript. She challenged me to think at the deepest level about the important issues articulated throughout the book, especially in the introductions preceding each section. Thanks, Patti! Seventh, I am grateful to my mother Leanne Adelson, to my brother Lyonel Orelus and to my sister Frida Orelus, to my sister-in-law Carline Orelus, and to my nieces and nephew for their support and love. Eighth, I want to thank my good friends and former professors, Mercure Jean Frankel, Lumumba Shabaka, Curry Malott, Pepi Leistyna, Herman Garcia, Marisol Ruiz, Sonia Nieto, Ann Withorn, Jerri Willett, Sangeeta Kamat, Donna Lecourt, Donaldo Macedo, Eva Lam, Milton Joshua, Andrew Hafner, Elick Eduard, Galette Jean Ronel, Noel Estephen, Gardy Guiteau, Deroy Gordon, Michelet Jacques, Emmanuel Vedrine, Paul Ascencio, Magaret Boykott, Kardine Higgins, Manal Hamzeh, Makie Jean Pierre, and Krista Glazewski, among others, who have been supportive to me, inspired me, and heightened my spirit through great teaching and conversations over the years. Finally, I want to thank my colleagues in the Curriculum and Instruction Department at New Mexico State University for their support. I am particularly grateful to Dr. James O'Donnell, for providing me with a small grant, which enabled me to hire a professional transcriber to transcribe all the interviews conducted for this book. Without this financial support, it would have been virtually impossible to finish the book—at least not this year. My obligation to teach three classes every single semester while serving on several committees, chairing the Post-Colonial Studies and Education Special Interest Group (SIG), and coordinating the Teaching English to Speakers of Other Languages (TESOL) and Bilingual Program, combined with my responsibility as a father of a young child, would have prevented me from finding time to transcribe all the interviews conducted for this book project. Thank you so much, Jim!

About the Interviewees

Eduardo Bonilla-Silva

Eduardo Bonilla-Silva is a professor of sociology at Duke University. His research has appeared in journals such as the *American Sociological Review, Sociological Inquiry, Racial and Ethnic Studies, Discourse and Society,* the *Journal of Latin American Studies, Contemporary Sociology, Critical Sociology,* and *Research in Politics and Society,* among others. To date he has published five books, *White Supremacy and Racism in the Post-Civil Rights Era* (co-winner of the 2002 Oliver Cox Award given by the American Sociological Association); *Racism without Racists: Color-Blind Racism and the Persistence of Racial Inequality in the United States* (2004 Choice Award); *White Out: The Continuing Significance of Racism* (with Ashley Doane); *White Logic, White Methods: Racism and Social Science* (also co-winner of the 2009 Oliver Cox Award); and *State of White Supremacy: Racism, Governance, and the United States* (with Moon-Kie Jung and Joao H. Costa Vargas). He is the 2007 recipient of the Lewis Coser Award given by the Theory Section of the American Sociological Association for Theoretical Agenda Setting. His current work is on a book titled *The Invisible Weight of Whiteness: The Racial Grammar of Everyday Life in America.*

Noam Chomsky

Noam Chomsky was born on December 7, 1928, in Philadelphia, Pennsylvania. He received his Ph.D. in linguistics in 1955 from the University of Pennsylvania. During the years 1951 to 1955, Chomsky was a Junior Fellow of the Harvard University Society of Fellows. The major theoretical viewpoints of his doctoral dissertation appeared in the monograph *Syntactic Structure* (1957). This formed part of a more extensive work, *The Logical Structure of Linguistic Theory*, circulated in mimeograph in 1955 and published in 1975. Chomsky joined the staff of the Massachusetts Institute of Technology in 1955 and in 1961 was appointed full professor. In 1976, he was appointed Institute Professor in the Department of Linguistics and Philosophy. Chomsky has lectured at many universities here and abroad and is the recipient of numerous honorary degrees and awards. He has written and lectured widely on linguistics, philosophy, intellectual history, contemporary issues, international affairs, and U.S. foreign policy. Among his recent books are *New Horizons in the Study of Language and Mind*, *On Nature and Language*, and *Hopes and Prospects*.

Antonia Darder

Antonia Darder is distinguished professor of educational policy studies and Latino and Latina studies at the University of Illinois, Urbana-Champaign. Her scholarship and teaching focus on comparative studies of racism, class, and society, as well as questions of culture, identity, language, and pedagogy. She is internationally recognized for her work in the field of critical pedagogy and her writings on education, racism, culture, and class. Her books include *Culture and Power in the Classroom*, *Reinventing Paulo Freire: A Pedagogy of Love*, *After Race: Racism after Multiculturalism*, *Culture and Difference*, *Latinos and Education*, *The Latino Studies Reader: Culture, Economy and Society*, and *The Critical Pedagogy Reader*. As a cultural worker, poet, and artist, Darder has been active in a variety of community grassroots efforts tied to education rights, workers' rights, bilingual education, women's issues, and immigration. In 2006, she established a radio collective that produces *Liberacion!* a public affairs radio program on WEFT 90.1, Champaign community radio. She is also a community journalist/editor with the *Public I*, an independent newspaper associated with the Independent Media Center in Urbana, Illinois, working to link local community issues and struggles with national and global concerns. Antonia was born in Puerto Rico and migrated with her mother and sister to California at age three. She was a teen mother, giving birth to all three of her children before she was twenty. She grew up in poverty and lived on welfare until she was twenty-six years old, when she graduated from Pasadena City College with a degree in registered nursing.

She went on to earn a license as a marriage and family therapist, working within the Latino community in the area of child abuse treatment and domestic violence. She earned a doctorate in philosophy of education at Claremont Graduate University. Antonia has lived in Los Angeles most of her life.

Richard Delgado

Richard Delgado is professor of law (emeritus) at the University of Pittsburgh and university professor of law at Seattle University, where he teaches and writes in the area of race and civil rights. He is the author of two hundred articles in law reviews and journals and twenty-eight books, eight of which have won national prizes. He and his wife, Jean Stefancic, who is also a civil rights scholar and teacher, live in Seattle, Washington, and have three grown children.

David Gillborn

David Gillborn is professor of critical race studies in education at the Institute of Education, University of London. Recently described as "one of Britain's leading race theorists," David has twice been a recipient of the UK's most prestigious education research award, the Society for Educational Studies (SES) prize for outstanding education book of the year, for his books *Racism and Education: Coincidence or Conspiracy?* and *Rationing Education* (coauthored with Deborah Youdell). David has also been honored for his work in promoting multicultural education by the American Educational Research Association (AERA) special interest group on the Critical Examination of Race, Ethnicity, Class and Gender in Education. He is founding editor of *Race Ethnicity and Education*, the leading international journal on racism and education, and coeditor (with Ed Taylor and Gloria Ladson-Billings) of *Foundations of Critical Race Theory in Education.* In addition to his research and teaching, David also works closely with policy and advocacy groups, including the Stephen Lawrence Charitable Trust, the Runnymede Trust, and the National Children's Bureau. David has held visiting posts at the University of Wisconsin–Madison and the Ontario Institute for Studies in Education (OISE) of the University of Toronto. He is an Academician of the Academy of Social Sciences and a Fellow of the Royal Society of Arts.

Carl A. Grant

Carl A. Grant is Hoefs-Bascom Professor of Teacher Education in the Department of Curriculum and Instruction and professor in the Department of Afro-American

Studies at the University of Wisconsin–Madison. His scholarship/research interest centers on curriculum and pedagogical development in multicultural democratic education for teacher candidates, classroom teachers, and college/university professors. Carl Grant was editor of the *Review of Education Research* (RER) from 1996 to 1999 and chair of the publication committee from 2003 to 2006. In 1993, he received the American Education Research Association (AERA) Distinguished Scholar Award, and at the 2009 annual conference, he was inducted into the America Education Research Association Fellows. Professor Grant has served AERA in numerous capacities, including member of AERA Special Interest Group: Research Focus on Black Education, and founding member of AERA Special Interest Group: Critical Examination of Theories of Race, Class, and Gender. He has reviewed conference proposals for several divisions. His most recent publications include: *Teach! Change! Empower!* (2009); a six-volume set on the *History of Multicultural Education* (2008, edited with Thandeka K. Chapman); *Doing Multicultural Education for Achievement and Equity* (2008, with Christine E. Sleeter); and *Pedagogy Toward a More Perfect Democratic Union: Re-envisioning College & University Teaching* (with Kim M. Wiezorek, under review). Professor Grant has written or edited more than 30 books and monographs and over 125 articles, chapters in books, and reviews.

Zeus Leonardo

Zeus Leonardo is associate professor in social and cultural studies in education, and an affiliated faculty of the Critical Theory Designated Emphasis at the University of California, Berkeley. Professor Leonardo has published several dozen articles and book chapters on race and educational theory. He is the author of *Ideology, Discourse, and School Reform* (Praeger), and he is editor of *Critical Pedagogy and Race* (Blackwell) and coeditor (with Corinne Martínez and Carlos Tejeda) of *Charting New Terrains of Chicano(a)/Latino(a) Education* (Hampton). His articles have appeared in *Educational Researcher*; *Race, Ethnicity, and Education*; and *Educational Philosophy and Theory*. Some of his essays include "The Souls of White Folk," "Critical Social Theory and Transformative Knowledge," and "The Unhappy Marriage between Marxism and Race Critique." His recent books are *Race, Whiteness, and Education* (Routledge, 2009) and the *Handbook of Cultural Politics and Education* (Sense Publishers, 2010).

Peter McLaren

Peter McLaren is professor in the Graduate School of Education and Information Studies at the University of California, Los Angeles. He is the author, editor, or coeditor of approximately forty-five books. Professor McLaren's writings have been translated into twenty-five languages. La Fundacion McLaren has been established by scholars and activists in Northern Mexico, and La Catedra Peter McLaren has been established by the Bolivarian University in Caracas. Professor McLaren is currently an invited professor at the Universidad del Salvador, Buenos Aires, and the Institute for Critical Pedagogy, Chihuahua.

Sonia Nieto

Sonia Nieto is professor emerita of education at the University of Massachusetts, Amherst. Her research focuses on multicultural education, teacher education, and the education of Latinos, immigrants, and other students of culturally and linguistically diverse backgrounds. She has written numerous journal articles and book chapters, as well as several books, including *Affirming Diversity: The Sociopolitical Context of Multicultural Education* (6th ed., 2012, with Patty Bode); *The Light in Their Eyes: Creating Multicultural Learning Communities* (10th anniversary edition, 2010); and *What Keeps Teachers Going?* (2003). She serves on several regional and national advisory boards that focus on educational equity and social justice, and she has received many academic and community awards for her scholarship, advocacy, and activism, including four honorary doctorates. She is married to Angel Nieto, a former teacher and author of children's books, and they have two daughters and eleven grandchildren.

Pedro Noguera

Pedro Noguera is the Peter L. Agnew Professor of Education in the Steinhardt School of Culture, Education and Development at New York University. He also serves as director of the Metropolitan Center for Urban Education and codirector of the Institute for the Study of Globalization and Education in Metropolitan Settings (IGEMS). Noguera is an urban sociologist, and his scholarship and research focus on the ways in which schools are influenced by social and economic conditions. From 2000 to 2003, Noguera served as the Judith K. Dimon Professor of Communities and Schools at the Harvard Graduate School of Education. From 1990 to 2000, he was a professor at the Graduate School of Education and the director of the Institute for the Study of Social Change at the University of California, Berkeley. Pedro Noguera has published over 150 research articles, monographs, and research reports on topics such as urban school reform, conditions that promote student achievement, youth violence, the potential impact of school choice and vouchers on urban public schools, and race and ethnic relations in American society. His work has appeared in several major research journals, and many are available online at inmotionmagazine.com. He is the author of several groundbreaking books, including *The Imperatives of Power: Political Change and the Social Basis of Regime Support in Grenada* (Peter Lang Publishers, 1997); *City Schools and the American Dream* (Teachers College Press, 2003); *Beyond Resistance* (Routledge, 2006); and *Unfinished Business: Closing the Achievement Gap in Our Nation's Schools* (Josey-Bass, 2006). His most recent book is *The Trouble with Black Boys and Other Reflections on Race, Equity, and the Future of Public Education* (Josey-Bass, 2008; winner of Critics' Choice Award of the American Educational Studies Association and the Schott Foundation Award for Research on Race and Gender). In 2008, Noguera was appointed by New York governor David Patterson to serve as a trustee for the State University of New York (SUNY). He is a frequent commentator on educational issues on CNN, National Public Radio, and other news outlets. He also serves on the board of several local and national education and youth development organizations.

Christine E. Sleeter

Christine E. Sleeter is professor emerita in the College of Professional Studies at California State University, Monterey Bay, where she was a founding faculty member. Currently serving as president of the National Association for Multicultural Education, she previously served as vice president of Division K (Teaching and Teacher Education) of the American Educational Research Association. Her research focuses on antiracist multicultural education and multicultural teacher education, and currently she is developing a new area, critical family history. With a team of researchers at Victoria University, New Zealand, she recently completed an evaluation study of a Maori professional development program for secondary schools. Dr. Sleeter has published over one hundred articles in edited books and journals such as the *Journal of Teacher Education*, *Teacher Education Quarterly*, *Teaching and Teacher Education*, and *Curriculum Inquiry*. Her recent books include *Un-standardizing Curriculum* (Teachers College Press, 2005); *Critical Multiculturalism: Theory and Praxis* (with Stephen May; Routledge, 2010); and *Doing Multicultural Education for Achievement and Equity* (with Carl Grant; Routledge, 2007). Awards for her work include the American Educational Research Association Social Justice in Education Award, the American Educational Research Association Division K Legacy Award, the California State University Monterey Bay President's Medal, and the National Association for Multicultural Education Research Award.

David Stovall

David Stovall is associate professor of educational policy studies and African-American studies at the University of Illinois at Chicago (UIC). His scholarship investigates four areas: (1) critical race theory, (2) concepts of social justice in education, (3) the relationship between housing and education, and (4) the relationship between schools and community stakeholders. In the attempt to bring theory to action, he has spent the last ten years working with community organizations and schools to develop curricula that address issues of social justice. His current work has led him to become a member of the Greater Lawndale/Little Village School for Social Justice High School design team, which opened in the fall of 2005. Furthering his work with communities, students, and teachers, Stovall is involved with youth-centered community organizations in Chicago, New York, and the Bay Area. In addition to his duties and responsibilities as an associate professor at UIC, he also serves as a volunteer social studies teacher at the Greater Lawndale/Little Village School for Social Justice.

Howard Winant

Howard Winant is professor of sociology at the University of California, Santa Barbara, where he is also affiliated with the Black Studies and Chicana/o Studies departments and is chair of the UCSB Law and Society Program. He is the director of the UC Multicampus Research Project in New Racial Studies, and he also founded the UCSB Center for New Racial Studies. Winant's work focuses on the historical and contemporary importance of race in shaping economic, political, and cultural life, both in the U.S. and globally. He is the author of *The New Politics of Race: Globalism, Difference, Justice* (2004); *The World Is a Ghetto: Race and Democracy since World War II* (2001); *Racial Conditions: Politics, Theory, Comparisons* (1994); *Racial Formation in the United States: From the 1960s to the 1990s* (coauthored with Michael Omi, 1986 and 1994); and *Stalemate: Political Economic Origins of Supply-Side Policy* (1988).

Introduction

There is often a tendency, particularly in the mainstream media, to focus on one form of oppression and pay less attention to or leave out others. For example, when political pundits refer to middle-class or working-class people, they speak as if factors such as race and gender do not fundamentally shape one's subjective and material conditions as well. What this precalculated dominant discourse does is privilege class over equally important issues like race, gender, and language, among others.

This book aims to counter this discourse, which has been circulated in the corporate mainstream media as well as in institutions such as schools. Specifically, drawing upon data stemming from interviews conducted with educators and cross-border intellectuals from different fields and foci (critical race theory, Marxism, multicultural education, sociology, critical pedagogy, and feminist and postcolonial theory), this book presents a novel and critical perspective on various forms of oppression such as racial, social class, gender, and linguistic oppressions taking place in schools and beyond. Too often, many scholars have privileged one form of oppression over others despite the fact that a vast body of research shows that all forms of oppression are interconnected (Matsuda et al., 1993).

Utilizing dialogue as a form of inquiry into the collective voice and innovative ideas of many educators and scholars, this book thoroughly examines the effects of intersectional oppressions, particularly on people who have been pushed to the margins (hooks, 1990) because of their targeted social identities. While this book does not cover all forms of oppression that women, poor working-class people, gays, students of color, female faculty, and faculty of color have faced in schools and in society at large, it provides the reader with a comprehensive view of the way racism, classism, capitalism, and sexism affect people's lives.

This book is the product of a collection of in-depth interviews and conversations carried out over the course of two years with committed social justice educators and scholars genuinely concerned with, and who have critically explored through their teaching, scholarly, communal, and activist work, race, class, gender, and language issues. I chose to engage these scholars through interviews and dialogues because I believe that through this genre, people naturally express innovative ideas and co-construct knowledge, which is sometimes hard to do through other genres.

This dialogical way of discussing important issues while at the same time co-constructing knowledge can be traced back to the time of Plato and Socrates who used dialogue as a form of inquiry to explore and analyze social, political, and educational issues facing the world. This dialogical framework has been carried over by prominent scholars like Paulo Freire, Michel Foucault, Noam Chomsky, and Howard Zinn, who have had many books emerge out of dialogues and interviews conducted with other scholars. This book follows a format similar to that used, for example, by Paulo Freire and Donaldo Macedo (1987) in their book *Literacy: Reading the Word and the World*. However, unlike Freire and Macedo's book, and others, this book covers many interwoven and pressing issues echoed through the authentic and dissident voices of many progressive educators and scholars.

Selection of Invited Educators and Scholars

I spent about two months thinking deeply about whom I should invite to take part in this book, as my goal was to invite scholars and educators who could contribute to the critical analysis of social inequality that is race, class, gender, and language based. Some educators and activist scholars came easily to mind, for I was already familiar with their scholarly and activist work. Others required some deep thinking; consultation with mentors, colleagues, and friends; and doing some research before deciding to invite them, because I was not quite familiar with their work. Hence, I had to read their work in depth to determine whether their research interests and focus matched the goal of the book.

I decided to revisit the recent writings of scholars with whose work I was familiar to make sure that their research focus and interests matched the overarching goal that this book aims to achieve, that is, to analyze the intersection of race, class, gender, and language and their effects on people, particularly marginalized people. Each scholar was invited according to his or her expertise, though many are cross-border intellectuals transcending many fields with their scholarly work. I invited thirteen scholars from different class, racial, gender, religious, and linguistic backgrounds. Moreover, I invited scholars who are nationally and internationally known and highly respected. Finally, scholars from different parts of the world contributed to this book as well, as I deemed it necessary to invite scholars beyond the U.S. border. Needless to say, the scholars contributing to this book were carefully selected.

Most of the scholars and educators welcomed the idea of being interviewed for this book project. The interviews were both face-to-face and phone interviews. A few, however, were engaged in what I call question-and-answer dialogue via e-mail. To those who chose this option, I sent them a set of questions to which they responded. In many cases, additional questions emerged from their responses, which I sent back to them. I went back and forth via e-mail asking them to clarify and expand their responses to the questions that were sent to them. As for those who were interviewed, I sent them the transcribed interviews for their preview and review. I asked them to read the interviews carefully to make sure that their original ideas were not distorted during the transcription process. Many added to the content of the transcribed interviews and sent them back to me.

I designed a different set of questions for the interviews according to the expertise and research interests of the invited scholars. However, it is worth pointing out that I primarily used these questions to guide me through the interview process. Many of these scholars are border crossers who have written about a wide range of issues in their scholarly work. Therefore I was able to engage them in discussions revolving around many interwoven issues like race, class, and gender. It is also important to note that I asked many scholars the same or similar questions, some of which overlapped. I did this because I wanted to hear various perspectives from different scholars on the same issues, and I thought the best way to do that was by asking them similar questions.

Intended Audience

This book is designed for a broad range of readers and scholars in various disciplines and foci, including critical race theory, women's studies, sociology, education, cultural studies, African American and ethnic studies, multicultural education, and postcolonial theory. However, this book is particularly suitable for courses on class, race/ethnicity, language, gender, and multicultural education at both the graduate and undergraduate level. The author hopes, therefore, to open spaces for genuine dialogue about these issues among others, in school and as well as other settings.

Given its interdisciplinary scope, readers interested in race/ethnic and gender/women's studies, social class, language, and identity issues will find this book germane to their needs and interests. Because of the critical lens through which these issues are analyzed throughout the book, readers will gain a sophisticated understanding of the intersection of racial, gender, social class, and linguistic oppressions. The dialogue with various scholars and educators about this intersection is presented in an accessible academic language.

I believe that the issues this book addresses are of great importance to people across racial, gender, linguistic, and social class lines, which fundamentally influence the way many of us behave, think, act, treat others, are perceived, and are treated in society. This book gathers in a single volume the thoughts and authentic voices of a myriad of respected progressive scholars and educators who have profoundly transformed many disciplines and have impacted many communities around the world. I am therefore hopeful that people will find this book helpful for social justice work in education and beyond.

Book Organization

This book is divided into several parts; some are longer than others. While some parts address issues like capitalism, neoliberalism, and democracy, others focus on the matrix of racial, class, linguistic, and gender inequalities on a broader scale. Still others explore multicultural, multiracial, and White supremacy issues. It is worth noting that each part critically examines a set of intertwined issues. While in some interviews I engage scholars in a deep conversation that revolves around the sociocultural and historical constructions of race and gender, in others we talk about the misguided ideas about the intricacies of social class and its relation to Western capitalism and neoliberalism. In subsequent interviews, we focus on the ways in which people have resisted racial, social class, linguistic, and gender oppressions. While each interview attempts to address a particular issue, the inevitable occurs; that is, race and gender issues run through interviews that focus on class and vice versa. Needless to say, the content of the book is a hybrid, so it is hoped that the reader will read it with a "hybrid" eye. A short paragraph precedes each dialogue, providing a brief overview of the content of the dialogue and the context in which it took place. A separate section provides some key background information on each invited scholar who participated in this book.

Part I

MAPPING AND ENGAGING THE DEBATE ON RACE, RACISM, AND OTHER "ISMS"

FROM SLAVERY TO THE CIVIL RIGHTS ERA TO BARACK OBAMA'S PRESIDENCY AND BEYOND

Race and racism rarely surface in political debates though they are among the leading factors that have led to people's racial and socioeconomic marginalization. Throughout history, race and racism have been used as a socioeconomic and political means to achieve specific ends.[1] During slavery, race was a powerful tool used by the White master to oppress and exploit the slaves. Though slavery is officially over, race has continued to be used in different contexts by dominant groups to oppress marginalized people, such as African Americans, Native Americans, and Latino/as.[2]

Despite the empty rhetoric of many American politicians, including politicians of color, we have yet to see a significant shift in the racial paradigm. Even though we now have a Black president, Barack Obama, after centuries of political domination and control by privileged heterosexual, Christian, and able-bodied White males, the United States remains racially divided and segregated. The symbolic and historical presidency of Barack Obama does not necessarily mean we are living in, or approaching, a post-racial era.[3] Race mattered during slavery and colonization in terms of how the slaves and the colonized peoples were treated. It continues to matter today and will most likely continue to matter for centuries to come unless there is a profound transformation of the unequally race-based political and economic system.

This system, which has been dominated by privileged and heterosexual White males, would not have been able to survive for centuries had it not been unequally race based. More specifically, the racist system that we have now has been able to survive for centuries because of the superiority myth that has been historically created about the White race. Hence, as long as marginalized and minoritized groups and Whites alike continue to believe in this myth, they will in tandem, consciously or not, continue to feed and support this system, which by now should be a dying system, for to sustain itself it relies on the exploitation and subjugation of people who happen to be embodied in black and brown skins. A system that racially isolates and economically exploits people because they are different is a weak system.

In addition, a system that targets a certain group of people because of their skin tone, social class, or sexuality is an intolerant and oppressive system that needs to be radically restructured. A system that privileges a small group of wealthy people over the starving and exploited majority is a decaying system. A system that punitively exploits the poor, including poor people of color and poor Whites, and yet refuses to grant them access to health care and other benefits is a sordid system. A system that is run by a small privileged group who lie to and mislead young people, including youth of color, and send them to war to kill and be killed for their own corporate interests is an immoral system that should be dismantled.

Transforming this system will require not merely the good intentions of individual Whites and empty rhetoric from White, Black, and Brown people, but rather concrete steps toward this transformation. Some of the steps need to entail raising social and political consciousness in individuals, particularly those who have been brainwashed to believe that this system is democratic and provides equal opportunity to each individual. Further steps should involve collective effort and struggle against many oppressive practices, such as racial profiling and putting teachers and students under surveillance. These are some of the oppressive practices to which many people of color, including professors and students of color, and other marginalized groups have been subjected.[4]

The limited number of faculty of color and students of color in the U.S. academy often have to work twice as hard as their White colleagues. However, they often do not receive the respect they deserve. Despite the hard work, competence, and high level of academic performance and achievement of faculty of color, they are often invisible in the eyes of many of their White colleagues and the institution itself. For example, the highly respected U.S. legal and critical race theory scholar Richard Delgado has experienced isolation and invisibility with some of his White colleagues. Delgado states, "Many of my White colleagues do not really know what a Latino is. Others know but barely tolerate me, even though I am one of the top legal publishers in the country and am well liked by my students" (as cited in this section, p. 11).

Outside the classroom walls, people of color, including professors of color, receive ill treatment from police officers because of their racial and ethnic backgrounds. This has been the experience of Professor Delgado:

> Even dignified, well-dressed professionals encounter police profiling and challenges at work. I have been stopped by university police for merely looking out of place in the law building during evening hours. The incident had nothing to do with my income or class, but with my color and race. On other occasions, highway police have pulled me over just to check me out, even though I was driving a sober-looking rental car sedately on my way back from an academic conference. (as cited in this section, p. 12)

Similarly, the acclaimed African American scholar Cornel West has been a victim of racial profiling. Professor West narrated his experience with racial profiling in the following terms:

> Years ago, while driving from New York to teach at Williams College, I was stopped on fake charges of trafficking cocaine. When I told the police officer I was a professor of religion, he replied, "Yeah, and I'm the Flying Nun. Let's go, nigger!" I was stopped three times in my first ten days in Princeton for driving too slowly on a residential street with a speed limit of twenty-five miles per hour. (p. x)[5]

There are countless stories like Professors Delgado's and West's that may not have been told publicly. These stories have been silenced. Institutions, such as high schools, colleges, and universities, where many students and professors have been targeted because of their race, gender, social class, and country of origin, have been complacent and complicit about the poor treatment of these students and professors.[6] This is not coincidental. Many of those who hold key positions at these institutions, such as presidents, deans, department heads, and directors, have been for the most part dominant White males who may have no interest in transforming the status quo from which they have benefited in terms of building their professional careers.[7]

It is not surprising then that institutional racism is rampant at many universities and colleges and has affected not only students and faculty of color but also White students and professors, though to a lesser extent in the case of the latter. It has been argued that racism is not merely a White or a Black/Brown person's problem; it is a societal problem. At any institution where racial tension exists, both people of color and White people feel this tension, though I believe the former feel it much more, for they are the targeted groups. The question that is then worth asking is, can equity and diversity ever be a reality on college and university campuses when Black and Brown students, faculty of color, and female faculty are frequently discriminated against because of their gender and racial background?

As many scholars have eloquently articulated in their work, race has been the determining factor leading to racial, socioeconomic, and political marginalization of people of color in the U.S. and beyond.[8] Despite sound evidence of the crucial role that race plays in the unequal power relations between Whites and non-Whites, many privileged groups, particularly heterosexual, Christian, and able-bodied White males have attempted to "whitewash" race.[9]

Of course, the socioeconomic marginalization of people, including people of color, can't and should not be merely reduced to their racial background, because factors such as social class, sexuality, gender, homophobia, and xenophobia also play an important role in their marginalization. However, it must be acknowledged that race shapes almost every faceted aspect of the life of people of color. Like other marginalized groups, including gays, lesbians, and transgender individuals, people of color have been denied housing, well-paid jobs, job promotions, quality education, and adequate health care because of their racial background.[10]

They face challenges at all levels and at different places, for their racial background seems to be a shadow that follows them wherever they go or happen to be. Yet they must continue to live their lives within the confinement of a racist system. But how can people of color resist the racial margins and do so in ways that are not harmful to their lives and the lives of others? This is a terrific challenge that they have before them as many are trying to earn a decent living and protect their human dignity at the same time. The authors featured in this section, Richard Delgado, David Gillborn, and Zeus Leonardo, shed light on these important issues by drawing on both their personal and professional lives. Though they have different life experiences and professional trajectories, they all acknowledge and examine the intricacies of race, racism, classism, and sexism and point out the extent to which these forms of oppression have affected the lives of many people, particularly people of color, women, and poor Whites.

Notes

1. Marable, M. (2006). *Living Black history: How reimagining the African-American past can remake America's racial future.* New York: Basic Civitas Books.
2. Grande, S. (2004). *Red pedagogy: Native American social and political thought.* Lanham, MD: Rowman & Littlefield; Alexander, M. (2010). *The new Jim Crow: Mass incarceration in the age of colorblindness.* New York: New Press; Haley, A. (2007). *Roots: The saga of an American family.* New York: Vanguard Press.
3. Bonilla-Silva, E. (2010). *Anything but racism: How social scientists limit the significance of race.* New York: Routledge.
4. Tatum, B. D. (2007). *Can we talk about race? And other conversations in an era of school resegregation.* Boston, MA: Beacon Press; Leonardo, Z. (2009). *Race, Whiteness, and education.* New York: Routledge.
5. West, C. (2001). *Race matters.* Boston, MA: Beacon Press.

6. Bonilla-Silva, B. (2003). *Racism without racists: Color-blind racism and the persistence of racial inequality in America.* Lanham, MD: Rowman & Littlefield.

7. Wise, T. (2010). *Colorblind: The rise of post-racial politics and the retreat from racial equity.* San Francisco: City Lights Publishers.

8. Winant, H. (2002). *The world is a ghetto: Race and democracy since World War II.* New York: Basic Books; Dyson, M. E. (2009). *Can you hear me now? The inspiration, wisdom, and insight of Michael Eric Dyson.* New York: Basic Civitas Books.

9. Brown, M., Carney, M., Currie, E., Duster, T., Oppenheimer, D., Schultz, M., & Wellman, D. (2003). *Whitewashing race: The myth of a color-blind society.* Berkeley: University of California Press.

10. West, C. (2008). *Hope on a tightrope: Words and wisdom.* New York: Smiley Books; West, C. (2010). *Brother West: Living and loving out loud; A memoir.* New York: Smiley Books.

CHAPTER 1

Unveiling Majoritarian Myths and Tales about Race and Racism

A CONVERSATION WITH RICHARD DELGADO

In this dialogue, Professor Delgado begins by talking about how his painful personal and professional experiences with institutional racism, as well as the experiences of his parents, have inspired him to explore racial issues throughout his career as a law professor. He goes on to describe the great contribution that critical race theory has made in helping people become aware of racism, which blights the lives of many people of color. In addition, he brilliantly establishes the interconnection between different forms of oppression such as classism, racism, xenophobia, and language discrimination. He argues that being a Chicano law professor with brown skin has not protected him from being racially profiled. Therefore, he challenges and refutes the color-blind discourse and the idea that we are living in a post-racial era because of the presidency of Barack Obama.

The Dialogue

Orelus: *You are among the distinguished scholars who are profoundly vested in critical race theory. Please, would you share with me what has inspired you to devote your professional and personal life to exploring racial issues?*

Delgado: Racism has always struck me as both perplexing and unfair. Growing up in the pre–civil rights era, I was on the receiving end of a good deal of mistreatment as a brown-skinned son of a Mexican father. We moved around constantly when I was young, whether because of my father's immigration status or for some other reason, I don't know. Usually, I was the only Mexican kid in my class. When I would transfer to a new school, the principal would usually look me over with a jaundiced eye and put me in the dumbest track, much to my dear mother's chagrin. In fact, I was an excellent reader and good at numbers. Because of my family's frequent moves, I had few long-term friends. To console myself, I became bookish. When we moved to a new location, I would locate the nearest library, where I would check out books by the dozen and read them in my room. It wasn't until seventh grade that a teacher noticed that I was reading many years ahead of grade level, and not until eleventh grade that one realized I was capable of challenging work.

I encountered racism in every aspect of life—in stores, school, even Little League sports. This was before *Brown v. Board of Education* and the civil rights era, so many Americans were old-fashioned, unapologetic racists who would make statements about Mexicans' intelligence, hygiene, and even proclivity to carry knives—to my face.

I grew up wanting to understand what made many of my fellow citizens so mean. In graduate school, I took courses that I hoped could help me understand how society worked. Later, as a law student, I hoped to use the law as a tool to combat racism. But my career took a slightly different direction. I did not become an activist lawyer but a law professor writing about race and civil rights. Looking back, I see that my interest in this field is a direct result of my own early experience with racism.

ORELUS: *In my conversations with other critical race theorists, I asked them to what degree they think critical race theory, starting with Derrick Bell in legal studies and Gloria Ladson-Billings in education, has contributed to the fight against institutional racism and White supremacy. How would you answer this question?*

DELGADO: Critical race theory addresses a number of issues that traditional civil rights scholarship leaves out, such as unconscious or institutional racism. It also helps us understand that racism is rarely accidental or a product of ignorance, but a means by which society maintains social relations. Critical race theory helps explain how breakthrough cases, like *Brown v. Board of Education*, arrive in response to a majoritarian need or interest and how antidiscrimination law itself reinforces racism.

Recently, the movement has begun examining the legal fortunes of non-Black groups. This scholarship shows how a Black-White binary paradigm of race can inhibit progress for Latinos, Indians, and Asian Americans. In order to invoke civil rights laws and theories coined with Blacks in mind, these other groups must analogize their mistreatment to a type that Blacks historically encounter. Discrimination that proceeds on the basis of immigration status, a foreign accent, or a foreign-sounding surname is difficult to redress under the prevailing approach. Critical race theory shows how this is so and what we need to do about it.

Critical race scholars have critiqued civil rights mainstays such as without intent-no discrimination and the idea that neutrality and color blindness are ideal approaches to controlling discrimination. They have shown how one can use storytelling and narrative analysis to challenge comforting majoritarian myths and tales. They have shown how liberal mainstays, such as the First Amendment, can shelter bigots and racists and how limiting hate speech, as other countries have done, can protect children of color from invective and abuse. They have analyzed the legal case for Black reparations, affirmative action, and an open border with Mexico. Recently, critical race theory has moved into other disciplines, such as education, sociology, and psychology. In education, for example, scholars on both sides of the Atlantic use critical race theory to analyze hierarchy in the schools, school discipline, the Western canon, and IQ and high-stakes testing. They use it to study migrant and bilingual education, affirmative action, and school tracking. Critical race theory has also jumped the Atlantic, with a lively contingent in England holding conferences, writing books, and challenging the educational establishment.

ORELUS: *To what extent has critical race theory contributed to the fight against institutional racism and White supremacy?*

DELGADO: The movement has jarred White complacency by showing that society needs more than color-blind attitudes and laws to reverse the legacy of a racist past. Critical historians have shown how seemingly neutral laws (like the GI Bill) and practices (like school choice) have enabled Whites to secure wealth, jobs, and influence at the expense of non-Whites, and to hang on to them. They have shown how White supremacy is more than the occasional practice of favoring one's kind, but an interconnected system of rules, customs, and privileges (such as union membership) that consistently enable the majority group to remain ahead.

Critical race theorists have been in the forefront of struggles to integrate the academy, including professional schools. They have been advocating new approaches to voting and voting rights, including cumulative voting. They have analyzed how the law helps construct race, the definition of Whiteness, and notions of criminality and delinquency.

ORELUS: *Race is pivotal to many aspects of our life. However, many people, particularly some White people, have refused to talk about it. In your view, what are some of the underlying reasons that might explain their refusal to do so?*

DELGADO: Many Whites are reluctant to talk about race because they are afraid that a verbal slip or gaffe will subject them to criticism. Some Whites would like to talk about race but remember receiving poor treatment by a Black or Latino who let them have it for an honestly held view or attitude. In my opinion, we should have more conversations about race. That includes Blacks speaking with Latinos, Latinos with Blacks, and Asians with members of both groups. We should ease up on our friends for minor slips or for using a wrong term (such as "Hispanic" rather than "Latino" or "Chicano") and try to get to the heart of a problem. Some White folks prefer not to talk about race because a neutral or color-blind approach helps conceal their own White supremacy and enshrines White normativity. As soon as they put race under the lens, their own White status comes in for examination, and the answer is not often pretty.

Orelus: *People are shaped by a multiplicity of identities. How would you link racial identity to other forms of identity? Why do you think it is crucial to establish such a link?*

Delgado: A Chicano, for example, can be gay, lesbian, or a single working-class mother. She can even be Black or Asian. The number of multiracial people is growing because of increasing intermarriage. Racial membership is no longer clear and pristine.

Moreover, to a large extent, we perform our identities, acting Black or Brown on some occasions (for example with friends), and speaking the King's English on others. Even if we think of ourselves as belonging to a certain group (say, Black), we perform our identity differently from one occasion to the next by our choice of clothes, music, manner, speech, and whom we hang out with. One can be very Black on one occasion, such as when hanging out with one's friends, and less so when in a mixed group.

Merely because racial identities are seldom fixed or simple, it does not follow that one can never make categorical statements in this area. White supremacy is ubiquitous, and wrong. Operation Wetback—which deported over one million Latinos, many of them U.S. citizens—was so as well. The case for Black reparations and an open border with Mexico is strong and compelling. Not everything is constructed, or just a matter of point of view. Racial identity may be complex and shifting. But American society still embraced the "one drop" rule under which a person with *any* detectible sign of Blackness was categorized that way, both socially and legally. During Operation Wetback in 1954, over one million Mexican-looking people were deported, even ones who were U.S. citizens born in this country. It did not matter that one was a fourth-generation American, of mixed blood, or a college graduate. Sometimes identity is very simple. You either look like one of "them," or you don't.

Orelus: *Many professors of color, including myself, have expressed great concerns about the way they have been treated at some institutions because of their racial/ethnic/linguistic backgrounds and country of origin. What has been your experience as a professor of color?*

DELGADO: My experience as a Chicano in academia has been, by turns, rewarding, amusing, and infuriating. I got into law teaching almost accidentally at a time when the number of Chicano law professors was smaller than twelve. Thirty-five years later, only about 3 percent of the legal academy is Latino, and even fewer are Chicano or Mexican American. Many of my White colleagues do not really know what a Latino is. Others know but barely tolerate me, even though I am one of the top legal publishers in the country and am well liked by my students. One of my most frustrating experiences, year after year, is advocating for more professors of color at my law school. If I propose an exciting junior scholar, my colleagues tell me they are looking for someone with more experience. If I champion a top senior scholar, I learn they are looking for an entry-level professor whose salary is more affordable. If I identify a good prospect in area X, it always turns out that our main curricular needs are in area Y. Sometimes students will ask me where I went to law school or whether I was on the law review. (The answers are, "Berkeley, although I was also admitted at Harvard," and to the second question, "yes"). These questions are aimed at finding out if I was an affirmative action hire.

ORELUS: *Depending on how language is used, it can be a liberatory or an oppressive tool. In your view, in what way might people's use of language lead to the perpetuation of racial stereotypes about people, particularly people of color?*

DELGADO: Language may not be the most powerful means of oppression—coercion, economic discrimination, and housing and employment discrimination rank higher—but it is an ever-present reality. It is also a key mechanism by which society orders social relations. Media stereotypes and images teach members of the majority group that minorities are lazy, stupid, and criminal. Minorities, too, internalize these messages, which are especially damaging for the young. Stereotypes limit what teachers expect from students of color and are a prime cause for underachievement and school dropout. Hate speech can break out at colleges and universities in the form of anonymous e-mail messages and graffiti. Some have responded by enacting student conduct codes penalizing the expression of racial hatred.

English-only laws and rules penalize people for speaking Spanish or other foreign languages at work. These laws are rarely enforced against people speaking high-prestige languages like French or Italian, or speaking with an upper-class English or French accent. Some school systems disdain bilingual education, even though studies show that this is the best way to prevent immigrant children from falling behind in school.

ORELUS: *Some scholars, particularly orthodox Marxists, have prioritized class issues over racial issues, arguing that inequality stemming from capitalism affects both Blacks and Whites. Where do you stand on this issue?*

DELGADO: For dark-skinned minorities or indigenous-looking Latinos, racism is a more significant barrier than is classism. One can change one's social class by earning or inheriting money or achieving a high educational level. One cannot change one's skin color. Many White people like to believe that if Black or Brown people only behaved like Whites—spoke good English, dressed conservatively, stopped listening to rap music—racism would abate. This is a fallacy. Even dignified, well-dressed professionals encounter police profiling and challenges at work. I have been stopped by university police for merely looking out of place in the law building during evening hours. The incident had nothing to do with my income or class, but with my color and race. On other occasions, highway police have pulled me over just to check me out, even though I was driving a sober-looking rental car sedately on my way back from an academic conference. Capital constantly mistreats workers, including ones who are Black and Brown. But capitalists and noncapitalists alike may be racists. The White cop who pulled me over was not a capitalist. He was not suspicious of me because of my middle-class status, but my brown face and indigenous-looking features.

ORELUS: *There have been a lot of debates about the so-called post-racial era, specifically in the U.S. context soon after Obama got elected as president. Where do you stand on this debate? What challenges have you faced in talking about racial issues?*

DELGADO: I have experienced several types of challenges. Early in my career, a number of well-meaning White colleagues advised me to "play things straight" in my scholarship. They urged me to stay away from civil rights and other ethnic subjects and develop an expertise in some conventional legal area, such as evidence or civil procedure. Why ghettoize myself, they seemed to say, when expertise in a mainstream area would serve me better in the long run? Even though the advice may have been well meant, it subtly suggested that one needed to deracinate oneself to get ahead in the legal profession.

In recent years, I have received fewer such challenges, but more of a different kind. This other, more frontal attack, which I experience most often while on the speaking circuit, accuses me of playing the race card. The accuser recites the panoply of civil rights laws this country has enacted, mentions the many institutions that still practice affirmative action, and declares that racism is now over. We have a Black president and several Black entertainers and athletes. Anyone calling attention to race problems is now a complainer who is asking for something he doesn't deserve.

I have found that critics who espouse this position are almost impervious to argument. If I point out that Blacks and Latinos earn less than Whites for the same jobs, they argue that the minorities are younger and have fewer years of seniority. If I point out that a high proportion of Whites express anti-Black sentiments in response to survey questions, these critics reply that that's because of statistical discrimination—Blacks, on average, commit more crimes than Whites, so a person who is leery of them is only responding rationally. By the same token, anyone who associates Latino men with drug dealing is not far off base, these speakers say, because the number of us who are drug dealers is higher than it is for Whites. A variant of this approach asserts that since the Obama election, America has entered into a post-racial era. Everyone has Black friends and likes Latino food and music. America has a Black president. Anyone who persists in treating racism as a problem is living in the past or resettling ancient scores.

But America has not entered into a post-racial era and is unlikely to do so anytime soon. Only about 43 percent of Whites voted for Obama, even though he was by far the superior candidate. Obama's election came about almost entirely from the large majorities he commanded among Latinos and Blacks. Race is such a powerful social organizing principle that it will never fade away entirely. It is hard to think of a single society where racial hierarchy, once deeply engrained, ceases to be so. Certain societies have done a better job than we have of reducing racial disparities of income, education, and longevity. But none has fully eradicated the mark of race; nor is ours likely to do so anytime soon.

Orelus: *Do you think that Obama's presidency will help many Whites see people of color differently, in a positive way? Or do you think the main problem for this country will remain the problem of the color line, as Du Bois put it about a century ago?*

Delgado: In one respect, Obama's election has made race relations worse. It has set off a shrill debate about whether America has turned socialist, whether it is losing its way, and even whether Obama was born in the USA. In that sense, the tone of discourse is worse since he took office. Some of the discourse comes accompanied with an implied threat ("We must take our country back!"). Recall how America went on a gun-buying spree as soon as it appeared Obama might win, and how many blogs and individuals (at town-hall meetings, for example) now talk openly about violence. For the first time in memory, we have seen disgruntled Whites brandish guns at town-hall meetings, or even outside the hall where the president is speaking. On the other hand, Obama's election may have improved the outlook for young Blacks and Latinos. Some early evidence shows that stereotype threat is diminishing for Black test takers. Latinos are beginning to feel that they, too, may aspire to high positions, including the Supreme Court!

Orelus: *Do you think racism affects Black people the same way it affects other marginalized groups, such as Latino/as and Native Americans?*

Delgado: Discrimination takes different forms for the three groups. Like Blacks, Latinos can come in for discrimination based on their appearance and skin color. But they can also suffer it based on a foreign accent or a foreign-sounding name, like Jésus or González. Their presumed immigrant status also subjects them to suspicion, even if their families have lived here for generations.

And they have to contend with a host of media stereotypes, including poor hygiene, laziness, stupidity, and hypersexuality. Native Americans have to cope with a different set of stereotypes, including the myth that the federal government provides endless amounts of scholarship money for Indian students or that Indian tribes are rolling in casino-generated wealth. All groups internalize some of the prevailing social attitudes, including disdain for darker-skinned members of their own group. And Whites, of course, are most comfortable with minorities who are light skinned, with Anglo features and mannerisms. Social science evidence is confirming this phenomenon in many settings, including jury verdicts and awards.

Some people believe that intermarriage will eventually blur racial lines so that we will all be a pleasing shade of brown. But this is apt to happen more slowly than most people think. Only a very small number of Black men marry White women. If racial preference were not a factor, the percentage would be around 70. Asian American intermarriage with Whites is higher than it is for Blacks, especially for Asian women marrying White men. Latinos intermarry at rates between those of Asians and Blacks. When intermarriage does occur, the minority person is apt to be light skinned, conventionally attractive, and well educated.

Orelus: *What do you imagine the world would be like if one's race were not an issue? What do you imagine it would be like living in such a world?*

Delgado: Derrick Bell has written that racism is apt to be permanent and that if society somehow magically solved the race problem, it would invent a different out-group. Jews, gays, lesbians, or foreigners might be next. For some, racism serves a need for domination or superiority. At a group level, the majority finds it profitable to subordinate members of minority groups. Doing so assures a pool of surplus labor. And it cuts down the competition for social goods, such as slots in elite university programs.

For these reasons, I have trouble envisioning a world where race is not an issue. I can envision settings where it might become less of an issue than it is in society at large. But I cannot easily envision a world without race anytime soon.

Orelus: *Let's briefly go back to history. It is unquestionable that slavery, colonization, and racism are interconnected. How do you see this interconnection?*

Delgado: Slavery was, of course, profitable, at least for many slave traders and plantation owners. In that sense, the institution was a product of capitalism and the search for profit. Colonialism stemmed from much the same impulses, although individual colonials and settlers may have been attracted to life in India, Africa, or North America for a mixture of motives. For some, it was love of adventure. For others, it was a search for religious freedom. For still others, it allowed them to escape a bad marriage or family or work situation. But the dominant motive was the search for power and profit. Racism and colonialism reinforced each other and were practically different sides of the same coin.

The colonial settlers needed to rationalize exploiting other people, raiding their resources, and replacing their leaders. Racist stereotypes and scripts painted the colonial subjects as stupid, hapless, and lazy, so that the settlers were doing them a favor by teaching them superior Western ways. White supremacy—the notion that the English or French deserved to rule the new territories—was the flip side of racism. Racism taught that the original inhabitants were inferior and savage; White supremacy that the cure was for the superior Whites to take over. Both forces—racism and colonialism—are profitable. Both provide the dominant society with profits, cheap labor, access to resources, and psychic benefits. They get to lord it over other people and consider themselves superior.

CHAPTER 2

The Fight against Racism and Classism

A CONVERSATION WITH DAVID GILLBORN

In this dialogue, Professor Gillborn starts by talking about how his experience as a working-class boy witnessing and personally experiencing racial and class divide in school and his native land, the United Kingdom, has shaped his consciousness of racism and classism. Such experience has consequently led him to dedicate his professional life to race and class issues. He goes on to point out the extent to which critical race theory has contributed to a high level of awareness among people about racial issues. In addition, Professor Gillborn talks eloquently about the challenges and resistance he has faced addressing race issues in school settings and beyond. Furthermore, he points out the intersection between race, class, and gender and explains how these forms of oppression are linked. Finally, Professor Gillborn challenges the color-blindness discourse and refutes the idea that we are living in a post-racial era.

The Dialogue

ORELUS: *You are among the distinguished scholars who are profoundly vested in critical race theory. Please, would you share with me what has inspired you to devote your professional life to exploring racial issues?*

GILLBORN: It has been a lifelong process. I can't point to any single experience or epiphany that opened my eyes; it was a growing realization of the amount of injustice in education. My starting point was my own experiences of injustice as a working-class boy attending a primary [elementary] school where there was a mix of kids, including some from middle-class backgrounds. That gave me an inside track on how labeling and low teacher expectations work in relation to class. It started when I was maybe seven or eight years old. I realized that teachers often looked shocked when I spoke—it was my working-class accent. My parents always made sure I was in full school uniform, and so my accent contradicted the image that the teachers had started to form based on my appearance. I could literally see their expressions change as their expectations *sank*. That hit me very powerfully.

As I moved through primary school, I started to work out what it was that teachers wanted from me. Some could be won over with a joke (I could remember comic routines from TV); others were impressed if I fed them back parts of the previous lesson (I thought it was a *game;* they thought it demonstrated *learning!*). I was already operating as a kind of ethnographer, observing the classroom and developing strategies to survive. My primary school was overwhelmingly White, and it was clear that the Black kids were treated less well. They were told off more than other kids and would receive much harsher punishments. They were often removed from the class and put in separate groups—what would now be termed "special needs." At first, my White friends and I couldn't understand why some teachers seemed so angry at the Black kids; what had they *done*? But as time went on and we got older, we pretty much assimilated to the racist messages on the TV and on the street. Over time, the anger—the racism—seemed normal. We—the White kids—learned to accept the racism as just part of the routine.

When I went to a much more racially diverse secondary school (at age eleven), the racial hierarchies were stark. Although my year group was the first generation to go to an all-inclusive comprehensive school (catering to all children regardless of their prior test results), inside the school, all the classes were rigidly organized by ability. As you looked at the lines of pupils entering the assembly hall, the pattern could not have been more obvious: from top to bottom, the classes moved from all White to all Black. The *only* place where Black kids were treated as having something to offer was the sports field. It sounds brutal, simple, and stereotypical, and it was!

When I started studying sociology (at age sixteen), there wasn't very much about race in the curriculum, but the more I read about *class* inequality (which dominated the field), the more obvious it seemed to me that racism should be right up there alongside it. The more I studied sociology, the more I found myself baffled by the silence about racism. Even at university, there was only one (optional) course that seriously addressed the issue.

When I finished my degree (in the early 1980s), British research on race and education was minimal. Writers talked about "West Indian underachievement," and they had a few statistics, but they simply hypothesized about what might lie behind it. Mostly they assumed it was the fault of the Black kids, their parents, or their communities. There were studies of Black families, arguments about race and "intelligence," and lots of books about Black "self-concept," but (at that time) there were virtually no studies of what White teachers do to Black kids in school. It seemed obvious to me that we needed research on racism *inside* schools, and so that was where I focused my application for postgraduate research.

The more I came to understand about how racism works, and the more time I spent with different community and activist groups, the clearer it became that this was what I needed to focus on full time. I couldn't step away from antiracist work—although lots of (White) people around me advised me to focus on something less political.

Orelus: *To what extent would you say that your scholarly work has contributed to our understanding of the racial issues that people, particularly people of color, have faced in Great Britain and beyond?*

Gillborn: I am determined that my work should not just sit on bookshelves and gather dust. It doesn't matter how many awards certain academics win; if their work does not add to the struggle against inequity in the real world, then, as far as I am concerned, their careers have not been successful. Consequently, I try to be what is sometimes called a "public intellectual"; that means I try to get my findings into the public realm. In addition to the usual academic things (like teaching and writing), I speak at community and activist meetings, I address policy makers and advisers, and I try to use the news media (including TV, radio, and newspapers). At all times, I try to combat the stereotypes that dominate general discussions of race and education.

As for whether I have been successful, you would have to ask other people. I know that I have influenced debate on some occasions. I am told by people who work behind the scenes in policy that I *have* had an impact, but it can't have been very big in view of the level of racism that saturates the British education system.

I know that some *individuals* have benefited a great deal (in lots of different ways), because people share those things with me. For example, teachers often tell me that my work has challenged their views and led to some life-changing decisions about what they wanted to do. People working in community groups and in activist roles tell me that they are often able to use my work in positive ways to validate and support the kinds of changes they are working toward. That is one of the things that keep me going—when people say that my work has affected their lives in positive ways.

Orelus: *In my conversations with other critical race theorists involved in this book, I have asked them to what degree they think critical race theory, starting with*

Derrick Bell in legal studies and Gloria Ladson-Billings in education, has contributed to the fight against institutional racism and White supremacy. How would you answer this question?

GILLBORN: In the UK, the fight against institutional racism has been advanced by communities of color, especially the Black (African Caribbean) community. This has involved prominent Black intellectuals (such as Stuart Hall, Sivanandan, and Gus John) and community figures. The single biggest contribution in recent times was the campaign for justice led by Doreen and Neville Lawrence, Black parents who fought for years to get justice for their teenage son who had been murdered by a gang of White racists.

Although Stephen Lawrence's killers have never been convicted, the case led to far-reaching reforms of British race equality laws, which, though flawed, have offered important new opportunities for antiracist action right across the public services (including education, the criminal justice system, and health service).[1]

Critical race theory (CRT) has only arrived in the UK quite recently, from around 2005 onward. In fact, CRT is growing rapidly over here. In just a few years, it has moved from something that was barely mentioned to quite a vibrant and challenging movement. Academically, CRT offers a major advance on race equality in education. It doesn't offer any easy answers, of course, but it provides a perceptive and highly sophisticated lens to help people move beyond the tired assumptions that had come to dominate the field in the UK.

I have found that the most receptive audience is people of color, including university students and community activists. Some activists had knowledge of CRT long before it entered the British academy, but even those who haven't read Bell, Crenshaw, Delgado, and others, when they hear about CRT, they often make direct and dynamic links with their own experiences and struggles. And that is really exciting—when you are involved in discussions between Black teachers and activists, applying CRT directly and strategizing. That is when the real promise of CRT starts to take shape.

ORELUS: *Race greatly influences our life. However, many people, particularly some White people, are reluctant to talk about it. How do you explain that?*

GILLBORN: White people refuse to engage with race-sensitive analyses for many reasons. The most obvious reason why White people refuse to see race is that it is in their *interests* to do so! White people gain from their Whiteness in countless ways. Of course, not all White people are *equally* privileged, but they do all gain to some extent. This is a point that most White people refuse to acknowledge.

Ricky Lee Allen has produced a wonderful article that reflects on how the argument "What about poor Whites?" makes a series of racist assumptions and operates to silence race-critical research.[2] Also, most White folk are oblivious to their racial advantage. The White supremacy that CRT identifies (in the everyday routine of business as usual) simply doesn't look like anything special to White people: they have experienced this all their lives and so they don't see it unless they undergo some sort of antiracist education. Someone once said that asking a White person to talk about White supremacy is like asking a fish to describe water; they have never known anything else and it is everywhere, so they are oblivious to it.

However, once White people begin to penetrate the façade of racism as business as usual, then life gets very uncomfortable for them. It is much *easier* for them to revert to denying the significance of racism. I use Derrick Bell's "Rules of Racial Standing" with my students, and the effect is very dramatic.[3] Often it takes White people a long time to gradually accept the truth: those that *do* understand have to constantly strive to be effective antiracists despite (or even because of) their privilege.

Bell argues that White antiracists will not be so easy for the system to ignore (because their views can't simply be written off as "special pleading"), but that puts an onus on White antiracists to constantly check themselves; are they giving due credit to people of color in their work? Are they working for race equality or their own career? The two are not always the same. This partly explains why so many White academics want to emphasize a class-based analysis: they *see* class in a way that they don't really see racism. Also, a class-based analysis is much more *comfortable* for White academics because they can assert some sort of direct link to the struggle—a strategy they don't have in terms of race.

ORELUS: *As you know, people are shaped by various forms of identities. How would you link racial identity to other types of identities? And why do you think it is important to establish such a link?*

GILLBORN: Serious work on *intersectionality* is one of the most important tasks facing critical race theorists. CRT has produced a very sophisticated set of tools for analyzing racism, but we still need to do more to understand how racism works in and through a relationship to other factors, such as class, gender, sexuality, and disability. I have written about the challenge with my colleague Deborah Youdell,[4] and we made the point that simply using the word "intersectional" is not enough: we have to do some serious work identifying (from concrete cases in the real world) how these different forms of inequity work with, through, and sometimes against each other. It's a long-term task—there aren't any easy answers, but it is necessary. However, I would sound two notes of caution.

First, we need to keep grounded and not get lost in a kind of extreme postmodernism where we imagine that we can be anything we wish simply by claiming a certain identity. In the real world, identity can be fluid and complex and unpredictable—but it can also get very simple and very fixed when power holders are in a position to assert their definition of your identity. For example, Jean Charles de Menezes was a Brazilian electrician living and working in London when, in 2005, he was shot dead by police and army officers.[5] Most Brazilian people I have spoken to describe Menezes as White, but in the eyes of the police and army he was a person of color who looked suspicious. *Their* definition defined him as a potential terrorist threat, and *their* definition led to him being shot dead with no warning.

Second, we must keep our nerve in placing racism at the heart of our analysis. I don't see feminists having to justify how they define themselves and their work, but every time I attend a CRT conference or seminar, there is someone (almost always a White person) challenging the fact that we start with a concern to identify and challenge racism. Kimberlé Crenshaw has written about similar attacks, right from the start of CRT; indeed, the very term "critical race theory" was chosen as part of a deliberate refusal of the accusation that a focus on racism is essentialist and simplistic.[6] We have to retain that core focus, or else there is a danger that a critical engagement with intersectionality could transform into a polite conversation about lots of other things where racism slips from the agenda (again).

Orelus: *What are some of the challenges you have faced in your classes and other settings talking about racial issues? How did you deal with these challenges, and what lessons have you learned from this experience that may have better informed and illuminated your professional and personal life?*

Gillborn: I have written about this a little in the appendix to my last book.[7] Several Black friends told me that I had to include a discussion of my own Whiteness and how it affects my work as an antiracist, because readers who don't know me would want this as background to the analysis. People are right to be suspicious of White antiracists—it's absolutely legitimate for them to want this kind of information: Does the author understand the position they are in? What does he think and do about it? However, I am also aware of the danger of White antiracists claiming some sort of special position on the basis of their Whiteness. So I made it an appendix so that it is there for readers who are interested, but it is not essential to the analysis in the rest of the book. In view of what I said earlier about the rules of racial standing, obviously my Whiteness is something that raises questions about my ability to be a good critical race theorist.

I have to make a conscious decision to keep questioning myself and listening to Black colleagues. I am very fortunate that I have some close colleagues (both at home and in other parts of the world) whose advice and insights keep me grounded and moving forward.

In fact, my overwhelming experience as a White critical race theorist has been the generosity of people of color; whether in activist movements, community groups, or the academy, most people of color listen to what I have to say and recognize a seriousness of intent and some validity in the work. I have rarely encountered any game playing from people of color when it comes to antiracism, though of course it does sometimes happen (just as Bell speaks about those who enjoy special status by criticizing other minoritized people).

Mostly I make my arguments on the basis of data (from statistics to ethnography), and data is stronger than my individual voice. However, just as CRT tells us to take seriously the experiential knowledge of people of color, so too it suggests a role for White theorists as offering an insight into the White racist imagination. I sometimes find myself using my Whiteness when I am addressing White audiences; I know what they are thinking when they try to shift the conversation from racism, so I can preempt that, and sometimes I can simply name it. A White person calling out Whites on racism can be very useful strategically.

ORELUS: *Language can be an oppressive tool depending on how it's used. In your view, in what way might people's use of language lead to the perpetuation of racial stereotypes about people, particularly people of color?*

GILLBORN: Race is entirely a socially constructed category, and so language is a vital part of the systems that create, sustain, and legitimate racial inequity. I don't have any earth-shatteringly original observations on this, but clearly it is vital that we always interrogate the *words* that people use and the *assumptions* that lie behind them. There are no hard-and-fast answers.

One of the key strategies of the Right has been to co-opt the language of the Left. For example, one of the most influential conservative think tanks in Britain is called the *Centre for Social Justice*. Anyone can claim a concern with justice or equal opportunity—what matters is what is said, the assumptions underlying the statements, and their likely impacts in the real world. So, if someone says they are in favor of equal opportunity, I want to know what that means, because they could be arguing for affirmative action, or they could be arguing for color-blind merit standards at all costs.

The word "culture" is especially slippery. The term can be used in very progressive ways (to identify distinctive and complex identities and histories), but it is frequently used as a kind of code word for regressive, even racist, perspectives. For example, in the UK, if a media commentator asks an education researcher about cultural differences, they are really asking about race differences; but by using the word "culture," there is an inbuilt assumption that any inequities must arise from differences within the minoritized groups themselves. A culturalist analysis often lapses into a deficit analysis, and racism disappears from sight.

Orelus: *Some scholars, particularly orthodox Marxists, have privileged class issues over racial issues, arguing that inequality stemming from capitalism affects both Blacks and Whites. Where do you stand on this issue?*

Gillborn: Let me state one thing very clearly: Social class inequality is immensely important. However, social class inequality is not the only form of inequality, and neither is it always the most significant. In the UK (as in the U.S.), some of the harshest critics of CRT have been people who are wedded to a pretty narrow and determinist version of a class analysis. This is not surprising; CRT started as a critique of the class-dominated vision of critical legal studies (CLS), and class theorists have a lot invested in their perspective. As I have already noted, a proper critical approach to the intersectional analysis of race and class is a vital project. However, there are certain things that need to be understood by those critics (who are mostly White people, by the way) who insist on the primacy of class and class-based analyses.

First, race inequality is neither secondary nor peripheral. As Charles Mills has argued, systematic racial exploitation predates capitalism and, indeed, provided the means for the industrial revolution.[8] The assertion that race inequality is simply a superficial form of "divide and rule" strategy, meant to divert people from their "real" shared interests as class-identified subjects, is both patronizing and racist. It's a view that elevates the concerns of White people and once again places the experiences of people of color on the margins.

Second, CRT does not, and never has, viewed all White people as *equally* privileged (see question 4 above). As Dave Stovall has argued, this assertion is a gross oversimplification and serves the interests of those people who continually peddle the same inaccurate and caricatured image of CRT.[9] Your question posits the idea that "inequality stemming from capitalism affects both Blacks and Whites"; I agree, class inequity *does* affect both White and minoritized people, but it does not affect them in *identical* ways.

This might sound like an obvious point, but I keep meeting White people (academics, politicians, media reporters, students) who simply can't, or won't, understand the point. They seem to believe that if class is important, it must be equally important for all—again, an assumption that is easy for White folk to make because it puts their experiences at center stage. But the evidence does not support their view; if we compare the attainments of White and Black boys who do and don't qualify for free school meals (an indicator of poverty), then the statistics show that *the outcomes for Black kids are more alike on the basis of their race inequity than in relation to their economic position.*[10]

Class is not equally important for all people—for some minoritized kids, the racism that saturates the system is the biggest obstacle they face, regardless of social class. Outside of the education system, you see the same things in operation; whether it's stop-and-search, the chances of being imprisoned for the same offense, or the chances of having your DNA stored in the national database—race inequity is frequently greater than the differences associated with class.

Orelus: *There have been a lot of debates about the so-called post-racial era, specifically in the U.S. context soon after Obama got elected as president. Do you believe we will ever be living in a post-racial era?*

Gillborn: I remember being at the annual AERA meeting a few years ago, and someone asked Zeus Leonardo whether we were in a post-racial state; he said, "I will talk about a post-*race* world when we have a post-*racism* world." Well, we are certainly not post-racism. A quick glance at official statistics (on education, unemployment, the criminal justice system, etc.) demonstrates that systemic racist inequities still characterize society. Whether these inequalities will *ever* disappear completely is a moot point. I don't know any serious antiracist who imagines that racism will be eradicated in their lifetime. Some think it will take a century or more; others don't think it will ever happen. But regardless of when or if they think we will ever achieve a nonracist world, they remain committed to doing everything in their power to work against racism in the here and now. In that sense, it is completely irrelevant whether we believe that racism is permanent or not.

Derrick Bell has famously said that he thinks racism is permanent, and a lot of people (especially, but not only, *White* people) have misinterpreted that to mean that CRT is somehow defeatist or pessimistic. Obviously such people have not read much if any CRT, because I don't know of any other perspective that makes activist involvement such a central pillar of its approach to scholarship. Bell, of course, has written a great deal about this issue and has demonstrated—through his actions as well as his words—his readiness to put political struggle ahead of his own safety and security.

The argument about Obama's election as a symbol of a post-racial society has many layers. On one hand, Obama's victory was incredible and thrilling. But it is a testament to the man and his political machinery; it is not evidence that racism has gone away. Please don't forget that in the South, Obama actually polled *fewer* votes than the last two Democratic candidates—John Kerry and Al Gore—and they lost their elections.

The United States, like Britain, remains a deeply divided country, and race continues to be a fault line that runs through the nation. For many commentators, the argument about post-race is a convenient repackaging of the old color-blind discourse. Except that now the argument runs, "Hey, you've got a Black president! How can you possibly hang on to the idea that racism is a problem these days?"

Orelus: *Given the historical significance of Obama's presidency, in what way and to what degree do think his presidency can set the tone for better race relations here in the U.S. and abroad?*

GILLBORN: Obama's election was certainly an important shift in the U.S. political paradigm. Obama's election could be the start of something very significant—and it is a wonderful achievement—but it is not an end in itself. Britain elected its first woman prime minister (Margaret Thatcher) in 1979, but the nation remains as deeply patriarchal and sexist as ever.

When Obama became president, there were celebrations all over Britain, and my sense was that the youth were especially energized—and not only Black youth. There was a real sense of a moral breakthrough, that the good guy *can* win and might just make the *world* a better place! But we have to remember that race/racism is infinitely complex and flexible. Just after Obama's victory, the British media featured lots of White commentators who were keen to argue that Obama is not Black. Regardless of how he chooses to identify himself, they asserted their own views on the matter.

Christopher Hitchens, a well-known journalist/commentator, appeared on BBC TV's flagship news program and said, "The great thing about Obama is that he's *not* Black; that he's as White as he's Black."[11] This is very revealing: first, it shows that White people remain convinced that *they* have the authority to decide what race a person *really* is. It also shows that people are still hanging on to a belief in race as something technical, encoded in bloodlines and genes. It is clear that to a great many people Obama is somehow *more* acceptable for being *less* Black.

A psychological study was published recently that used digitally altered photos to explore the relationship between how voters view biracial/mixed-race candidates (including Barack Obama). They found that people tend to think of politicians they dislike as having darker skin tones, and yet they lightened those with whom they agreed. Even people who identify themselves as Obama supporters tend to choose artificially lightened pictures of him as the true representation.[12] There's a long way to go.

ORELUS: *What do you imagine the world would be like if one's race were not an issue? What do you imagine it would be like living in such a world?*

GILLBORN: I can imagine it quite easily—a place where skin tone is meaningless—but I don't expect to ever live to see it. Because racism is not only about people's perceptions; it is also about deep-rooted structures of oppression that are not going to change easily. My friend and colleague Dr. Nicola Rollock captured it well when she was speaking at a conference in France and was asked about how much better things are getting. She said, "We might fool ourselves into thinking we have reached an equality ideal, that the color of your skin doesn't matter or is beginning to matter less. But the question I would put to you is this: Where in this world can I live and my children live as persons of color where we won't experience disadvantage in education, in employment, in outcomes across *all* the key areas of social policy?"

Orelus: *Let's briefly go back to history. Slavery, colonization, and racism are linked. How do you see this link?*

Gillborn: You would need an entire book-length response to begin to answer this properly. Slavery, colonialism, and racism are deeply intertwined, historically and psychologically. Of course, that's not something that most White folk acknowledge. They imagine that because slavery has been abolished, it is no longer an issue. But the historic structures of slavery are everywhere, and the legacy lives on in the attitudes of White people who simply expect to be able to do and say pretty much whatever they please (under the banner of freedom of speech).[13]

The constant complaints about political correctness, for example, are usually caused by White people being told they have to change their behavior. It is not something they are used to hearing, and they don't like it. Obviously I am not talking about every single White person, but it is remarkable how quickly such attitudes emerge when the freedoms of Whites are challenged.

Orelus: *A similar question would be, do you think capitalism has given birth to slavery? Or do you think that racism is the root cause of the enslavement of Black people?*

Gillborn: This is another topic where a book-length response would be appropriate. In one sense, however, there is a simple answer: slavery predates capitalism. The industrial revolution and capitalism were built on the wealth and trade produced by the transatlantic slave trade. It is important to break out of the either-or type of thinking that often happens in academic debate about race and class.

The idea that race or class is *always* the most important issue, in *every* situation, both historically and contemporarily, is just not sustainable. We know that class and race oppression (and sexism, and ableism, and heteronormativity) tend to work in different ways in different contexts. I'm saddened by the amount of time that some academics spend arguing about the ultimate dominance of their chosen issue (usually class) rather than getting on with the real work of interrogating how different oppressions work with and through each other, as a means of resisting them. I have to say that I find the assertion by some class theorists that social class is supreme (while racism is dismissed as false consciousness and a diversionary tactic of capital) to be superficial, patronizing, and racist. It is no coincidence that this seems to be the preferred view of *White* academics. It puts *their* issue and *their* voice center stage and marginalizes other concerns.

Orelus: *Like in the U.S., racism is pervasive in the UK. So how would you compare these two countries in terms of how people of color, especially Black people, are treated?*

GILLBORN: There are a lot of similarities between race exploitation in the U.S. and the UK. A few are the following:

- The scale of race inequity across society.
- The fact that policy rhetoric (around equal opportunities) far outweighs real action for race equity.
- That the interests of the White elite always come first in policy, but are assumed as the normal, center ground of common sense.
- That "model minorities" and poor Whites are used as a blocking discourse to silence race equality moves. On both sides of the Atlantic, policy makers and commentators claim to worry about poor Whites and hold up high-achieving minorities as evidence that racism has disappeared, while their actions continue to demonize the poor and ignore the daily experiences of racism and alienation that are experienced by people of color regardless of their economic situation and educational achievements.
- That in the academy, CRT constantly has to fight for legitimacy. In addition to the conservative attack that we are revolutionaries bent on destroying standards, we also have to face postmodernists asserting that our theories are essentialist and simple, plus the incessant cry from some Marxists that we have simply misunderstood the world, and it is all about class.

There are also some important differences between the U.S. and the UK. One of the most important is that in the U.S., there is at least some public space for legitimate discussion of race issues (unless you are watching Fox News). Of course, in the U.S., race inequity is frequently marginalized, misrepresented, or simply ignored, but on the whole you don't have to justify focusing on race as a key issue. In the UK, the public discourse around race is a lot more subdued on a superficial level, and behind the façade, it is quite difficult to get racism taken seriously.

In the UK, the dominant trope is about class. With some very rare and hard-won exceptions, racism rarely makes the headlines in the UK. Race issues tend to be seen as specialized and tangential to most ordinary people. Over the last few years, however, the two nations are coming closer together on this front; the cry of political correctness is mobilized against antiracism on both sides of the Atlantic, and White folk are getting increasingly strident in their attacks on minority issues and minoritized people.

ORELUS: *Do you believe that someday a Black man will be elected to the highest elected office in the UK? If so, what would make you believe so?*

GILLBORN: Interestingly, there was a political argument about this shortly after Barack Obama's presidential victory. The most prominent Black man in British politics is Trevor Phillips, who currently runs the Equalities and Human

Rights Commission (EHRC), which has the official role of helping to police equalities legislation (e.g., around race, age, sexuality, gender, and disability).

Phillips said that he didn't think that "even somebody as brilliant as him [Obama] would have been able to break through the institutional stranglehold that there is on power. . . . The parties and unions and think tanks are all very happy to sign up to the general idea of advancing the cause of minorities but in practice they would like somebody else to do the business."[14] Phillips' comments were attacked by people on the political Right and Left. The UK generally maintains this myth that Britain is a tolerant place and imagines that racism is very rare over here—but much more common in the States.

So people at both ends of the political spectrum were stung by a prominent Black man saying that, in effect, the system over here is even more racist than the U.S. Personally, I *can* imagine a Black person becoming prime minister, but, as a critical race theorist, I imagine it would happen under circumstances where there was a perceived benefit to elite White interests, and I doubt very much that having a minoritized person at the top would have a significant impact on the daily realities of racist inequity across society.

Notes

1. Lawrence, D. (2006). *And still I rise: Seeking justice for Stephen.* London: Faber & Faber; and Gillborn, D. (2008). *Racism and education: coincidence or conspiracy?* London: Routledge, especially chapter 6.
2. Allen, R. L. (2009). What about poor White people? In W. Ayers, T. Quinn, & D. Stovall (Eds.), *Handbook of social justice in education* (pp. 209–220). New York, NY: Routledge.
3. Bell, D. (1992). *Faces at the bottom of the well: The permanence of racism.* Chapter 6. New York: Basic.
4. Gillborn, D., & Youdell, D. (2009). Critical perspectives on race and schooling. In J. A. Banks (Ed.), *The Routledge international companion to multicultural education* (pp. 173–185). New York: Routledge.
5. See chapter 2 of Gillborn, D. (2008). *Racism and education: Coincidence or conspiracy?* London: Routledge.
6. See Crenshaw, K. W. (2002). The first decade. *UCLA Law Review, 49,* 1343–1372, esp. 1357.
7. Gillborn, D. (2008). *Racism and education: Coincidence or conspiracy?* London: Routledge, pp. 197–203.
8. Mills, C. W. (1997). *The racial contract.* London: Cornell University Press; Mills, C. W. (2003). *From class to race: Essays in White Marxism and Black radicalism.* New York: Rowman & Littlefield.
9. Stovall, D. (2006). Forging community in race and class: Critical race theory and the quest for social justice in education. *Race Ethnicity & Education, 9*(3), 243–259.

10. In relation to the proportion of boys achieving the "benchmark" of five or more higher grade passes when they leave compulsory schooling, there is a difference of 11.7 percentage points between Black Caribbean boys who do and do not receive free school meals (27.1% and 38.8%, respectively). But the difference between Black and White boys who do not receive free school meals is 17.2 percentage points (38.8% and 56%, respectively). Source: Department for Education & Skills (DfES). (2006). *National curriculum assessment, GCSE and equivalent attainment and post-16 attainment by pupil characteristics in England, 2005/06*. SFR 46/2006. London: DfES, table 32.

11. You can see video of this at http://www.huffingtonpost.com/huff-tv/arianna-on-bbc-newsnight_b_141651.html (accessed December 2, 2009).

12. Caruso, E. M., Mead, N. L., & Balcetis, E. (2009). Political partisanship influences perception of biracial candidates' skin tone. *Proceedings of the National Academy of Sciences of the United States of America, 106*(48), 20168–20173.

13. I've written about "freedom of speech" and how it operates in favor of White interests here: Gillborn, D. (2009). Risk-free racism: Whiteness and so-called "free speech," *Wake Forest Law Review, 44*(2), 535–555.

14. BBC News Online. (2008). Bias "would hamper British Obama." http://news.bbc.co.uk/1/hi/uk_politics/7717149.stm (accessed December 23, 2009).

CHAPTER 3

Unmasking White Supremacy and Racism

A CONVERSATION WITH ZEUS LEONARDO

In this dialogue, Zeus Leonardo brings to the forefront what escapes many people, including intellectuals: the inextricable link between multiple forms of oppression. To this end, Professor Leonardo draws on the moving story of W. E. B. Du Bois' personal and professional journey to slowly and critically build his arguments about race and class oppressions in education. Using critical race theory (CRT) as his primary conceptual framework, Professor Leonardo challenges the color-blind discourse and unravels the pervasive nature of institutional racism and its negative impact on racial minorities, including professors of color. While recognizing the serious racial challenges that students and professors of color have faced in academia and beyond, he encourages us to be defiant in order to avoid being demoralized by institutional racism rooted in slavery and the continuing legacy of colonization. Professor Leonardo rejects the tendency of many orthodox Marxists to privilege class issues over race issues, arguing that all forms of oppression are connected. He therefore argues for a *race-class* analysis to signal the way that race and class disparities reinforce each other. Likewise, he questions the naive idea or propaganda that we are living in a post-racial era, taken in its most literal sense, and contends that critical race understanding in education is crucial in circumstances where racism continues to limit the lives of intellectuals of color. He wrestles away the post-race argument from conservatives and introduces the concept of *race ambivalence.*

The Dialogue

ORELUS: *To what extent do you think race has affected the learning of students of color as well as the performance of professors of color who teach and do research in predominantly White institutions?*

LEONARDO: On a recent trip to Harvard University, I couldn't help but remember that W. E. B. Du Bois once walked the halls and paths of that elite setting. As I ascended to street level from Harvard Square's Red Line train depot, heard the bells of the First Church of Cambridge, and continued past Radcliffe College, Du Bois' avatar haunted my steps on the well-worn sidewalks on the outskirts of campus. As I ventured into the campus and peered into buildings erected by the Massachusetts Bay Company in the middle of the 1700s, I wondered how it felt for Du Bois to navigate what is generally acknowledged as one of the world's most exclusive institutions. Du Bois wrote about his educational experience as the first Black doctoral candidate eventually to receive a degree from Harvard.[1] One senses that he enjoyed his experience without excess resentment concerning the racism that he was well aware of. This excess resentment would have destroyed his spirit as I have witnessed many faculty of color today become consumed by it.

Du Bois clearly took pleasure in being among the brilliant thinkers of his time, feeling a sense of his own entitlement with having earned a spot on the Ivy's roster, sharing time and space with the likes of James and Santayana. He knew he was a Black man in a White place, a tenuous position at best, but he was among his intellectual peers, even the elite, and this came with some satisfaction.

I bring up this narrative because race is a limit situation that scholars of color face in the academy, but it should not be more of a limiting experience than it has to be. There is a difference between engaging a battle and becoming embattled. The academy is so racial and precisely racializing that many scholars of color feel under siege and constantly under the White gaze. Some of us react with a heightened sense of embattlement, which affects our sense of equilibrium. Some even begin to think that *they* are the problem, and Du Bois' question—"How does it feel to be a problem?"—becomes their mantra. They may assume qualities they have always disliked in other people: suspiciousness, negativity, even pessimism.

Becoming embattled is a downward spiral as it begins to gnaw away at our ability to maintain good relationships with colleagues. It begins to affect our emotional and mental well-being. This is not our fault and even less our doing. But it reminds us that we must find a collective way to deal with the alienation that scholars of color experience in the academy like an illness that threatens personal and intellectual development.

Du Bois' example confirms the reality that in the academy, scholars of color are always targets insofar as they have to earn their legitimacy over and beyond proving their intellectual mettle, for which there is no medal. They have to earn their right to be there. True, every person has to show his or her merit in order to enter the academy's competitive climate. My point is that, for people of color, *being there* is always tenuous and comes with racial considerations.

For most scholars of color, this comes with intense existential anxiety, not to mention self-doubt. This is not evidence about their insecurity but about the institutional predicament of being thrown into a racist project called the academy. It actually testifies to their strength in surviving a process that was not meant for them, a condition that professes to welcome, while merely tolerating, their presence. It means that they are always marked by their identity, whereas White scholars are assumed to pursue intellectual, even universal, matters. For scholars of color, studying Du Bois suggests that we are interested in our lives, advocating for our histories, and indulging ourselves in what we already know. For White scholars, studying European civilization or thought is just a matter of intellectual interest. It does not occur to them that they are also studying themselves.

So this is the dilemma of being a scholar of color in the academy, wherein the question of one's legitimacy is always in play. For even the most grounded scholars, it is crazy making, and the frustration alone may get the best of them. Calling it "becoming jaded" is an understatement as they feel the intense racialization that weighs on them: from the subtle offenses that Solorzano[2] calls "racial microaggressions" to the more explicit attacks, such as the UC–San Diego incidents involving the Compton Cookouts, where White students mocked Black people by dressing up as caricatures of them (much like minstrelsy) and Arizona's attacks on ethnic studies and allied fields. In these public spaces, upwardly mobile people of color feel surrounded by Whites like never before and negotiate Whiteness daily. This is always true, no matter the industry, as people of color who ascend the leadership structure find themselves around more Whites. From the corporate boardroom to the classroom, educated people of color will find themselves reflected less in their surroundings, occasionally becoming the only minority at the table. Calling it tokenism also misses the mark, for they have usually earned their rightful place.

People of color begin to doubt that they belong in such a place for two reasons. I have known perfectly well-adjusted scholars of color experience disequilibrium so acutely that they no longer feel they can go on. Mentoring in the academy is of utmost importance, but senior scholars of color, already overextended, feel the double burden of intellectual production and a commitment to the community. Junior scholars also feel the pinch as they advise student groups of color at either the undergraduate or graduate level.

The level of mental and emotional isolation gets the better of some of the best. One, institutionally they receive the subtle and sometimes overt message that their study is important to them but not to the academy in general. It is advocacy work, which it may in fact be. But it is denigrated for that very reason because it is not objective, scientific, or detached. It is not accorded universal status but only a particular, narrow, and perspectivist standing. I do not want to trivialize the problem of advocacy work without scholarly engagement; obviously the work has to embody academic richness. That said, I have witnessed some of the most elegant interventions by scholars of color dismissed by White professors as wanting seriousness. Two, because of this perceived intellectual guerrilla warfare in the academy, scholars of color fail to develop further the coping mechanisms that got them there in the first place. The academy's heightened racial politics, with which there is sometimes no apt comparison, begins to break them down emotionally, and resilience becomes even more important. In some respects, these are real distractions from the otherwise rich experience that may be gained from the academy, the wealth of knowledge that may be exchanged, and the networks that may be cultivated with others. Despite these distractions, Du Bois' tale tells us that although the academy may at times be completely inhospitable to scholars of color, it offers a liberal experience that minorities rarely find elsewhere.

Being an academic means that we are around our intellectual peers, similarly educated colleagues, and a shared disciplinary discourse. As much as we would like to romanticize our communities, it is also a fact of the matter that we no longer fit into their general populations and feel painfully our difference from our families and friends who may not share our educational experience. We cannot return there either, at least not without a great sense of nostalgia. We are that group of intellectuals that Said calls "exiles."[3] Like Freire and Faundez,[4] Said considers the exilic condition a productive (not a synonym for positive) and tensioned experience that is full of knowledge. Never feeling quite entitled to be at home in the academy and having left their communities, exiles of color do not belong in either space.

Too much of color for the academy and too educated for their communities, scholars of color experience a twoness that they struggle to resolve. They understand the offerings of the academy and therefore share in its mission. They bring with them their lived histories and want only to be allowed to be both an academic and a person of color. The academy perceives them as a qualified former as it reduces them to the latter. The intellectual of color is in exile, somewhat chosen, to some measure imposed.

ORELUS: *Many professors of color, including myself, have expressed great concerns about the way they have been treated at some institutions because of their racial/*

ethnic/linguistic backgrounds and countries of origin. What has been your experience as a professor of color?

LEONARDO: A professor of color is a marked intellectual. Much of the time, race and diversity are considered our domain of interest even if that is not actually the case. Not all faculty of color study or are interested in these lines of inquiry. But the day we walk into the halls, it is assumed that race is our preoccupation, or worse an obsession. For some scholars of color, it is rather awkward as they are asked to profess their expertise on a topic they may experientially know something about, which does not suggest that they have a command of the intellectual area. This rarely happens to White scholars.

The burden is sometimes so great that scholars of color eventually turn to race studies as a way to understand that lived, problematic experience of which they want to make sense. In other words, they become further racialized, the prophecy is fulfilled, and they wind up as race scholars. On the other hand, scholars of color may enter the academy precisely to conduct research on race but fail to find mentors who support this endeavor, being that the academy is White dominated, which does not mean that White scholars do not produce worthwhile studies of race. But an ingredient of experience is now missing, the pursuit becomes purely intellectual, and the lived dimensions of their academic existence become abstract.

So scholars of color spend years being derailed from their original interest. This is not time lost, as many of them may do excellent work, thrive, and go on to have productive careers in non-race-related intellectual pursuits. Be that as it may, they feel a certain void, and a faint voice calls them. They return to race, as it were. This happened to Charles Mills, once trained as an analytical Marxist, who then used those skills to construct one of the most elegant race theories the academic scene has witnessed in the last twenty years.[5] This happened to Eduardo Bonilla-Silva (personal communication), whose materialist theory of race and racism is an outcome of his sociological training and a critical reflection over its limitations. This happened to me as well. Trained as a critical theorist in the midst of the furious debates between materialist and discursive analyses in the 1990s, I have been *creolized* to think of race through multiple theoretical lenses.[6]

As a professor of color in the academy, I sit in that tensioned space of having a command of the Eurocentric field of critical theory and a race-oriented analysis. I know how to think on both sides of the aisle, which is perhaps evidence of what Du Bois once called "double consciousness."[7] Indeed, it is a peculiar experience of twoness, made rich by the duality of having a foot in both places, but also a burden of having to be authentic in two warring subjectivities. It can be a cruel condition because one risks being inauthentic in both communities: too engaged with Whiteness to be authentic to intellectuals of color on one hand, and too minoritized for White scholars on the other.

I am marked on both sides of the debate because I refuse to be cordoned off in a corner by virtue of the fact that I am a scholar of color and therefore am soiling critical theory with minority perspectives on the effects of racism. On the other hand, I have found that critical theory has much to offer race analysis, and I have labored to bring its relevant insights into antiracist and multicultural education. To the extent that critical theory is White dominated, I have tried to color it for race analysis, building what I call an *analytics of color*. It has been a rich experience, but not one that is obvious to many intellectuals who do not enter the critical project of appropriation. Like Essed and Goldberg,[8] I have found solace in making both race and critical theory strange, racializing the second and making critical the first.

ORELUS: *How do you see race being connected to education? What are some other factors you would connect race with? And how do you see them being connected?*

LEONARDO: As Omi and Winant[9] never tire of reminding us, race is never not in play, particularly in the U.S. It has become the main trope or guiding metaphor in our society. Charles Mills calls it the main "contract" that we enter into.[10] It explains our preferences for certain movies on one hand, and building our social movements on the other. In what Bonilla-Silva[11] calls a "racialized social system," the entire social edifice is driven by race, rather than the more obvious history of enslavement and land takeover to which many color-blind pretenders reduce it. In short, race explains every facet of our livelihood.

In schooling, as critical race theorists argue, race implicates every nook and cranny of the educational enterprise. Its ostensive, public face came to us in the crescendo known as the cultural wars of the 1990s, where multiculturalists and more or less Eurocentric scholars waged a war over the national curriculum's fate. According to Buras, it appears that the multiculturalists have won and the traditionalists (not in terms only of politics, since they include liberals) have acquiesced to a form of rightist multiculturalism.[12] The war of position rages on, this time guided by what kind of multiculturalism schools should have, not whether or not they should respect racial difference.

Few self-respecting educators would be card-carrying Eurocentrists in today's climate, though that does not prevent some from going underground. Only the most rabid, and therefore ineffectual, conservatives carry on the torch for a "White man's curriculum." This does not suggest that the war has been won once and for all, but the battle switches to new terrains requiring a new politics. This also does not suggest that the otherwise multiculturalized curriculum is what the insurgent scholars of the 1970s had in mind, as they have had to make accommodations to reactionary policies. It simply means that multiculturalism has become hegemonic, confirmed by an impression that it is the new common sense. It has morally persuaded the public that diversity is good for students, from its more authentic form of social transformation to its commodified T-shirtization of heroified people of color.

This is the most sweeping racial change the schools have seen in the last twenty years, thanks largely to its founding fathers and mothers, such as James Banks, Sonia Nieto, Geneva Gay, Carl Grant, and Christine Sleeter. It is not without its critics on the Right as well as the Left.

The Right's critique is well rehearsed, but from the Left, Marxists lament multiculturalism's compatibility with postmodernism, or what Jameson calls the "cultural logic of late capitalism."[13] Although not incompatible with multiculturalism, critical race theorists push back against multiculturalism's apparent lack of militancy. This was Ladson-Billings and Tate's challenge in 1995 when their *Teachers College Record* essay sparked a new school of thought under the banner of critical race theory of education.[14] Taken historically, this is the trade-off that multiculturalism, or any racial discourse for that matter, faces when reaching the mainstream, where Whiteness waits to co-opt it and converge it with its own interests. Critical race theory currently may be the more radical voice on the matter of race and education, but the lessons of multiculturalism's struggles with Whiteness should not be lost on us. There are already telling signs, as Ladson-Billings warns, that CRT is already becoming "mainstreamed." It is not far-fetched to imagine the day when CRT's radical spirit is domesticated, much like Freirean dialogics have become synonymized with discussion-based pedagogies.

Like many other racially progressive platforms, multiculturalism works with Whiteness as a limit situation. In schools, a mostly White female teaching population would have to be convinced that Whiteness needs to be under intense scrutiny, not to mention depedestalizing it. Indeed, this has been a tough sell, and the question becomes, "Is it a White or minoritized form of multiculturalism? Likewise, is it a White CRT or an endarkened one?"

ORELUS: *What are some of the challenges you have faced teaching courses on race and multiculturalism? How have you dealt with those challenges? What have you learned from them?*

LEONARDO: As a professor of color teaching critical race perspectives, my experience has largely been specific to a history with which Americans only awkwardly know how to deal. Being a Filipino American in the U.S. academy is a peculiar experience.

On one hand, I am not African American, but on the other I am not from a visible Asian group, such as Japanese, Chinese, or Korean. Let me be clearer. I am pretty successful at tackling difficult issues concerning race and pedagogically cultivating a space where real dialogue and exchange of ideas may take place. But it is not as simple as that. Personality aside, as a scholar who teaches and researches race relations, I am located in a precise positionality that has its share of anxieties. Because I do not look Black, I am not perceived as a militant or radical Black male, despite the fact that I may share similar politico-intellectual positions with some Black scholars. For example, I may confront and write on themes such as White supremacy. But to the extent that my race becomes known (it is not always transparent in my writing), the work is not received in the same manner, and the reception of my ideas is softened by the fact that I am not a Black intellectual. Scholars whom I have met for the first time sometimes inform me that I do not write from a typical Asian voice; rather I write more from a Black or Latino perspective. Some have told me that they thought I was Black because usually "my people" are quiet about issues concerning racism.

These statements are often meant as a compliment, and I take them as such, but the upshot is that my race teachings are perceived differently because of my race. That said, we should notice a distancing move in effect here, whereby I am separated from "my people" in the same moment that I am apparently accepted as a race scholar through ideological Blackening.

I am also given credibility as someone who is brown skinned and has the presumed legitimate history with racism that puts me closer to the Black experience on the color line. In other words, commonsense race discourse does not give much weight to a Yellow narrative on racism, and my Brownness provides me with certain political credentials. The problematic assumption that certain Asian groups have achieved Whiteness leads to their suspect status as having reliable experience with racism. So for me it becomes a dual process. Because I am not Black, I am taken seriously as having something objective to say about racism, but because I am Brown I carry some legitimacy in saying those things. It seems my positionality provides a particular entry into race discourse that regulates what I have to say and write.

This dynamic becomes most obvious when I teach courses on race. Although it may seem like a good mix, this combination of not-Black and therefore more objective and "Brown enough" and therefore racially legitimate produces racial regulation that disciplines everyone involved insofar as it creates multiple interpellations.

The situation is more like a perfect storm. It means that students respond with learned expectations of the boundaries that we may negotiate when it concerns race. Looming in the background of it all is the ghost of Whiteness that disciplines Asians as not-White and not-Black at the very same time. It is tempting to trace the source of the problem as having to do with being not-Black within minority discourses (i.e., proximity to Blackness is what counts), but as Ladson-Billings points out, the problem is precisely a group's proximity to Whiteness within specific historical conditions without necessarily gaining entry into the White house.[15] If this is correct, then passing as White is a broader phenomenon than we recognize, and every racial group has tried to pass as White at some point in order either to be accepted by White society or to protect oneself against its violence.

Without an understanding of Whiteness and its extreme gravitational pull, "minoritized groups" (Gillborn's phrase) judge one another as either suspect at best or collaborationist with Whiteness at worst. We fundamentally misunderstand and look down on one another because we are not critically *looking up* at Whiteness. As a result, Black students may perceive Asians as cozying up to Whiteness; Asians and Latinos suspect that Blacks do not treat the racism they suffer seriously enough; and Native Americans may resent even being lumped into the race discourse altogether.

This development, or what I call elsewhere "inter-minoritarian politics," is very serious. Klor de Alva, Shorris, and West have written about the Black-Brown unease,[16] Vijay Prashad documents Afro-Asian relations,[17] Lerner and West collaborated on their understanding of the Black-Jewish condition,[18] and the Los Angeles uprisings in the 1990s sparked attention to the Korean-Black conflict. One may notice, however, that these tensions seem to focus on minority group relations with Blacks in the U.S. context. This lends some credibility to the idea that the Black-White paradigm of race relations is alive and well and still structures some of the important racial dynamics of our time. The second half of the film *Color of Fear* captures this tendency when, in tackling what the participants call "inter-ethnic racism," the narratives revolve around Black/not-Black minority tensions.

Orelus: *With Obama's ascendency to the U.S. presidency, race has surfaced to a great extent in the political scene. Do you think Obama's presidency will help many Whites see people of color differently, in a positive way? Or do you think the main problem of this country will remain the problem of the color line, as Du Bois put it about a century ago?*

Leonardo: More than one hundred years after Du Bois pronounced the problem of the color line, race is definitely still an issue in the United States despite Obama's rise to leadership. In fact, one is tempted to suggest that he was elected despite his Blackness rather than because of it. In other words, he did not become president *by virtue of being Black*, but by having all the other special attributes that a great leader ought to have, which Obama had to possess over and beyond a comparable White candidate: charisma, intellect, good looks, and campaign and political skills. One should also mention that Obama raised monies comparable to any Republican in recent memory. In short, race was in play during Obama's election, not to mention many examples of racism, from the Clintons' antics, to the question of White workers' votes, to racially motivated death threats.

What interests me about Obama's rise is the tension that intellectuals cannot seem to resolve. We hear two types of arguments. One, Obama's inauguration surely signals the end of U.S. racism as we know it. If a Black person can become president, then racial disparities are explainable through differences in effort and random chance and not through structural racism. This rationalization has rightly been called color blindness and boasts an excess of racial optimism.

Two, and opposing this view, to some intellectuals Obama's victory represents the latest (not the last) chapter in White supremacy because it is predicted that Obama will neither radically change the racial landscape nor advocate for race-based initiatives. The upshot is that a Black man for president becomes another alibi for White tolerance, and we should be suspicious of White interests that converge with the Black plight. This sentiment may rightly fall under racial realism, even pessimism.

I would like to suggest that Obama's rise represents two conflicting trends in the fight for racial hegemony. On one hand, breaking through the color barrier represents racial progress, nothing more, but also nothing less. What was unimaginable, even for Obama's early supporters, has now become a reality, and pinching oneself to make sure it is real is still appropriate.

Less than fifty years after the march to Washington, many Black kids can imagine themselves as president of a leading nation. It is no longer only an abstract idea. This does not mean that the likelihood for success is on their side, but neither is it with most White kids who aspire to the presidency. It is statistically more achievable for Whites to become president, but it is still like winning the lottery. And although all eyes are on Obama, and his every move is racialized as the average White citizen waits for him to slip up in order to confirm the Blackness that his White supporters would like to forget, his inauguration is nothing short of remarkable. And yes, it represents racial progress, and Whites' excessive optimism cannot take that away from him or his supporters of color.

On the other hand, we are uneasy about the nation's direction after hundreds of years of White leadership and eight recent years of Bush, and we wonder if a Black man in the Oval Office is enough to change the legacy of racial oppression. Of course, no one credible or reasonable believes in this, but a lot of pressure falls on the first non-White president. In his image is contained the excessive hopes of people of color and racially progressive Whites. In a sense, he has one shot, perhaps two shots if he is reelected, to change our course. Already, pundits and scholars exhibit excessive pessimism about the likelihood of this happening. The bets are on.

Orelus: *Some scholars, particularly orthodox Marxists, have prioritized class issues over racial issues, arguing that inequality stemming from capitalism affects both Blacks and Whites. Where do you stand on this issue?*

LEONARDO: This is a theoretical theme that is central to my work. As mentioned, having been trained as a Marxist, I find too much utility in historical materialism to support or build a bourgeois understanding of race. But as a race scholar, I struggle against what Ricky Allen[19] calls a "White Marxism" that treats racism as a phenomenon that can be reduced to the machinations of capitalism and the internal dynamics of class warfare. Some even consider race analysis either incompatible with or deleterious to class analysis.

In fact, I consider race and class issues so central to my understanding that I have recently argued for a *race-class* analysis.[20] Like Einstein's revolution of space and time as two fabrics that cannot be separated and hence are expressed as *space-time*, race-class analysis cannot imagine ending racism without a simultaneous critique of capitalism. They are the two hands of a five-hundred-year-old clock that marks the beginning and potential end of the abjection that so many people of color suffer.

How does a scholar account for racism without critical attention to the disproportionate national proletarianization of the labor force with minorities in the United States and the exploitation of countless nations across the globe, many of which are populated by people of color? It is a bit like looking at a situation with one eye closed. Though you may still see the images in front of you, they are less clear, and one's vision is impaired.

I am arguing what in thermonuclear physics is called fusion. Briefly, in the center of stars, the temperature is very hot (in our sun alone, a yellow dwarf's interior is 10 million degrees), and the pressure is immense due to the density of hydrogen atoms in that region. The hydrogen molecules collide with such speed and force that they fuse into one molecule and emit energy as a result; this was the concept of the atomic bomb.

In our social universe, revolutionary moments heat up contradictions to such an extent that race and class fuse into race-class, and our ability to discern which one is responsible for the other becomes unreliable, perhaps even praxiologically undesirable. Race and class become one unified force, much like what physicists find among the four elementary forces of gravity, electromagnetism, the strong force, and the weak force, which begin to behave as one dynamic when high temperature is achieved.

So my task has been to theorize the ways that social environments enable intellectuals to think of race and class analyses as inextricably linked. When we think of racial oppression, its compatibility with capitalist exploitation, particularly within a U.S. context, is indisputable. When we study the globalization of capital, we notice the disproportionate burden that nations of color, from India to Indonesia, from Central America to South America, and from the Pacific to the Caribbean, bear in order to gain the patronage of first-world powers like the United States.

The argument is less about a happy middle ground, which can be intellectually disingenuous, or as I like to say to my students, a "liberal cop-out." It may seem self-evident that inequality takes many shapes that crosscut each other to produce the necessity of an intersectional perspective. It is only after long and critical engagements with race and class analysis that I have arrived at some beginnings of a synthesis.

Many race scholars in education are open to a class analysis, for it is readily apparent to them that capitalism is not exactly working for people of color. True, some fail to engage Marxism, which is not merely a position against *classism* and then valuing a denigrated working-class culture and milieu. Unlike multiculturalism, which highlights racial diversity, there is no valuing of diverse classes within Marxism, which is less about continuing a class-based system, even one that values the differences among them, and more about abolishing class distinctions altogether.

Marxism is an elegant and multifaceted systematic theory about tying together various levels of social life into (1) an overarching explanation and (2) a praxis-oriented intervention. Marxists are correct to show their frustration when class analysis is reduced to studies of differential class privileges without so much as a nod to the productive system that makes this possible, or capitalism. So an analysis of class is not a synonym or replacement for an analysis of capitalism.

That said, many scholars of color who study race and might not otherwise be inclined to turn the bourgeois cheek to Marxism, wind up resisting academic Marxism because they perceive academic Marxists (not to be equated with Marxism) as just another tool of Whiteness. At worst, they replicate in intellectual form the White chauvinism that reifies the smartness of Whiteness, their insatiable desire always to be in charge, this time in the realm of theory. Books abound that decry the introduction of identity politics (read: race analysis), in the 1960s and on, for having fragmented and splintered the Left. It does not occur to them that they romanticize a so-called unified past that functioned under Jim Crow in both practical and intellectual life. The ironies are quite obvious. Scholars of color, once open to Marxist intellectuals of color from Césaire to Fanon, from Che to Cabral, turn their backs on academic Marxism for minimizing racist structures.

Most insurgent scholars of color understand that capitalism has wreaked havoc on communities and nations of color. They may not have an intimate knowledge of Marxism, academic or otherwise, but their sensibilities and organic experiences already accept the social fact of economic exploitation. But in appreciating the awesome reach of Whiteness and racial supremacy, they are also reminded that racism seems to work both in capitalist America and communist Cuba. Centuries after the introduction of raciology, scholars of color have designed sophisticated explanations of how it works to their detriment and to the advantage of Whites.

Now that critical race theory, Whiteness studies, and other allied theories have walked onto the intellectual scene, it seems at least bad timing, if not bad faith, for Marxists to announce the declining significance of race relations and the decreasing utility of race analysis. It reminds me a bit of the criticisms laid at the doorsteps of postmodern thinkers whose critique of large-scale movements and pronouncement of fractures in identity arrived on the scene precisely when identity-based movements were gaining hold in the 1960s.[21] Now that critical race analysis is informing educational research, White academic Marxism is happy to wage war against an oppressed group, against another insurgent theory. It is at least ironic that those who suffer the brunt of economic exploitation are not given the right to name that injury based on their lived experiences.

This is enough for some critical race scholars to turn their backs on academic Marxism. Who could blame them? They are attacked from both the Right and the Left, both parties reminding them of the errors of their ways. The former informs them of their inferiority; the latter patronizes them. Critical race scholars respond by distancing themselves from Marxism and not incorporating its insights into the nature of oppression. As Ward Churchill once noted, it remains to be seen if Marxism is a friend or foe of people of color.[22] As a result, the intellectual tie is severed. I believe this is a mistake. Race scholars have much to gain from Marxism in terms of a richer analysis of race. Its systematic description of the inner workings of capitalism is still unmatched by other discourses, and Charles Mills remarks that race philosophy has yet to achieve the same systematicity.[23] In fact, my work on the abolition of Whiteness is informed by a certain Marxist dialectic brought to bear on the material structures of race.

If I am correct about the continuing utility of Marxism for the study of race, then it is a predictable symptom of race relations that race scholars' interaction with White Marxism discourages them from appropriating Marxist insights. Against what Freire (1994) once called "Marxist smugness" in *Pedagogy of Hope*,[24] abdicating Marxism to Whites surely gives Whiteness more power than it deserves. Whiteness once again limits our options for action.

ORELUS: *Let's briefly go back to history. Slavery, colonization, and racism are interconnected. How do you see this interconnection?*

LEONARDO: Slavery, colonialism, and racism are basically synonyms. Slavery may have ended, and official colonialism has seen its last kicking days fade into history, but this does not mean that new forms of enslavement and what Quijano calls "coloniality" cannot survive.[25] True, the specific structures of slavery and colonialism are no longer around, and we should celebrate this. We cannot equate today's race structures with the ones from yesteryear on that level, just as the phrase "American apartheid," which Massey and Denton popularized,[26] should not lead Americans to conclude that we function under apartheid. We may have an undeclared apartheid or de facto apartheid in the United States, but that is not the same as a declared or de jure apartheid. In fact, as helpful as that phrase is, it works primarily as a metaphor or an appropriation.

The structures of slavery and colonialism have been dismantled, and we should be glad that the last nails have been pounded into their coffin. But the fact that the nails have secured the box does not mean that the memories of what we buried in the 1860s and 1950s, respectively, have faded. And one may argue that remembering them is precisely the point in order to remind us of what Whites are capable of doing *at any minute.*

What people of color have earned through struggle and the protections they count on could easily be taken away. The law may exist to protect citizens from harm, but if minorities have learned anything from history, they cannot count on its enforcement when they need it most. If this smacks of conspiracy theory, David Gillborn reminds us that a conspiracy is not necessary.[27] The situation is worse than that.

If racialized societies and the schools that reproduce them behave as they normally do, the results are as predictable as if there were a concerted effort. The way societies are set up—the United States in particular—laws, policies, and common sense favor White advantage so that a select group of conspirators do not need to act deliberately to produce unequal outcomes. In fact, a conspiracy would simplify the matter such that educators could ferret out the guilty party; a racialized social system is more difficult to dismantle. All of this means that the memories of people of color for the recent past are as fresh as if it happened yesterday. Slavery, Jim Crow, genocide against native peoples, and immigration acts that Ian Haney Lopez[28] reminds us physically (i.e., racially) created what Americans look like, are not relics of some cruel past but events that have heretofore created a colonial situation known as the United States of America.

For some, the colonial discourse is outdated, referring to something that happened to someone somewhere else in some other time. But decolonial scholars, from Annibal Quijano to Nelson Maldonado-Torres,[29] Ramon Grosfoguel,[30] Chela Sandoval,[31] and Linda Tuhiwai Smith,[32] remind us that the colonial-educational project is still in effect, and there are traditional colonial subjects as well as colonial immigrants who navigate what Althusser[33] once called the "ideological state apparatuses," such as schools. It means that a colonial situation is in place and awaits newly arrived immigrants who then take their seats in the master's house. It also means that Whites' racial memory has not faded either. That they assume they are smarter and better than people of color is still in effect.

The logic of slavery and colonialism is still intact while their practice has certainly changed. A new form of enslavement and colonialism has taken their place, one that is more difficult to discern because of the distorting effects of the neoliberal project that Henry Giroux[34] has spoken so well about, as well as the regressive forms of color blindness that reduce life chances to just that—random chance. Centuries later, the fact of slavery and the stubbornness of colonization haunt every person of color.

ORELUS: *Race and ethnicity fundamentally shape many aspects of our life. However, many people, particularly privileged Whites, have refused to talk about race and ethnicity. In your view, what are some of the hidden reasons that might explain their refusal to do so?*

LEONARDO: Whites refuse to admit to their racialization for a few obvious reasons. One, to admit having a racial experience compromises their presumed universality. In *White*, Dyer describes this process well when he documents the history of Whites' self-representations, a saga of portraits that project Whites into a human history with no limits.[35] Like Jesus, Whites have that much more to fall but that much to aspire to. On the other hand, people of color are stuck in our specificity, our mediocrity as racialized beings, and we have little to accomplish as a result.

Two, Whites refuse to acknowledge race because recognizing their own racialization means they would have to recast themselves as full and knowing participants in what Omi and Winant call the "racial formation."[36] This has several consequences. First, they become less the spectators and more the actors in the formation. Their presumed ignorance and innocence are exposed as bogus stories. Not only do they know a lot about race, as I have suggested elsewhere, based on their daily racial interactions that are hard to avoid, but they discover that racism does not happen without agents.[37] They may prefer an argument that conjures up what Bonilla-Silva calls "racism without racists,"[38] but this is becoming increasingly difficult to maintain with a straight face. Whites are like dogs trying to avoid their tail, sometimes even pretending it is not there. Second, that Whites are full participants in race suggests that racism is not the problem of a select and evil fringe group of racist Whites. In fact, although these groups may inspire terror in people of color, the daily institutional forms of racism come from average, even some well-meaning, Whites.

Three, Whites avoid racial analysis because it would bring into question their very livelihood. For example, it would force difficult conversations around merit if worth is bound up with racial identity and structures. If racism is a fact of life—and I am suggesting that it is—then White achievement, and its opposite in the failure of people of color, is not duly deserved. This does not suggest that Whites do not have much to bring to this world, but that the synonymous equating between Whites and civilization, and people of color and backwardness, is too patterned, too predictable. That this is not random at all points to the inequality that is structured, as well as to the circulating narratives that constitute it.

Fourth, related to the previous point, admitting to racialization implies that Whites have some divesting to do. If they have not earned their social position fairly, then Whites may not welcome the remedy with open arms. Their debt to people of color cannot be underestimated, and hundreds of years of takeover, legal or illegal, must be accounted for.

Whites have it better because people of color do not. True, there are Whites who are not successful, who suffer, and who are marginalized. But they do not incur these misfortunes because they are White but precisely because of other ideologies that intervene into their Whiteness, such as gender, class, or sexuality. Their Whiteness is not the cause of their oppression and misery but precisely what mitigates them in terms of what Du Bois (1998) once called their "public and psychological wages."[39]

Now there is a tendency to interpret Du Bois' phrase as only concerning ideational processes, be they psychic or emotional ones. When we marry Du Bois with Nancy Fraser,[40] we understand that there is no politics of recognition without a simultaneous politics of distribution. The White workers' wages that we are fond of psychologizing as a form of social honor convert to actual, material wages. Whites edge out Black workers for leadership positions that come with pecuniary rewards or provide access to job networks, are assimilated into the job market more quickly as a surplus army of laborers, and are promoted at higher rates than workers of color. The wages of Whiteness are not merely psychic forms of prestige but material advantages that Whites accrue by virtue of being constructed as White. Within the abolitionist pedagogy that I have developed over the years, which takes seriously Roediger and Ignatiev's insights, *Whites must now take a radical furlough.*[41]

ORELUS: *Many transnational subjects of color have been minoritized in the West, that is, racially defined and labeled. What is your opinion about these labels that have been imposed on transnational subjects of color?*

LEONARDO: As I described in the introduction to my book *Race, Whiteness, and Education*, I had to learn to be a Brown Yellow in the United States.[42] I was not an Asian American until I stepped foot onto U.S. soil. Many subjects of color, to differing degrees, enter the United States unprepared for what awaits them: an undeclared apartheid system. They spend a transitional period hanging on to their previous identity and may even resist racialization American-style. Transnational subjects, immigrants, and refugees of color are introduced to a bizarre system that hails them to choose one of the four or five main racial categories. At first the process makes no sense to them as they assimilate the assumptions and expectations of generalized racial discourses into their specific ethnic histories and self-understanding. It does not take them long to realize (or even admit) that the current of racialization is stronger than their upstream paddle.

Usually for purposes of protection, scholars of color begin to accept their imposed racial identities. Not only does American culture transform them into racial beings, but fighting against racialization ironically means taking up racial identification and affirmatively answering the hail.

Entering the racial struggle requires that people of color subject themselves to racial grouping, that is, become subjects of a violent interpellating system. The irony of this moment should not be lost. Our way out of racialization is finding our way in. Entering the domain of race is the first step to dismantling the master's house. Insofar as racialization was created to oppress people of color—and there is compelling evidence for this—turning a color-blind cheek to it ensures that race continues at the level of social behavior and policy. This is something color-blind pretenders do not fully comprehend. Expurgating race from our vocabulary does not address its durability as an organizing principle throughout society. Race does not disappear because we stop using its overt referents, while material disparities accompanied by a politics of recognition stay in place.

All of this suggests that race is an objective fact of social life, particularly in the United States. True, it is a social construction. True, it is a daily reified concept. And true, it was an invention. But centuries later, race is as real as it gets. I have been in bizarre situations where I witnessed Spaniard intellectuals inform Latinos that race is not a factor in Spain, or where a light-skinned Brit tells a dark-skinned Indian that caste, rather than race, is the main struggle in India. Only historical amnesia that Spain colonized what are now Spanish-speaking countries and Great Britain colonized India could explain this facile move. After years of inculcating raciology into the minds of colonized peoples from all corners of the world, Whites may now flippantly disregard race's consequences.

After people of color have finally figured out what this thing called race has done to us, Whites may cut out the rug from under us and call it a vacuous concept. The irony is not just laughable; it is downright cruel. The upshot is that, with all the essentialisms that race thinking unwittingly reinforces, there is very little detour around it if we expect to deal effectively and honestly with what we have become as a result of race and to which we no longer consent.

ORELUS: *What do you imagine the world would be like if one's race were not an issue? What do you imagine it would be like living in such a world?*

LEONARDO: Imagining the end of race is difficult because it happens within a racial mind-set. That is, one cannot imagine the end of race from a position outside of race, but from within. So our ability to conjure up a post-racial world is a projection from within a racial imaginary. This fact alone does not disrecommend it. For now, race has no outside, but it may have an elsewhere. In fact, if my assertion is correct that race is an organization that takes away from, more than it gives to, people of color, it is more than a little ironic that we hold on dearly to it. Of course, this does not speak to what Lipsitz[43] calls the "possessive investment in whiteness," which is the strongest form of investment in race in general.

If it is a hierarchical system invented in order to oppress people of color and elevate Whites, then as a mode of social organization, a racialized system has little to recommend it. If race has never existed without racism, then a racial utopia without racism is precisely a raceless utopia. Now this is different from suggesting that race is only practiced in order to promote racism. Whiteness may be nothing but false and oppressive, as Roediger[44] correctly puts it, but political race has been deployed by people of color for liberatory purposes against falsification and oppression. "To be liberated from what?" is precisely the issue at hand.

Racially organizing against race organization is not an oxymoron. A people free from racism may fight against the yoke of a racially organized society, which is not the same thing as the obliteration of the history, memory, and pain of racial oppression. It means living an existence without structural racism. In addition, it is not the end of groups as we know them, Black, Latino, or otherwise. The issue is whether or not they are racial groups. That Blackness, for example, constitutes a culture does not suggest it must remain a race, or skin-based collective. Escaping raciology's essentialisms may be a secondary consequence to the primary goal of ending racism, but rigid racial boundaries are an impoverished sibling of White supremacy. In opposition to this, we may conjure up the possibility of nonessentialized racial understandings. But is this race any longer?

Post-racial arguments are a woefully misunderstood species. As a visceral reaction to color blindness, progressive U.S. scholars have categorically rejected post-racialism. There is good reason for the suspicion that Whiteness is up to its old tricks again. At a time when race consciousness has made gains in terms of both social policy and common sense, post-racial ruminations arrive on the scene. It is not unlike the modernist suspicions about the unfortunate timing of postmodern announcements of fragmentation, the death of metanarratives such as justice, and local antagonisms at a time when the Left was struggling for cohesion, universal rights, and global social movements. But just as setbacks may be opportunities for further advancement and reflection, so I believe that certain post-race interventions are worth considering.

The versions that argue for either the waning effect of race or its moribund status are not helpful. Even more problematic are the species that consider race as an outdated category through which to think about social patterns. This is patently false, but not because race is a tight concept; in fact, it can be quite flimsy as ideologies go. Race-conscious scholars would probably be happy to announce the end of racial trends, such as profiling, job discrimination, and educational disparities. That we announce their disappearance does not make them vanish right before our eyes, which does not prevent people from pretending that the problems are invisible. As Paul Warmington notes,[45] race is a mediating tool, and as long as it functions that way, its ideological status notwithstanding, the question of whether or not race is real becomes an abstraction. At the level of social practice, race is clearly real.

But as I (in press) have said elsewhere, "race ambivalence" is an opportunity. As race theory gains mastery over its subject matter, it reaches maturity and establishes distance from it. Again, the irony should not be underestimated. People of color have fought for so long to be considered human that hanging on to its racialized articulation now seems a bit bizarre. It strikes me as a curiosity that invoking the end of race has been all but left to conservative thought. The critical Left must wrestle the discourse away from this tendency. Of course, conservatives may annunciate the end of race, but they have neither the will nor the means to abolish it. On the contrary, conservative denial of the continuing fact of race merely hides its machinations and conceals its inner workings, which is to say, perpetuates it. Critical race intellectuals have an opportunity to dislodge this conservative hold on the post-race imaginary, to reclaim our human right to stop the five-hundred-year-old madness.

Notes

1. Provenzo, E. (2002). *Du Bois on education.* Lanham, MD: Alta Mira Press.

2. Solorzano, D. G. (1998). Critical race theory, racial and gender microaggressions, and the experiences of Chicana and Chicano scholars. *International Journal of Qualitative Studies in Education, 11*, 121–136.

3. Said, E. (2000). *Reflections on exile.* Cambridge, MA: Harvard University Press.

4. Freire, P., & Faundez, A. (1989). *Learning to question: A pedagogy of liberation.* New York: Continuum.

5. Mills, C. (1997). *The racial contract.* Ithaca, NY: Cornell University Press.

6. Leonardo, Z. (2009a). *Race, Whiteness, and education.* New York: Routledge.

7. Du Bois, W. E. B. (1989). *The souls of Black folk.* New York: Penguin Books. First published in 1904.

8. Essed, P., & Goldberg, D. T. (2002). Introduction: From racial demarcations to multiple identifications. In P. Essed & D. T. Goldberg (Eds.), *Race critical theories* (pp. 1–11). Malden, MA: Blackwell.

9. Omi, M., & Winant, H. (1994). *Racial formation in the United States: From the 1960s to the 1990s* (2nd ed.). New York: Routledge.

10. Mills, C. (1997). *The racial contract.* Ithaca, NY: Cornell University Press.

11. Bonilla-Silva, E. (2005). Introduction—"Racism" and "new racism": The contours of racial dynamics in contemporary America. In Z. Leonardo (Ed.), *Critical pedagogy and race* (pp. 1–36). Malden, MA: Blackwell.

12. Buras, K. (2008). *Rightist multiculturalism*. New York: Routledge.

13. Jameson, F. (1991). *Postmodernism, or, the cultural logic of late capitalism*. Durham, NC: Duke University Press.

14. Ladson-Billings, G., & Tate, W. F., IV. (1995). Toward a critical race theory of education. *Teachers College Record, 97*(1), 47–68.

15. Ladson-Billings, G. (2005). The evolving role of critical race theory in educational research. *Race Ethnicity & Education, 8*(1), 115–119.

16. Klor de Alva, J., Shorris, E., & West, C. (2000). Our next race question: The uneasiness between Blacks and Latinos. In R. Delgado & J. Stefancic (Eds.), *Critical White studies* (pp. 482–492). Philadelphia: Temple University Press.

17. Prashad, V. (2007). The darker nations: A people's history of the third world. New York: New Press.

18. Lerner, M., & West, C. (1996). *Jews and Blacks: A dialogue on race, religion, and culture in America*. New York: Plume.

19. Allen, R. L. (2002). The globalization of White supremacy: Toward a critical discourse on the racialization of the world. *Educational Theory, 51*(4), 467–485.

20. Leonardo, Z. (2010). Whiteness and New Orleans: Racio-economic analysis and the politics of urban space. Afterword to K. Buras, with J. Randels, K. ya Salaam, & Students at the Center (Eds.), *Pedagogy, policy, and the privatized city: Stories of dispossession and defiance from New Orleans* (pp. 159–162). New York: Teachers College Press.

21. Hartsock, N. (1987, Fall). Rethinking modernism: Minority vs. majority theories. *Cultural Critique, 7*, 187–206.

22. Churchill, W. (2005). *Since predator came*. Oakland: AK Press.

23. Mills, C. (2003). *From class to race: Essays in White Marxism and Black radicalism*. Lanham, MD: Rowman & Littlefield.

24. Freire, P. (1994). *Pedagogy of hope* (R. Barr, Trans.). New York: Continuum.

25. Quijano, A., & Ennis, M. (2000). Coloniality of power, Eurocentrism, and Latin America. *Nepantla: Views from South, 1*, 533–580.

26. Massey, D., & Denton, N. (1993). *American apartheid*. Cambridge, MA: Harvard University.

27. Gillborn, D. (2008). *Racism and education: Coincidence or conspiracy?* New York: Routledge.

28. Lopez, I. H. (2006). *White by law*. New York: New York University Press.

29. Maldonado-Torres, N. (2007). On the coloniality of being: Contributions to the development of a concept. *Cultural Studies, 21*(20–23), 240–270.

30. Grosfoguel, R. (2007). The epistemic decolonial turn: Beyond political-economy paradigms. *Cultural Studies, 21*(2), 211–223.

31. Sandoval, C. (2000). *Methodology of the oppressed*. Minneapolis: University of Minnesota Press.

32. Smith, L. T. (1999). *Decolonizing methodologies: Research and indigenous peoples*. London: Zed Books.

33. Althusser, L. (1971). *Lenin and philosophy* (B. Brewster, Trans.). New York: Monthly Review Press.

34. Giroux, H. (2010). Neoliberalism, pedagogy, and cultural politics: Beyond the theatre of cruelty. In Z. Leonardo (Ed.), *Handbook of cultural politics and education* (pp. 49–70). Rotterdam, The Netherlands: Sense Publishers.

35. Dyer, R. (1997). *White*. London: Routledge.

36. Omi, M., & Winant, H. (1994). *Racial formation in the United States: From the 1960s to the 1990s* (2nd ed.). New York: Routledge.

37. Leonardo, Z. (2009b). Reading Whiteness: Anti-racist pedagogy against White racial knowledge. In W. Ayers, T. Quinn, & D. Stovall (Eds.), *Handbook of social justice in education* (pp. 231–248). New York: Routledge.

38. Bonilla-Silva, E. (2003). *Racism without racists: Color-blind racism and the persistence of racial inequality in the United States*. Lanham, MD: Rowman & Littlefield.

39. Du Bois, W. E. B. (1998). *Black reconstruction in America, 1860–1880*. New York: Free Press. First published in 1935. See also Roediger, D. (1991). *The wages of Whiteness*. New York: Verso.

40. Fraser, N. (1997). *Justice interrupts*. New York: Routledge.

41. Roediger, D. (1994). *Toward the abolition of Whiteness*. New York: Verso. Ignatiev, N. (1997). The point is not to interpret Whiteness but to abolish it. Talk given at the Conference on The Making and Unmaking of Whiteness, University of California, Berkeley. Available online at http://racetraitor.org/albolishthepoint.htm (accessed July 26, 2007).

42. Leonardo, Z. (2009a). *Race, Whiteness, and education*. New York: Routledge.

43. Lipsitz, G. (2006). *The Possessive Investment in Whiteness: How White People Profit from Identity Politics* (Rev. and expanded ed.). Philadelphia: Temple University Press.

44. Roediger, D. (1994). *Toward the abolition of Whiteness*. New York: Verso.

45. Warmington, P. (2009). Taking race out of scare quotes: Race-conscious social analysis in an ostensibly post-racial world. *Race Ethnicity & Education, 12*(3), 281–296.

Part II

AGAINST THE MATRIX OF OPPRESSIONS

TOWARD A MORE HUMANE WORLD

Oppression is a theme that has been the center of the scholarly work of many scholars, particularly those who have explored such issues as social class, race, gender, sexuality, language, and inequality in schools.[1] However, what seems to be missing in the literature is a deeper analysis of the ways in which people, especially historically marginalized people, have been victims of multiple forms of oppression whose layers are often difficult to uncover and whose language can be too limiting to name.

This section examines in what way and to what degree these groups have endured these types of oppression. At the outset, it is worth pointing out that it is virtually impossible to understand how one is a victim of various forms of oppression without having a sound understanding of unequal power relations between the oppressor and the oppressed.[2] Stated otherwise, oppression needs to be configured within the power structure, which is by and large unequal, antidemocratic, and inequitable.[3] Such a structure, of course, was not created by itself. It was created by those who historically have had a monopoly of the wealth of the world, which has placed them in key positions to control many institutions, such as the media, schools, churches, and the socioeconomic and political structure of a country.[4]

Here I am not alluding to power with, but rather power over the "subaltern," as Spivak eloquently puts it.[5] I am not referring either to Michel Foucault's definition of power, that is, something that circulates through institutions and one's body and is not necessarily oppressive by nature. Foucault states that power "reaches into the very grain of individuals, touches their bodies and inserts itself into their actions and attitudes, their discourses, learning processes and everyday lives" (p. 39).[6]

Specifically, the type of power to which I am alluding here is oppressive politically, economically, emotionally, and psychologically to people; that is, it is the one that those on the higher scale of the socioeconomic and political ladder use to subjugate and dehumanize those who have been forced to be at the bottom. Proponents of the oppressive capitalist machine have used this type of power for centuries to coerce people and maintain the status quo, which needs to be challenged and resisted. As Simone de Beauvoir put it, "We must put a brake on the machinery of power, rather than go on oiling its wheels" (p. 98).[7]

It is important to emphasize that it is challenging to find an encompassing language that clearly spells out different kinds of names by which people have been oppressed. The reason is that language, as a mediated and communicative tool used to name things, namely various forms of oppression occurring in hidden ways, is sometimes too restrictive. In other words, there are some forms of oppression that one has yet to find a language to name, for many hidden layers embedded in these oppressions are often difficult to reveal.

For example, how does one fully capture and name the type of oppression a parent of a lesbian, gay, transgender, or even a biracial child experiences? Likewise, how does one call the oppression a child of a gay or lesbian couple encounters in schools and in society at large? Further, how does one fully capture and name the multiple layers of racial aggression, such as being accused of "acting White," that some people of color, including those adopted by White families, face? One can claim that the forms of oppression these parents and children experience are racism and homophobia. However, the question is then begged: to what degree does naming these two forms of oppression fully reflect what these parents and children experience and feel daily? How about the underlying forms of oppression that they may be experiencing which do not surface? How does one name those?

Besides the fact that language is sometimes too limiting to adequately capture the complexity of human oppressions, the difficulty of doing so lies in the fact that those in power have used all kinds of semantics, euphemisms, and political rhetoric to put a mask on people's suffering, gaining their consent to dupe and make them become docile citizens in order to continue oppressing them. This fundamentally explains why, as I will argue later, many people who have been oppressed in many ways may not have yet developed a keen awareness of various types oppression, or a language to name them.

Being Victims of Multiple Forms of Oppression

Being victims of multiple forms of oppression—racial, socioeconomic, sexual, and linguistic—is linked to one's individual existential experience. Some people are oppressed in ways that are not often obvious to others. Therefore, only those who are victims of this type of oppression feel and suffer its psychological and emotional damages. For example, some students, such as biracial students, female students of color, queer students, and students of poor working-class backgrounds, have been victims of various forms of oppression because of their multiple identities.

There are many levels and forms of oppression. For example, the institutional oppression from which professors suffer is not the same as the type of oppression that migrant, factory, and sweatshop workers have endured daily. Likewise, the level of oppression that students, especially female, queer, and students of color, face may be worse than that of a heterosexual White male. Although all forms of oppression hurt, some people feel or are oppressed at a deeper level than others. Oppression does not only occur through physical violence. There are oppressed people who may have been mostly subject to symbolic violence, to which I turn next.

Symbolic Violence: A Concealed Form of Oppression

To further illuminate what is meant by a concealed form of oppression, I want to borrow Pierre Bourdieu's phrase "symbolic violence," which is a form of violence that may not be obvious to many people, including, paradoxically, those who have been victims of it, but has damaging psychological and emotional effects on individuals.[8] This type of violence can damage someone physically, psychologically, and emotionally to the same extent as physical violence, if not at a much greater degree. In fact, in some cases symbolic violence may be worse than other forms of violence. For example, a person of color who has been told all his or her life that he or she is of an inferior, uncivilized, and weak race; that people like him or her have low IQ; and that he or she is deficient intellectually and morally would most likely be worse off in the long run than someone who is physically beaten by a stranger on the street. Those who have been victims of these types of symbolic violence end up internalizing them. As Carter Woodson eloquently put it,

> When you control a man's thinking you do not have to worry about his actions. You do not have to tell him not to stand here or go yonder. He will find his "proper place" and will stay in it. You do not need to send him to the back door. He will go without being told. In fact, if there is no back door, he will cut one for his special benefit. (p. 43)[9]

Likewise, a woman who has been told all her life that she is weak, that she is not as intelligent as men, and that she is only good for sexual pleasure and for giving birth and raising children would be worse off in the long run than someone who is subject to physical violence, except rape, which also entails a great level of coercion.

Not too many people realize or fully realize that they are victims of many forms of oppression. Part of the reason is that those in powerful positions use all kinds of tactics to gain the consent of those they oppress. As the Italian critical thinker Antonio Gramsci explains, hegemonic control of one's mind by those in power is achieved through one's consent.[10] Gaining the consent of anybody is a way of zombifying that person, for he or she will end up doing things that go against his or her own interests in order to protect, consciously or not, the interests of those in power, thereby maintaining the status quo. Consent is usually obtained through ideological propaganda circulated in the media and institutions, such as schools, churches, and even families. Without this ideological trap, dictatorial governments, oppressive institutions, and manipulative corporations would not have been able to lie to and exploit people. In short, consent, which in my view is an ideological sleeping pill, has allowed those in power to keep people in a dormant state so that they can continue being in control of people's lives. Needless to say, consent has played a major role in the oppression of people.

In short, people, particularly people of color and women, who have been targeted, labeled, and pushed to the margins because of their skin tone, social class, sexuality, accent, or country of origin have experienced varying forms of oppression because of these biological, historical, and socially constructed identities. The various ways by which people have been oppressed should challenge one to look at human oppression from different perspectives. To this end, the following dialogues with Professors Howard Winant, Christine E. Sleeter, Sonia Nieto, and Carl A. Grant attempt to illuminate the various ways people have been oppressed. Specifically, these scholars unravel hidden and overt ways in which many people have been victims of multiple forms of oppression and propose alternatives to these oppressions.

Notes

1. Marx, K. (2010). *Capital: A critique of political economy.* Charleston, SC: CreateSpace; Kozol, J. (2006). *The shame of the nation: The restoration of apartheid schooling in America.* New York: Broadway; Gramsci, A. (1971). *Selections from the prison notebooks* (Q. H. G. N. Smith, Trans. and Ed.). New York: International Publishers; McLaren, P. (2005). *Capitalists and conquerors: A critical pedagogy against empire.* Lanham, MD: Rowman & Littlefield; hooks, b. (2006). *Outlaw culture: Resisting representations.* New York: Routledge; Butler, J. (2006). *Gender trouble: Feminism and the subversion of identity.* New

York: Routledge; Freire, P. (2000). *Pedagogy of the oppressed.* New York: Continuum; Wa Thiong'o, N. (2008). *Decolonizing the mind: The politics of language in African Literature.* New Hampshire: Heinemann.

2. Freire, P. (2000). *Pedagogy of the oppressed.* New York: Continuum.

3. Zinn, H. *A people's history of the United States.* New York: HarperCollins; Žižek, S. (2010). *Living in the ends of time.* UK: Verso.

4. Chomsky, N. (2010). *Hopes and prospects.* Chicago: Haymarket Books; Giroux, H., & Giroux, S. (2006). *Take back higher education: Race, youth and the crisis of democracy in the post-civil rights era.* New York: Palgrave Macmillan.

5. Spivak, G. C. (1988). Can the subaltern speak? In C. Nelson & L. Grossberg (Eds.), *Marxism and the interpretation of culture* (pp. 271–313). Basingstoke: Macmillan Education.

6. Foucault, M., & Gordon, C. (1980). *Power/knowledge: Selected interviews and other writings, 1972–1977.* New York: Knopf Doubleday.

7. de Beauvoir, S. (1984). In Alice Schwarzer, *After The Second Sex: Conversations with Simone de Beauvoir.* New York: Pantheon.

8. Bourdieu, P. (1999). *Language and symbolic power* (John Thompson, Trans.; Ginau Raymond & Matthew Adamson, Eds.). Cambridge, MA: Harvard University Press.

9. Woodson, C. (2000). *The mis-education of the Negro.* New York: African American Images.

10. Gramsci, A. (1971). *Selections from the prison notebooks* (Q. H. G. N. Smith, Trans. and Ed.). New York: International Publishers.

CHAPTER 4

Unpacking Racial and Socioeconomic Marginalizations

A CONVERSATION WITH HOWARD WINANT

In this interview, Professor Howard Winant, a leading American scholar whose work has focused on social inequality, particularly inequality that is race and class based, addresses socioeconomic and racial issues that confront many in society. Professor Winant starts by sharing his experience of being involved in the civil rights movement as a teenager and how his Jewish parents inspired him to be involved in this movement. While he acknowledges that the civil rights movement has opened doors to a few people of color and contributed to some socioeconomic and political changes, he argues that structurally and fundamentally not much has changed. Professor Winant maintains that the income and wealth divide between Whites and people of color persists, that Blacks, Latino/as, Asians, and other marginalized groups are still at the bottom of the economic ladder, though at varying degrees. Professor Winant, therefore, argues that there is a lot more left to be done to combat inequality that is race and class based. He says it is a great thing that the United States elected Barack Obama as president. However, he does not believe we are living in post-racial era, and he has been disappointed with the decision that Obama took to escalate the war in Afghanistan.

The Dialogue

ORELUS: *Professor Winant, you are a highly respected scholar who has dedicated your professional career to social justice issues, including racial issues. Please, would you explain what or who has inspired you to focus on these issues throughout your career?*

WINANT: My work on racial issues really goes back to an early part of my life and my career. I was involved in civil rights movement activity from around the age of thirteen, like picketing Woolworth's to protest segregation in the South. This was at the time when the civil rights movement was developing in the late 1950s and early 1960s, during the Greensboro sit-ins in 1960 for example. I was a middle-school student then and was living in the North. We had a Woolworth's where I was living, and we picketed it—a bunch of teenagers, Black and White.

So those are some of my earliest experiences. I have to say that my parents were a big factor. They were Jewish refugees from Hitler. They recognized the civil rights movement as a democratic, and in some ways antifascist, movement. They were able to compare it with the struggle against anti-Semitism. They contributed in small ways to the Black movement, like to the NAACP. At an early age, this was a factor for me. Then later on, of course, I was an activist in college, a child of the 1960s: antiracist and antiwar, a new leftist, and a community activist as well. I was very involved in civil rights movement activities throughout the 1960s. It is a familiar story for many people.

ORELUS: *Some have argued that racial issues are not discussed enough in U.S. mainstream classrooms. What would you say about this?*

WINANT: Well, I am not sure if racial issues are not discussed in classrooms. I guess you have to talk about what classrooms, what disciplines, and what fields. Ethnic studies programs around the nation—Black studies, Chicano studies, Native American studies, and so on—have made a big impact as far as racial issues are concerned. And the existence of diversity programs of different types and multicultural centers has contributed to awareness about racial issues in a big way. There are many racist incidents as well; these mobilize people and bring a lot of attention to the ongoing racial conditions that exist in the country and the world. But beyond that, I would say that even in mainstream disciplines—I know better the social sciences and I guess the humanities to some extent—there is quite a bit of discussion about race.

ORELUS: *What advice would you give to people, particularly educators, who are trying to address racial issues in their classrooms?*

WINANT: In terms of talking about race, there is reluctance, particularly among White faculty and students, to come to terms with the unresolved issues that race presents for them. There is a sort of a consensus in the country now that racism is bad, that to be prejudiced is bad, and that we want to get beyond that. But does that mean racism is a thing of the past, as neoconservatives and the Supreme Court want to claim? This is a very mainstream viewpoint, which tends to deny the deeper problems. The idea of color blindness—my students (especially my White students) will tell me, "I don't see color," "A person is just a person to me," "I know everyone is equal." This view is a willful type of self-deception. It points to the difficulties people—especially but not only White people—experience in confronting issues of racism.

The color-blind discourse is full of limitations, but at the same time it offers opportunities for teaching people about racial issues, "teachable moments," as they say. It indicates that people are conflicted in ways that they don't really understand. You say that you are color-blind and that you treat everyone alike. But how would you describe the neighborhood you live in, in terms of race? Who are your friends? What is your orientation toward issues of racial poverty, racial inequality, unemployment, housing, discrimination, or the subprime lending crisis? The subprime crisis has plunged the entire economy into recession; do you see that as a racial issue? America's wars in Afghanistan and Iraq, do you see those as racial issues? How do you view immigration? If you get into anything specific, it provides an opening rather than a closing down of the discussion on race.

ORELUS: *There are some orthodox Marxists who have privileged class issues over race issues. Where do you stand on this issue?*

WINANT: I have real sympathy for the Marxist perspective. I see myself as someone of the Left. But I have argued that it is very important that race not be reduced to some supposedly more fundamental contradiction or problem such as class or culture, as has been done in ethnicity theory. That is also true of Marxism, which sees class as the most basic conflict. This is more an article of faith than an analytically defensible position.

In practical terms, class cannot always be so easily distinguished from race, or from gender either for that matter. Economic determinism, class reductionism—these are endemic in Marxist thought. In the long run, they are politically ruinous. Stuart Hall sought to address these problems in late-1970s England, with his famous formula that "race is the way that class is lived." While that may be a little bit trite, a formulaic response, it does make the point that these are conceptual matters, experiences that are lived out every day, as well as social structural matters and theoretical concepts. What we really have to think about more deeply is the actual lived experience, the patterns of inequality, and the patterns of exploitation that exist. In this regard, it is very difficult to draw clear boundaries between race and class.

ORELUS: *Since Obama was elected, there has been a post-racial discourse circulated in the mainstream media. Do you believe that we will ever be living in a post-racial era?*

WINANT: I have been a long-standing supporter of Obama, and I also worked in his campaign. I have seen many of his positions in terms of governing as opposed to campaigning, necessary pragmatic alternatives to the purer arguments he offers in his books and speeches. Although of course he must be pragmatic, he is far too cautious, often reluctant to lead. He often abandons essential ideas and positions far too easily, in my view. His caution, if not timidity, on the economy has led to lost opportunities. That was an instance where he abandoned anticorporate popular sentiment—there's some class consciousness for you—to the authoritarian populist right wing. That was a big mistake. His war in Afghanistan is another big mistake.

In terms of the "post-racial" transition that you speak about, it is simply another word for this idea of color blindness, this notion that we can somehow by an act of will or a good definition reconcile ourselves to fundamental patterns of racial formation—structural racism—that continues to exist in the United States. Obviously I do not accept that. But neither are those patterns fixed entirely, immutable and incapable of reform. They are not so rigid as to resist all reforms or changes.

Although there is clear evidence of racial progress over the past half century, it should also be clear that we have not overcome the deep racism that has structured the United States and the modern world as a whole. The U.S. Civil War was not sufficient to do that. It was a massive blood-drenched affair. The end of the old colonial era was not sufficient to do that on a world scale either, even though it was an even more massive bloodletting. So if the organized murder of half a million Americans in the 1860s when the total population was only around 40 million, was not enough to generate racial democracy, let us call it, despite the best efforts of Black people themselves and their Radical Republican allies, then perhaps it is less surprising that the civil rights and Black power (Brown power, Yellow power, Red power, and antiracist Whites as well) movements of the mid-twentieth century could not do it either.

Obviously it is a big task to overcome racism, but at the same time, the civil rights movement, the antiapartheid movement, and other similar movements (like the immigrants' rights movement in the U.S.) have shown that there are possibilities for significant reform to happen. It is in this real world of racial contradictions that Obama's election and presidency must be viewed. In that regard, his election was a fairly momentous event. The fact that the United States could elect him was an encouraging fact. Are we living in a post-racial era? The answer is obviously no.

ORELUS: *I have been living in the United States for about fifteen years, so I didn't really get to witness the brutal forms of racism that occurred here, especially in the 1950s and the 1960s. So, given that you lived in this sad era of U.S. his-*

tory, would you say that people of color are better off today than they were, say, fifty years ago?

WINANT: First of all, let me say I was born in 1946. I am sixty-three years old now. What I witnessed in the 1950s and even the early 1960s, I saw as a child and as an adolescent. So I am not a great personal tribune of what happened during this era. But the question as to whether people of color are better off is a problematic question. From the sociological standpoint, we can measure standard indicators: unemployment rates, life expectancy, infant mortality, and so on. In the area of residential segregation, we find that while there has been significant improvement, it has been uneven, spasmodic, and far less than a dramatic change. Most of the reductions in White-Black inequalities, and many improvements in the socioeconomic status of Blacks as well, have occurred only for the upper strata of the Black community. That is, some middle-class Blacks and more established Blacks have been able to leave the ghetto to move into more integrated middle-class neighborhoods or Black suburbs, and have obtained professional or semiprofessional jobs, or white-collar jobs, government jobs, and the like.

These are significant changes, but they represent a very limited transformation in the overall socioeconomic picture. It is remarkable looking at the data to see how steady socioeconomic inequalities, health and income disparities, and unequal distributions of wealth have been. They have remained largely constant for many decades. Unemployment among Blacks remains higher than among Whites—about double. In almost any indicator you choose, you can find that steady reproduction of Black-White inequality. We can find similar patterns among other racially defined minority groups.

The U.S. racial system is a deeply rooted social structure, grounded in slavery, conquest, immigrant exclusion, and the like, and rationalized and justified by an all-pervasive political socialization: we are the "land of the free and the home of the brave, don't you know?" Obviously there are all kinds of variations: among Asian Americans for example. Certain Asian American groups have prospered tremendously in terms of socioeconomic status, equaling or exceeding some Whites, while others still fall very far behind. Latinos are in a very similar situation. Cubans are much better off than Mexicans. Mexican Americans are tremendously stratified, both better and worse off: there is increased socioeconomic disparity among this group, with a tremendous number remaining at the bottom of the socioeconomic scale, while a significant middle class has also emerged. Puerto Ricans more closely resemble Blacks. So it's a complex pattern, which must be examined closely and analyzed quite thoroughly. In sum, in the aftermath of the civil rights movement, there has been minimal though real improvement in the socioeconomic status of racially defined minorities in the United States, largely skewing toward the upper strata of these groups.

Orelus: *Broadly speaking, would you say that racism has affected Blacks more than it has affected other marginalized groups?*

Winant: These are difficult questions. They are also problematic. In what way do you mean something like "racism affects Blacks"? Racism is what Black people *are* and what White people *are*. It shapes us. It is something we are bathed in, marinated in, boiled in, like a stew. It is indistinguishable in many respects from the social structure as a whole. So, not to be affected by it would be extremely difficult even to imagine. Perhaps what you are trying to get at with your question is the following: Is racism more of a Black-White bipolarity, so to speak, or is it a multipolar situation in which there are more than two groups who are deeply involved?

Of course racism plays a greater part in the everyday life of Black people than it does in the life of White people because it is something that Black people can ignore only with great difficulty, whereas for White people it is still possible to normalize Whiteness by saying, "I am not a White person; I am just a person." There are many Black people who live in a largely Black world; their interactions with Whites are very limited. They can watch Whites on TV, deal with Whites to a very limited extent in the marketplace, try to handle the armed White occupiers of their neighborhoods—i.e., the police—and that's about it. To an even greater extent, there are millions of Whites who have very little contact with Black people, who see Blacks as the perpetrators on TV crime shows, and that's about it. Racial segregation is such that American experiences are often confined to a same-race milieu in which—especially for Whites—race can be largely ignored or set aside in terms of everyday life. Again and again we have to say it: there is a deep structural racism in the United States.

Racial segregation is a self-reinforcing process, but it hasn't always been there. It was basically built into U.S. society over certain quite identifiable periods of time, as a matter of policy, by favoring Whites and neglecting (and overtly excluding) Blacks. Look at housing policy, employment and labor policy, and education policy as they were organized after World War II. Of course there were earlier manifestations as well.

To overcome segregation will require a very large, concerted effort. It is an enormous, difficult problem, one that continues to exist because segregation benefits Whites in many ways. But yes, it is also self-reinforcing, and so it creates disadvantages for Black and Brown communities—clear difficulties. For example, it limits the quality of education in Black and Brown communities; it limits employment opportunities for residents of those communities. These patterns then act back on the overall structure—of segregation, or structural racism—to maintain it. It's not entirely that people are choosing to live in given communities, although the vast majority of Whites have no interest in living in any close proximity to Black people.

If you say personal choice, it reduces the problem to more of an individual or experiential dimension, when in fact it is a structural problem. The only interesting thing about personal choice, in my view, is when people master the ability, the insight, and the capacity of making an unusual choice or challenging an existing situation. When people decide to fight racism, that is the time to talk about personal choice.

For many Black people, especially Black middle-class people, the right choice is not so obvious. Is it to pursue an "integrated lifestyle" or to live within a segregated environment? There are attractions and disadvantages on both sides. To what school is one going to send one's kids? How much tension can you stand: with the neighbors, the police, or the high school guidance counselor? What about gangs, drugs, and police violence? What opportunities are available for your kids in the ghetto or barrio? So, in this context, the framework of integration still has some relevance for these folks.

But as I said, there is in practice a much more complex pattern than we are discussing here. We can't talk as if it were a single Black community and a single White community when in fact there are many areas all around the country that are border areas, transitional areas, contested areas, and even integrated areas. Where are you located?

Orelus: *Las Cruces, New Mexico.*

Winant: New Mexico. Okay. You would find that there are many integrated White and Latino neighborhoods there. You'll also find integrated neighborhoods in large cities of the Northeast and Midwest, and to some extent the West Coast too. You will find border areas as well, residential "racial frontiers." In suburban areas, for example, there are many integrated spots within a residential geography that remains largely segregated. In a few particular districts, there are very high levels of integration. Consider Rogers Park in Chicago, the Mount Airy neighborhood of Philadelphia, or Takoma Park outside Washington, D.C.

There are wholly segregated suburbs, like Mount Vernon, just north of New York City. In the San Fernando Valley of Southern California, there is a large Latino influx into what were previously all-White suburbs. The list can go on and on. In the United States, racial identity and racialized social structures remain unstable and contentious. While the deep structure of race and racism endures, it is constantly being challenged in fundamentally political ways.

CHAPTER 5

Reexamining Social Inequality in Schools and Beyond

A CONVERSATION WITH CHRISTINE E. SLEETER

In this interview, Professor Sleeter analyzes unearned privileges attached to Whiteness, which she argues many individual Whites fail to acknowledge. She goes further to look at the pervasiveness of White supremacy and the extent to which it has affected people of color, preventing, for instance, biracial and multiracial people from claiming and honoring their multiple identities. Professor Sleeter also talks about other forms of oppression such as sexism, capitalism, neocolonialism, and U.S. imperialism. She uses the examples of marginalized groups such as indigenous peoples, women, and poor Blacks and Whites here and abroad to point out how these forms of oppression have affected these marginalized groups. Professor Sleeter connects her analysis of these issues to the current political context, including Obama's presidency. While acknowledging the historical significance of Obama's presidency, Professor Sleeter particularly argues that merely electing a Black president does not necessarily guarantee fundamental socioeconomic and political changes. Instead, Professor Sleeter reinforces the idea that changes need to take place at a whole range of institutions, including schools.

The Dialogue

ORELUS: *Throughout your scholarly work, you have made a strong case for tolerance, acceptance, and respect for diversity and people's multiple identities. But we continue to witness a lack of tolerance toward people who are different, particularly people who share multiple identities. How do you explain this lack of tolerance?*

SLEETER: That it has to do with the benefits that White people have in a racist society. Essentially, White people don't want to give up the benefits and the privileges that go along with Whiteness. That gets to the root of it. People end up being afraid that they are going to lose something, which I don't think is the case. But people are afraid of that, and in some ways they are aware of advantages that they have being White, and they just don't want to give that up. Institutionalized White supremacy is the main root of this.

Take, for example, housing patterns. White people grow up in segregated communities more than any other racial ethnic group. It usually doesn't get put that way; White people think it is people of color who are segregated, but in many ways it is White people who are segregated, who choose to live in segregated communities. White kids and adults growing up in segregated communities don't have very much firsthand contact with people who are different from them. So they end up relying on what they see on TV, what they see in movies, and what they hear to form their impressions of people who are different from them both racially and ethnically.

Similarly, if you connect this with social class and poverty, affluent people develop their understandings of people who are poor by viewing people who are poor at a distance, and hearing explanations for poverty through mainstream media as well as stories about people who worked their way up the ladder of success, or people who didn't do so but presumably could have. Living within this kind of structural arrangement feeds acceptance of the system, and it leads White people to blame people of color for their problems rather than looking at themselves and the institutions that White people dominate.

I was talking about this just this last week with a White teacher who retired a few years ago. She found out that the work I do is multicultural education, which I don't think she really understands very well. She then said, "Well, let me tell you my feelings about your work. A number of years ago, when I first started teaching, our students were mostly White here in Salinas." That's where she was teaching. And then she said, "As the student population became more diverse, and teachers started working with multicultural education and bilingual education, the academic standards just dropped." From her perspective, it probably would have been okay to have a more diverse student population if everything would have remained the same.

But teachers, especially bilingual teachers, started, at least to some extent, looking for ways to make the system more responsive to pluralism. Some such attempts were weak, such as schools hiring teachers for bilingual programs when the teachers themselves were not fluently bilingual and therefore were not able to implement bilingual education well. But the issue of looking at how the system itself works in favor of White middle-class nonimmigrant students, with an eye to making it work better for a wide range of students, is, to my way of thinking, moving in the right direction. But to the teacher I was talking with, quality education was being sacrificed in the process.

Schools are one place where we can start, although the problems are embedded in the whole range of social institutions. But since schools are where I work, then the schools became the place where I do my multicultural education type of work. But we need to think of how schools are connected with the network of social institutions. People who are working in housing need to break up housing segregation. People who are working in media have a lot of work to get done regarding media representation. I don't think schools are the only place where we as a society necessarily need to start, but since education is where I work, that is where I locate my work.

ORELUS: *Let's talk about an equally important issue: biracialism. People who are half White/half Black are often forced to identify themselves as Black. What is your position on this issue?*

SLEETER: I actually have a stepson who is in that situation. And it is the larger society that keeps identifying him as Black. Other people will look at him and see him as Black. I am just using him as an example here. He is actually very capable in many ways to walk in multiple worlds. But the rest of society, especially if they don't know him, when they look at him, they identify him as Black. Because he experiences the kind of racial discrimination that people who are categorized as Black in the United States experience, he identifies more strongly as Black than he does as White.

But when you look at the history of the United States, which probably most White people don't understand—some people of color may not know either, but certainly most White people don't understand it—racial categories were constructed initially by the U.S. government, partly through the census-taking process, but also as a way of solidifying slavery and legalizing White privileges. And after slavery, after emancipation, the one-drop rule that was written into the laws of most of the states in the United States legalized the idea that if you have any Black ancestry at all, any Black blood, regardless of how you look, you are classified as Black and could legally be denied access to White institutions such as White schools, labor unions, jobs, and so forth. So we're living with a legacy of something that White people created. Now, White people will say, "Well, we didn't come up with that." Well, yes we did!

ORELUS: *What do you think needs to be or should be done to create space for a multiracial/multicultural society? What should this society look like?*

SLEETER: Probably the best example in my own work that seemed to get somewhere was work that I and my colleagues were doing with teachers in our master's program at California State University in Monterey Bay. We had very diverse groups of teachers who we recruited so that we would have diverse cohorts of educators taught by a diverse faculty, with an explicitly multicultural-antiracist curriculum all the way through the program.

People from different backgrounds would be talking about issues related to race, ethnicity, language, and social class, and the historical construction of these issues, and how they play out in their own personal lives as well as how they play out in schools. Instead of just doing it in workshops, we made it sort of a systematic focus of the whole program. As students were going through the program, as I was hearing from both White students, students of color, and multiracial students, I saw that the dialogues and assigned readings helped them learn to see and respect other people's points of view. I saw developing in them the capacity to be able to go into the classroom with their own kids that they were teaching and start to have some more open conversations about racial and cultural issues. In our classrooms, they were engaged in conversations where in some cases people would get really upset or people would be crying. But you stick with it instead of backing off from it. We would sometimes have some really uncomfortable times in the classroom, but you stick with it, you work through it rather than running away and getting scared. When I would go into some of the classrooms and see the teachers doing with their students similar kinds of things that we had done in the graduate program, I would think, "Okay, yes, this is getting somewhere!" Although it is important to recognize that kids are less threatened by these conversations than adults are, some of our teachers found that students could plunge into issues better than they had anticipated.

Orelus: *What roles do you think those forms of oppression play in subjugating and marginalizing women and people of color?*

Sleeter: I have heard and often used the term "pyramid of power," which is a helpful way to think of it. In the larger society, we have this pyramid of power that has intersecting axes of oppression. People are located in various places within the pyramid of power depending on the various identities that they bring, who they are, and how they are constructed socially within a complex web of power relations. From my point of view, talking about and studying these issues may help people to link their own oppression with somebody else's whose background is different from theirs. An instructor may help them do this, but it doesn't usually happen. For instance, White women who understand gender oppression can be helped to see the connection between that and racial oppression. They don't automatically make the connection because White women will very often disclaim racial privilege. But it can provide an opening there.

In a class that I was teaching this last semester at San Francisco State University, I deliberately used multiple lenses to look at multiple forms of oppression. In many ways I opened up spaces for conversation where students discussed these issues. Two of the students in the class talked particularly about oppression on the basis of sexual orientation. Another one looked at oppression primarily from a gender perspective. These discussions helped form richer ways of conceptualizing and analyzing how power and identity play out rather than only using one lens of analysis.

Interestingly, at the end of the semester, as they shared where they were going with their dissertations, I remember listening to two who were looking at education leadership from a perspective that started with an analysis of racism, and two from an analysis that started with sexism. Although their starting place and the literature they drew on were different, the issues they brought up and the way they framed leadership were remarkably similar, and I asked them to think about connecting their work. Later, one of the White women e-mailed me and said that point hit home with her, and she was reworking her thinking to look at the nature of oppression through multiple lenses.

ORELUS: *What about U.S. imperialism and capitalism? Those are other forms of oppression, aren't they?*

SLEETER: Well, yes, that's a big part of it. I don't know if they are afraid, but a lot of people in the United States don't want to talk critically about capitalism. They will sometimes say, "Oh, well, that's so well institutionalized that you can't do anything about it." I believe that the Right has so successfully linked the idea of socialism with communism, with the countries the U.S. regards as national enemies, that most people in the United States have a knee-jerk reaction that if you criticize capitalism, you are being anti-American.

Without giving students a critical lens and critical language for looking at capitalism, they make assumptions about it, such as assuming that capitalism and democracy are the same thing, which they are not. It is a big part of the overall structure of oppression. To me, it is kind of like the big elephant in the room that doesn't get talked about.

One of the things I like to do when I teach is to historically look at how racism and capitalism in the United States were constructed in tandem with each other. Historically, you could not really pull them apart because they did go together so much. Today, we put capitalism in the background when talking about it, and yet the whole way that the global economy has been restructured around global capitalism becomes the modern-day way of doing colonialism. That desperately needs to be part of what we look at, part of what we talk about critically.

ORELUS: *Speaking of colonialism. Do you believe that we are living in a postcolonial world? Or do you think it is a revived and renewed form of colonialism?*

SLEETER: A renewed form of colonialism. It depends on who one is talking about. For instance, indigenous people of the Americas aren't living in a postcolonial world. White people—descendents of the colonizers—haven't left. White people haven't given back land and autonomy to the indigenous people. Indigenous people are still colonized. And the forms of colonialism that were used to colonize the Americas are still at work. Look at, for instance, the U.S. presence in Iraq, in the Middle East. That is a form of colonialism even if we don't go in and set up the government. Well, we have handpicked who is in the government and that kind of thing. Whether we go in and primarily control the economy or the military of a country, or a combination of both, or do so from more of a distance, that is still a form of colonialism.

ORELUS: *Now let's speak a little bit about Obama. Since he is biracial, there has been a lot of talk about biracialism since he has been in power. Do you think Obama's presidency could help people develop some level of acceptance toward people who are biracial?*

SLEETER: The potential for that is there. What I am finding very disheartening, however, is a rise of blatant expressions of racism, on at least two fronts. First, President Obama is being attacked in ways that I do not recall previous presidents being attacked. There is a mean-spiritedness to many of these attacks, such as comparing him with Hitler, questioning his citizenship, and that kind of thing. And the Republican Party seems to be stoking potential fears that White people have of having a Black person in charge while the nation is experiencing huge economic problems—that was actually leaked as a strategy in a PowerPoint presentation at a Republican strategizing meeting. Second is the number of blatant expressions of racism in society and on college campuses. We are seeing nooses hung, swastikas drawn, and racist epithets hurled at Black students.

So, although I would like to think that his election can change perceptions, there is a backlash that is frightening. I don't think just him being elected and becoming president will necessarily change that. It depends on what sorts of polices flow from his election. Look at the recession and what people are dealing with. I am not sure there has necessarily been any improvement in people's conditions of life yet. I hope he is around for eight years so that we can see what happens. But just electing one person to a high office alone does not change things, especially when the policies he tries to advance are attacked as strongly as they are.

ORELUS: *Going back to the multiracialism issue, are you hopeful that someday multiculturalism will be accepted by people? If so, how do you think that will happen?*

SLEETER: I don't think it is ever going to be like just one happy harmony. People are going to be continually struggling. The more hierarchical the distribution of wealth and resources in the society, the more people struggle and fight with each other because the hierarchical system sets that up. Scott Page[1] has just recently completed statistical studies looking at the benefit of diverse organizations making constructive decisions, all the way from corporations to schools and other kinds of institutions. Apparently, he found that when there is a diverse group making the decisions, the decisions end up being better and working better than when it is a homogeneous group. I sort of knew that from my own life experience, but when a White guy comes out with a book like this, then people think, "Well, maybe some people probably hadn't really thought of it before. Oh! It's a different perspective."

Note

1. Page, S. (2008). *The difference: How the power of diversity creates better groups, firms, schools, and societies.* Princeton, NJ: Princeton University Press.

CHAPTER 6

Unveiling and Fighting against Discrimination in Schools and Society

A CONVERSATION WITH SONIA NIETO

In this dialogue, Professor Sonia Nieto, a leading figure in multicultural education, addresses challenges that mixed people face in a society that often places them in a rigid "racial identity box." Nieto points out the lack of tolerance and respect that multiracial people face in a society that does not allow enough space for people who differ from the majority. She argues that opposing forces such as institutional racism and White supremacy play a major role in the lack of tolerance and respect for, and the marginalization of, mixed people. Professor Nieto also talks about Whiteness, from which, she argues, especially privileged Whites benefit. Along with Whiteness, she talks about the privileges that sometimes come with one's light skin. She talks about the poor treatment dark-skinned people often receive, especially those who live in poverty. Professor Nieto argues that having light skin has allowed many people, including light-skinned professors of color, to have an easier time in academia than those who happen to be dark skinned. Moreover, she challenges the color-blind discourse, contending that race and skin color matter. After identifying and analyzing the racial and socioeconomic challenges that marginalized people, including mixed people and other people of color, have faced in society, she makes an appeal for equal treatment and opportunity, and respect for everyone regardless of their ethnic, racial, cultural, sexual, and socioeconomic background.

The Dialogue

Orelus: *In your first book,* Affirming Diversity, *you made a strong case for people to be who they are. Please, would you expand on this?*

Nieto: People should have the right to be who they are, that is, to affirm their identities, even though those identities may be different from year to year, or even from day to day. For example, take a look at you. You are Haitian, but you are different from your parents, right? Your daughter will probably be different from you. You are different generations, different experiences, different contexts, and she is also bi-ethnic and binational (Haitian and Venezuelan). I would not say that your daughter has to be exactly like you. She has the right to choose who she wants to be, and that means not having her culture denigrated or her languages denigrated so that she can feel that she can be who she is while at the same time recognizing that no culture is pure or stays the same way all the time.

Orelus: *I recently had a conversation with someone who happened to be biracial. He said that what is important is not so much being allowed to claim your multiple identities, but for marginalized people, be they biracial or not, to be united to fight against White supremacy. What is your take on that?*

Nieto: That is an important goal, but I don't think it should be the only thing people fight against. I am trying to think of how to answer that. I don't think it is just a struggle against White supremacy. It is a struggle against the forces of the dominant culture, which is not only White. Just like our identities are shifting and becoming more hybridized, culture in general is changing as well. So yes, while we have this struggle against White supremacy, we also have to understand that it is not the only struggle there is.

That term, "White supremacy," is so overarching that I see it on different levels. Although White supremacy affects all of those levels (personal, institutional, and ideological), and I have often talked about those levels in my work, I see claiming or developing identity as more than just a struggle against White supremacy. In the case of your daughter, for example, she will no doubt also have to fight against patriarchy, and if she were to live in poverty, against classism as well.

Orelus: *How would you envision a multiracial world? What do you think it should look like?*

Nieto: That is an interesting question, because we don't have many models for such a world. Even Hawaii, for example, which many people say is a multiracial society, is not necessarily the best model, because the power structure is still White. There is an overall context that we are all living in, and it influences everything we do. I would not just call it White supremacy, because that is limiting. It is all sorts of situations, which include White supremacy, but which also include patriarchy, classism, and other political, social, and economic pressures. So it is hard to envision what a multiracial society would look like. I guess it would be a color-blind society in the best sense of the word.

Orelus: *What do you mean by a color-blind society "in the best sense of the word"?*

Nieto: Usually, when people talk about being color-blind, they claim that they don't see differences. They say, "I don't see differences, so all my students are the same to me." I don't think that is possible. We *do* see differences, and we need to acknowledge them because differences are not necessarily negative. But to be "color-blind" in the best sense of the word means that you don't see those things as getting in the way, but rather as being additive, that is, as adding to who people are. So I would see it as not merely being color-blind but being color-blind conscious. People should not be held back because of who they are. Who they are should not determine their place in the world. And that is what I mean by being color-blind in the best sense of the word.

Orelus: *For example, people who are half Black and half Japanese, or half White, are often forced to claim only their Black identity. They are identified as Black. How do you explain that since you claim that the ultimate goal shouldn't be about fighting only White supremacy, but also against other forms of oppression?*

Nieto: This is mostly a cultural thing. It is because of how we have constructed identities in this society; in other societies, it is not the case. In Brazil and in Puerto Rico, for example, people can be mixed and still be seen as White, or seen as something other than Black. Now, that is not to claim that there is not racism in those societies, because of course there is. Because of laws that we have had that determined who people are simply by one drop of blood, people are constrained. So I guess that White supremacy can explain this. But other social, political, and economic forces, especially patriarchy and class discrimination, are also at work here.

Orelus: *In countries in South or Central America, a mixed person can pass for White. Why do you think some mixed people do not want to be called Black?*

Nieto: Obviously because it is seen as a negative thing. However, if you have money, even if you are dark skinned, you can claim Whiteness. This happens in a few cases. But even in those cases, it is still negative to be Black. I always give the example of my sister's ex-boyfriend. He is Puerto Rican and dark skinned, or what we call *trigueño*, that is, "wheat colored," or brown skinned. My sister was talking to my mother one day and said something like, "You know, Joe is Black." My mother said, "He's not Black." My sister was telling this to Joe's sister, Carmen, and Carmen said, "You know, the more they like us, the lighter we become!" How we classify people is a social and cultural issue. If people want to see you in a positive way, they claim you are not Black, even if you are dark skinned and can't pass for White. So yes, Black is usually seen as the most negative.

ORELUS: *So in that sense, it is not the person who claims something other than Black. Rather, it is society.*

NIETO: Yes, absolutely. People who are mixed have a right to claim every part of who they are. Many times, it is not because they are ashamed of one or the other. But because they come from two parents, they want to claim all of who they are; they want to be fully who they are, but they are not allowed to do that. It is very tricky. Let's take Tiger Woods, for example. He is apparently willing to see himself as mixed, and more Asian than Black, and the African American community has been very upset with him or even angry with him because of that. They say, "You look Black, you are Black." I can understand both sides. But we have to get to the point where people can say, "Look, Asian or White is also a part of who I am."

For example, in *Affirming Diversity*,[1] we interviewed Linda, a young woman, almost twenty years ago. She claimed that she was "half Black" and "half White." At that time, very few people were claiming that identity. If you looked like her, you were Black, and that was that. Even the woman who interviewed her, who was one of my doctoral students, was surprised by the identity that this young woman claimed. Linda said, "You know, I get upset when people tell me who I am. I am Black and White American. That is who I am. Sometimes people think that I am Hispanic; other times they even thought I was Chinese." She went on to say, "They should ask because they have no right to tell me who I am. It's not that I am ashamed of being Black or White, but I am both of those things."

It took a lot of courage for an eighteen-year-old girl to talk like that twenty years ago. We are hopefully coming to a new age when people can do that. However, there is also a problem with claiming multiracial identity because right now the way people are counted in most situations is pretty standard. You are either Black, White, Asian, Native American, Hispanic, or whatever the categories are. That doesn't allow space for any kind of multiracial identity. So that is upsetting to a lot of people.

On the other hand, when people do claim all these identities—for example, on the new census forms—it dilutes some of the problems that we are facing. For example, we don't see the depth of poverty in the African American community and the Latino community when people claim all these different identities. I don't think people's identities should be determined for them. White supremacy and racism have a lot to do with how people claim their identity. I have a friend who is multiracial. She never says she is half this or half that. I have another friend who is Japanese and Danish American, and he says, "I'm not half of this and half of that. I'm double."

This woman who's a friend of mine is Puerto Rican and African American. She told me one day, "You know, many members of my family have become Indian." They have registered in a Native American Nation, but they were never raised as Native Americans. They can prove that they are. They are like one-quarter Native American. Native American is perceived in a more positive way. She felt her family members did this to get away from being Black, which is always considered much more negative in our society.

ORELUS: *Speaking of avoiding being Black, what role do you think colorism plays in the whole biracial dynamic?*

NIETO: It plays an important role, especially in terms of Latinos. In Puerto Rican and Dominican families, the color range is incredible, from very light skin to very dark skin, and every kind of combination in between. For example, I have always thought how interesting it is that the Puerto Ricans that I know who are in higher education are mostly light skinned. We didn't come from middle-class families. Most of us Puerto Ricans who are in this country started out as working class in poor communities. It is another example that the lighter you are, the better chance you have of getting ahead, not necessarily because you are smarter, but because of colorism. Within one family, you can see that too. Piri Thomas has written about this in *Down These Mean Streets*.[2] Thomas is Puerto Rican, and he was the darkest one in his family. He grew up in Harlem. His father was also dark, but he hated Piri the most. He had the most trouble with that son because he was the darkest.

ORELUS: *I recently interviewed a young lady who is half Black and half White. Her father is from Trinidad, and her mother is a White Jew. She said that when she is among her Black friends, she is not treated with fairness because she is light skinned, and when she is among her mother's family, she is the dark child. What would you say to her?*

NIETO: Well, that's really interesting. Linda, the young woman I mentioned before whom we interviewed about twenty years ago, and other mixed-race people who are light skinned have said that they don't really feel comfortable in a White group or in a Black group but in a mixed group. They said they feel most comfortable among people who can understand them, that is, how they feel, who they are, and what their experience has been. Linda said, "I would hang out with my White friends, and I felt like I was one of them, but I know they felt like I was different. Or I would hang out with my Black friends, and they treated me as if I was different." So this is where the movement to claim a multiracial identity is a positive thing, because people who are multiracial are sometimes marginalized from all communities. It is going to take a kind of movement like the Black Power movement or the ethnic studies movement for multiracial people to really claim for themselves a place at the table.

ORELUS: *Do you think that someday people who are multiracial will be allowed to claim their identities and choose whoever they want to be?*

NIETO: I don't know. That is a good question. If you look at White ethnics, for example, most don't claim all their cultural identities. I would say that most people are mixed. They don't claim all their identities. That is why when people look at me they see a light-skinned woman or a White woman. That is what they see. So when I have the opportunity to check off all those things on the census, I do so because I know that my heritage is mixed. I claim that identity. But I know that a lot of people don't. So I don't know if by the time we are so hybridized this will happen. That is, I don't know at what point people will say, "You know, I'm this, I'm that, I'm this," or if they will say, "You know, I'm American." And I don't think that is a bad thing. It would be good to say "I'm American" and include all those identities, because right now that is not happening.

ORELUS: *If I say, "I'm an American," in a way isn't that denying my Caribbean and Haitian roots?*

NIETO: No. We should all be able to get to the point where we can say, "I'm an American," and "American" should be inclusive of all our identities. I don't think we are there yet. This is a fanciful scenario that I am claiming. I wrote a book chapter about it called "Becoming American." It is complex. I was born and raised here, and I don't say I am American unless I am in a different context. If I am outside the United States, then I claim it. But I feel like I should be able to say, "I am an American of Puerto Rican descent," meaning I am of Spanish, African, and Native descent. Africans are very mixed, so are Native people, and so are Spaniards.

Your identity really is how you were raised. That is why my friend who is African American and Puerto Rican feels that her relatives "became Indian," even though they were not raised with that culture, with those values, and those traditions. So that is why she feels it is sort of a sham. Again, your identity is how you have been raised, the kinds of experiences you have had, and the values that you have developed as a result. So it's is a complicated thing.

I remember I had a young woman in a workshop I gave who was ethnically Korean. She was crying after the workshop, and she said, "You know, I am Korean, but I am White, because I was adopted by 'White' people, and I don't know what it means to be Korean. I can't speak the language. I don't do anything that is Korean." She was right. She is identified by others as Asian, but everything about her is "White." That is why it is so complicated.

ORELUS: *Earlier you stated that, "in academia, you find mostly light-skinned Puerto Ricans." What does that really tell us about racism and White supremacy?*

NIETO: Well, that is my experience. I am not saying that is true of everybody. White supremacy operates everywhere. It operates everywhere even in a country that is so mixed. It is still there. We see it all the time. It tells us that White supremacy is alive and well. But there is also patriarchy, sexism, classism, and homophobia.

ORELUS: *Do you think president Obama's legacy or presidency might contribute to the multiracial movement that has been taking place in the United States?*

NIETO: It might help. But he made it a point not to make a very big issue of race. But even if he doesn't make a very big issue of it, it's an issue. I do think it's interesting that it took a biracial president whose Black heritage is from Africa rather than an African American to be elected the first Black president. Although he may claim that biracial identity, people are saying he's Black. They identify him as "our first Black president." So it may give support to people who want to claim a biracial or multiracial identity, and that will be good for the movement probably.

At the same time, this opens the door for others. Look at the fact that he has appointed a Puerto Rican woman to the highest court. I'm thrilled about that. Had Obama been only African American rather than biracial, it would have been harder. But he is a different kind of Black leader from the Black leaders we have had in the past, who focused a lot more on race. This is just a different time, and you could never be a Black man focusing on race and expect to win the presidency of the United States. You can't be. Maybe in twenty or thirty years you can, who knows?

ORELUS: *Do you think it was a conscious choice that Obama made not to talk so much about his biracial identity?*

NIETO: Yes. You know why? Because he was raised by "White" people. That is what I was saying before. That is his background. That is how he was raised. He was not raised as a Black man in America. Basically, he was raised by his White grandparents in a "White world." He was the only person of color in that world. So I understand why he did not talk much about race. It was a choice not to focus too much on his Black heritage, because he recognized that is a difficult discussion to have for a lot of White people. On the other hand, the talk he gave on race was wonderful. He really confronted these issues, and nobody else had. So it was a step forward. I really do think so.

ORELUS: *So what advice would you give people who are biracial or multiracial?*

NIETO: I would say to be fully who you are, but at the same time recognize the sociopolitical context in which you live. That context will want to define you, and you will have to understand why. I would say to them, have solidarity with people who are mixed as well as with those who are not mixed. Of course, everybody is mixed; that is my own opinion. So, if you are biracial—say, Black and White—it is important that you have connection with the African American community. That is what Obama consciously did when he went to and got out of college. When he went to live in Chicago, he immersed himself in the African American community, joined an African American church, married an African American woman, and got into her family. So that kind of solidarity is also important, because even though you may claim a certain identity, you know you are also part of another.

ORELUS: *Anything else you want to add?*

NIETO: I really floundered at the beginning talking about White supremacy. It is not that I didn't want to talk about it. It is so overpowering that to name it so directly is sometimes hard. But it is something that we have to do. So the more I thought about it as you were talking, the more I realized, yes, it affects all these levels: our lives, the context in which we live, institutional norms. It affects all these things. So yes, White supremacy is still a major enemy.

ORELUS: *What about patriarchy?*

NIETO: Patriarchy is huge too; so is social class ideology. That is why I don't want to focus on just one form of oppression. Because it is not just discrimination; it is the ideology, so I can't say which one is more prevalent. I guess for different people, patriarchy is more prevalent; for others it might be social class issues. But I would have to say, from everything I have seen, read, and done, if you are Black, that is usually an overriding issue. For example, if you are Black, a woman, and working class, those are three kinds of issues that you have to deal with. From what I have heard, many people who have all these identities say that for them, being Black is the most difficult to deal with. But others might disagree and say that gender is more difficult.

ORELUS: *If women had been the ones in power for centuries instead of White men, do you think they would have created more space for people to claim their multiple identities and the world would have been a better place to live in?*

NIETO: I don't know. That is a very hard question to answer. People have said, "The world would be different if women were in charge," but I don't know. There have been women in charge in some places, not structurally, but "one" woman, and I haven't seen very many changes. "Power" is powerful. No matter who you are, when you have power, you tend to use it in ways that are not always to the benefit of the majority of people. I don't know if things would have been different if women had been in power. I would like to think that, but I don't know. I tend to think that they might not have been that different.

ORELUS: *I have seen many White women with men of color, but not so many White men with women of color. How do you explain this phenomenon?*

NIETO: The only way I can explain it is that the image of beauty that is out there in society, not only in our society, is White. Since men have more power than women, men are the ones to go for that image. So even Black men will go for that image of beauty. It would be good if we could say it is just love, that it has nothing to do with color or anything. But all of us are affected by all the images around us of what is desirable. Whiteness is one of those things. Also, power and prestige are part of those things. So we are all affected by those things.

In Puerto Rico, there is a saying that shows how racism operates even in a multiracial society: people are encouraged to marry lighter-skinned people themselves to *mejorar la raza*, that is, to improve the race. I am sure you have heard that term. When you think about that, it is pretty devastating, right? There are a lot of other sayings like that. The difference between Puerto Rico and the United States is that in Puerto Rico people are much more blunt about these things. They say them more directly. Maybe it is because we are so mixed. But like I said before, being mixed doesn't mean that we don't harbor racism. We were all raised with those images, whether we are Black or White or anything in between.

ORELUS: *Do you think that had you been Afro-Puerto Rican, your career in academia would have been different?*

NIETO: I bet it would have. I make White people comfortable, because when they see me come into a room, they think, "Oh, she's like us, we can talk to her. She looks like us. She sounds like us." So, if I had been a Black woman, it would have been much harder for people to deal with. Therefore, the reception I would have gotten would have been different, and my reaction to that reception would have been different. I didn't have a hard time in academia, like a lot of other people of color had, and that part of it is because of my physical appearance. I did not have a hard time because a lot of people could look at me and feel very comfortable with me because they could claim me as one of them. And in a lot of ways, I was.

ORELUS: *Is it fair to say that because you grew up socializing with Whites, that made it easier for you to interact with them?*

NIETO: As a kid, I did not socialize with White people. Until I was a teenager, we lived in Puerto Rican communities. But from early on, by being exposed to a few White people, I knew that there was something different. I was a working-class Puerto Rican and was brought up in Puerto Rican neighborhoods; my sister and I spoke with an urban Black, Puerto Rican kind of English. We used to say "mines" for "mine" and "ain't" and all of that. I knew from a very early age that I had to drop that if I wanted to be someone else. So that is social class; it is not only race and ethnicity. I wrote about this in my book *Language, Culture, and Teaching*.[3] Yeah, early on I knew that I had to learn how to speak differently than I used to if I wanted to get ahead.

ORELUS: *In your class as a White Puerto Rican, do you think that you received better treatment than those who were not White?*

NIETO: I'm sure. But that doesn't mean that this alone helped me become a really good student. I was a very good student. But my sister, who is very smart, wasn't as successful, probably because of learning disabilities, and she is lighter than I am. So it is a combination of factors. It is what you look like, who you are, your disposition, and certainly your color. All my teachers until I went to graduate school were White, except for one Black teacher I had, Mrs. Phillips; she was my fifth-grade teacher. She was a wonderful teacher, and I loved her. In all my classes, I was always the teacher's pet because I was always a really good student. I did all my homework, and I excelled. But there were other kids who looked like me who didn't excel. It was probably easier for me than for others. I have plenty of cousins who are also light skinned who didn't do well in school because of other socioeconomic, family, and personal issues. We can't just always point to one thing; it is more complicated than that.

Notes

1. Nieto, S. (2004). *Affirming diversity: The socio-cultural context of multicultural education*. Boston: Pearson Education.
2. Thomas, P. (1997). *Down these mean streets*. New York: Vintage.
3. Nieto, S. (2002). *Language, culture, and teaching: Critical perspectives for a new century*. New York: Lawrence Erlbaum Associates.

CHAPTER 7

Multicultural Education Matters More Than Ever

A CONVERSATION WITH CARL A. GRANT

Through this dialogue, Professor Carl Grant, a leading figure in multicultural education, talks about the role multicultural education has played in creating space for multiplicity of voices, acceptance, and respect for differences in schools and beyond. More importantly, he spells out the role multicultural education has played in promoting social justice for everyone. Professor Grant also talks about the challenges that many teacher practitioners face in trying to help people, including students and teachers, understand what multicultural education stands for. These professors, particularly Professor Grant, talk about the importance of taking into account the context in which multicultural education philosophy and ideas are implemented. Drawing on his experience leading workshops and giving talks abroad on multicultural education, Professor Grant states that multicultural education ideas and philosophy can be applied in any country as long as the context in which these ideas are being implemented is taken into account.

The Dialogue

Orelus: *You have been writing extensively about multicultural education for years. Have you seen any change in people's attitudes and actions toward students who are from multiracial and multicultural backgrounds?*

Grant: I would say there has been some change. People are not nearly as resistant as they used to be in a classroom twenty-five years ago. Back then, if you had five people who would be interested in really listening, that would have been a good sign. But today, you can probably have, in a classroom of twenty-five students, more than half of them very interested in multicultural and social justice issues. But the question remains: what will they do with the knowledge they acquire about these issues?

Orelus: *The world is changing with the new wave of immigrants coming from all over the world and with technology. So, has your philosophy of multiculturalism changed? Or does it remain the same?*

Grant: Yes, it is constantly growing. Recently, I was in Athens, Istanbul, and Cyprus. The people in those countries are dealing with issues of multiculturalism. They may call it intercultural education, but it is very similar to multicultural education. So you see it operating in different cultures and different contexts around issues like religion, and people's ideas and movement grow along with that. People's ideas grow. You begin to understand how multicultural education is being defined, conceptualized, and placed, or not placed, in a government policy. In some places, it is being put into government policy.

In this country, multicultural education is between two camps that focus on teacher education. In one camp you find those who are arguing for greater teacher compatibility and the professionalization of the teaching community; they definitely articulate multicultural education in what they say. Among those who are interested in the deregulation of the hiring of teachers, you don't see this that much. Regardless, one's awareness is increased about the way multicultural education plays itself out in the general public and in many fields in different countries, including the United States.

Orelus: *Have you incorporated in your recent work some of the feedback you have received from people in the United States and abroad?*

Grant: I include some of that in some papers that I am working on now. I haven't done that as a formal study, but I have in my work anecdotal statements people share with me about the type of multicultural work they are doing.

Orelus: *In your view, to what degree and in what way can multiculturalism be used as an educational tool to fight against racism and other forms of oppression?*

Grant: That is its purpose. Multiculturalism needs to be included in the curriculum and in whatever subject matters teachers are teaching. For those people who want to teach, having a clear understanding of what multicultural education stands for can help them become better teachers of all students. So ideas embedded in multicultural education are enlightening for students, teachers, and parents. We have a lot of White teachers who are increasingly supporting multicultural education. I would say that multiculturalism is a counter to White supremacy, which is based on an ideology that things should not be multicultural. But that is a journey of a thousand miles.

I would say that in the United States, we don't have what is called a *national curriculum*, although the textbooks we use may in some ways lead one to believe that. So it is a struggle at each school district in each town and each state to help people become more responsive to issues related around multicultural education. It is a journey, but as I say, increasingly different school districts are aware of it. Now, the extent to which they actualize it in the classroom is not as far along as I would like it to be.

ORELUS: *In your view, what should multiracial and multicultural society look like?*

GRANT: Well, it should be a society that is advocating for democracy, a multicultural democracy—a democratic society that does not merely believe in consumerism, but a democratic society that makes sure that people not only learn how to engage in citizenship, but also in doing things that help them to have a flourishing life. It is much more than just economics; much more should be involved in that. All of these things should be possible in a multicultural and multiracial society.

ORELUS: *So what role do you think multiculturalism should play in the fight against capitalism?*

GRANT: This capitalistic system in which we live needs to become more democratic. What multicultural education would work at is, how do we exercise some of the fundamental principles that people like Thomas Jefferson and Dr. King talked about so we can have democracy within this capitalistic system? I mean democracy for everyone. Every system that you go into will have some problems. Part of what we have to work at is how to reduce or eliminate as many problems as possible in order to open things up to more and more people.

ORELUS: *It is understood that no system is perfect. But capitalism is about maximizing one's profits. So how can a capitalist system be democratic and equitable?*

GRANT: Right now we are living in kind of a heightened period of attention to economics and moneymaking. But if you were to go back into the history of this country and read some of the literature that talks about how we used to live, you would see that the system was attentive to the common good of people; you would have a different take on this issue. But you are right; in the last twenty years, we have taken our eye off the ball of striving toward equality for everyone. We have become much more a consumer nation, concerned much more about money. But you can find this within a lot of systems. Capitalism has its problems, but it is like any other system of government that has its own problems.

ORELUS: *Can you share with me how you started being involved in multiculturalism? Who inspired you? And how did you start?*

GRANT: I was raised thinking, "How do you help your fellow human beings? How do you apply in your daily life the fundamental Christian beliefs and principles like, 'Do unto others as you would like them to do unto you?'" That is very much a foundation that a lot of us in multicultural education believe in. It is not a question of power and privilege. It is a question of sharing. It is a question of fairness. It is a question of cultural recognition. These things basically are fundamental and central premises that come from a number of different world religions. That is what got me involved in multicultural education types of work.

ORELUS: *What role do you think multiculturalism should play in building a community in school and beyond?*

GRANT: There is a woman named Diana Eck[1] at the Harvard Institute of Religion who talks about pluralist engagement. The whole notion of pluralistic engagement means to have people who come from different backgrounds be able to meet on equal footing, to meet and discuss problems and issues as they see them and also to inform people about their background, their history, and their contribution to this society. Multicultural education makes you realize that there is no model of being an American. We all contribute to the fabric of this country.

ORELUS: *Often there is a gap between home and school. So how can multiculturalism play a role in bridging that gap?*

GRANT: Much of what multicultural education talks about and advocates for is a strong positive relationship between the home and the school. What we have to work at is, how do we foster that relationship? How do we encourage parents to know that as simple a thing as a parent-teacher meeting is important for community and school building and the learning growth of their children? How do we make sure that when parents come, they are not expected to come and sit there and be quiet while the teacher talks? How do we help the parents and the teachers understand that the interaction between them is taking place because both of them are talking about someone that they care about and they love—that is, that parent's son or daughter? This is the type of awareness that we as educators have an obligation to help both teachers and parents have about the teaching profession, because it is for the benefit of all students, parents, and teachers.

ORELUS: *What are some of the limitations that you think people should be aware about regarding multiculturalism?*

GRANT: One of the limitations is getting people to understand it. Another limitation is that we don't know how it operates in all particular situations because there has not been money to fund studies that look at how multicultural education works or does not work in certain situations. A lot of what we are doing is talking about it theoretically, which is from opinions. What we need is to research it out. This would better inform us about some of the tentativeness of multicultural education.

OReLus: *Do you think that globalization, or, to be precise, the Western form of globalization, has somewhat impacted the multicultural education movement?*

GRANT: There is an influence. When I was in Greece and Istanbul, I was able to witness that intercultural education is a big thing, and it is very similar to multicultural education. The world's multiculturalism and globalization is in this very paradoxical form. Multicultural education can help people be aware about the positive and negative challenges of globalization. And globalization lets us know more fully that we live in a multicultural world.

ORELUS: *The way multicultural education is understood and applied in the United States might not necessarily work in other countries. Would you agree with that?*

GRANT: Yes. It would have to be modified. Some of the principles would hold up, like cultural recognition and fairness, but some of the other principles would have to be worked out conceptually in the country they are being tried out in. In other words, it cannot just be blankly transported.

ORELUS: *Where do you see the multicultural movement going from here?*

GRANT: Well, there is a lot going on. As I said, in those countries that I visited and this country, there are a lot of things going on related to multicultural education. It is very active and alive. But that doesn't mean it is not going to be criticized. We live in a global world, which is multicultural, and that is exciting.

Note

1. See The Pluralism Project's CD-ROM (1997), *On Common Ground: World Religions in America.*

Part III

REDEFINING DEMOCRACY, SCHOOLING, AND SOCIAL JUSTICE IN THE SUPREME STATE OF WESTERN NEOLIBERALISM AND U.S. IMPERIALISM

Is democracy possible in a neoliberal and capitalist state? Can we have a democratic school system within such a state? This section and the dialogues that follow attempt to shed light on these questions. The concept of democracy has been at the center of many political debates and can be traced back as far as the time of Plato. This concept occupied a central role in Plato's work, namely in his book *Republic*.[1] Specifically, through this book, Plato advocated for democratic values and principles, which he argued should be the cornerstone of any society or government.

Furthermore, Plato emphasized the great value and role of democracy in the construction of an equitable society. Moreover, he argued that embracing and implementing democratic values and principles in any given society can be conducive to the political stability of a country and the overall well-being of its citizens. Finally, Plato was against oligarchic and authoritarian forms of government often ruled by the wealthy at the expense of the poor.[2]

Many scholars from various fields and with different foci, such as education, philosophy, and political science, have taken on Plato's work on democracy and expanded it. For example, John Dewey, the prominent American philosopher and educator, was a champion for a democratic school system. Dewey advocated for creating democratic space within the U.S. school system. He believed such a place was essential for the creation of good citizenship. Dewey also believed that students and professors should be allowed to discuss social and political issues in schools without the intrusion and infringement of the government.[3] In other words, Dewey believed that students' and professors' voices should not be silenced if democracy is to exist. As Maxine Greene eloquently put it, "Without a Dewey, there would have been little concern for 'participatory democracy,' for 'consensus,' for the reconstitution of a public sphere" (p. 92).[4]

Taking Dewey's view on democracy and schooling a few steps further, I argue that in order to have a democratic school system, students should be allowed to voice their opinion about what kind of education they feel they deserve to receive. Also, students should be given the opportunity to actively participate in the co-construction of knowledge with their teachers. In my view, a school system within which students are expected to merely receive and regurgitate the information that their teachers pass on to them is not democratic. As the Brazilian educator Paulo Freire pointed out in his seminal work, *Pedagogy of the Oppressed*, students should not be passive recipients of prefabricated knowledge that professors pour into their heads. Freire called this form of teaching practice a banking form of education. Freire explains what this form of education entails in the following terms:

(a) the teacher teaches and the students are taught;
(b) the teacher knows everything and the students know nothing;
(c) the teacher thinks and the students are thought about;
(d) the teacher talks and the students listen—meekly;
(e) the teacher disciplines and the students are disciplined;
(f) the teacher chooses and enforces his choice, and the students comply;
(g) the teacher acts and the students have the illusion of acting through the action of the teacher;
(h) the teacher chooses the program content, and the students (who are not consulted) adapt to it;
(i) the teacher confuses the authority of knowledge with his or her own professional authority, which she and he sets in opposition to the freedom of the students;
(j) the teacher is the subject of the learning process, while the pupils are mere objects. (p. 73)[5]

Freire's notion of a banking form of education is not an obsolete one. It has been a recurring practice in the U.S. school system, especially with the passage of the No Child Left Behind mandate. Because of this mandate, many teachers have been pressured to teach to the test with the hope that their students would meet state and federal standardized test benchmarks.[6] Consequently, the teaching practices of many public school teachers have been reduced to mostly rote and drill test practices, leaving limited space for creative and critical work conducive to student growth and learning. The question that is then worth asking is, can one talk about democracy when these teaching practices are commonplace within the U.S. school system, whose goal should be to prepare students to become good and critical citizens?

School and politics are not two separate entities. Therefore, what is happening in school needs to be situated and configured within a country's political system. Cornel West and Noam Chomsky, among others, who have been very critical of the U.S. political system, concur that in a democratic society, people, including students and teachers, should be able to assert their voices without any fear of governmental repressive measures. These two public intellectuals similarly argue that citizens should be allowed to actively participate in the political decision-making process and that they should not merely be passive spectators of this process. Critiquing the U.S. system of democracy, West has stated,

> The American democratic experiment is unique in human history not because we are God's chosen people to lead the world, nor because we are a force for good in the world, but because of our refusal to acknowledge the deeply racist and imperial roots of our democratic project. We are exceptional because of our denial of the antidemocratic foundation stones of American democracy. (p. 41)[7]

Similarly, questioning the U.S. notion of democracy, Chomsky states, "That's mostly mythology. It's ideology. It's just not a fact. In fact, this has been well studied by scholars here. So there are good studies of this so-called democracy promotion movement" (Chomsky as cited in this section, p. 112).

In a country where workers have been exploited and are afraid of speaking up against their inhuman conditions and where students have often been rewarded for being silent, the concept of democracy becomes more of an illusion than a reality. Furthermore, one should not talk about democracy in a country where a small group of wealthy people control the information circulated through TV and radio stations that they own. Nor should one talk about democracy without the equal and representative voices and active participation of all citizens in political decisions concerning and affecting their lives. Moreover, democracy is an illusion in a capitalist state where profits are the priority, not the people.[8] Finally, democracy is yet to become a reality for those, namely poor Blacks and Latino/as, who are unjustly and massively incarcerated and have been treated as the "wretched of the earth" in the prison system.[9]

Unfortunately, this democracy myth has been ingrained in the minds of many people in many countries, including the U.S., which has dubiously been called a democratic country. Like Chomsky and West, de Tocqueville and Grant and Myrdal unveiled the contradictory nature of the U.S. political system.[10] As these authors observed, while the U.S. has earned a democratic reputation worldwide, many groups, such as African Americans, Native Americans, Latino/as, and Asians, among others, have historically suffered brutal forms of discrimination.[11]

Thus, one must ask, who exactly has been benefiting from the U.S. form of democracy?

The noble idea of democracy needs to be a reality, not only for those who own the means of production and control the U.S. political apparatus, but also for those whose voices have been silenced. As Chomsky notes in the interview that follows, democracy is a mythology when a minority group in powerful positions has accumulated the wealth of a country and has used the corporate media and the police to manipulate and silence the voice of the majority so that they will not revolt against social injustice. These practices violate the core values and principles that shape and constitute the spirit of a democratic society. As Eric Williams has pointed out, "Democracy means the obligation of the minority to recognize the right of the majority. Democracy means responsibility of the government to its citizens, the protection of the citizens from the exercise of arbitrary power and the violation of human freedoms and individual rights" (p. 266).[12]

Williams' definition of democracy is yet to be meaningful to those who have been marginalized and exploited in a capitalist state, where the wealthy, including CEOs of major corporations, have influenced many institutions, such as the workplace, the government, and even universities. These issues are central to the arguments that Professors Noam Chomsky and Peter McLaren make in the following dialogues. Specifically, Noam Chomsky and Peter McLaren critically examine the impact of U.S. neoliberalism and imperialism on people's lives, including students, teachers, and factory workers. Challenging U.S. foreign policy and the neoliberal agenda, Professor Chomsky argues that this policy and agenda have allowed the rich to become richer and worsened the socioeconomic conditions of the poor both in the United States and in the so-called third world. Chomsky questions the common myth that the United States is a democratic country. Similarly, Professor McLaren takes a radical position against Western transnational capitalism and U.S. imperialism, pointing out the extent to which they have impacted many people, including factory workers and students, and institutions such as universities.

Notes

1. Plato. (1992). *Republic* (G. A. M. Crube, Trans.). Indianapolis: Hackett.
2. Baird, F., & Kaufmann, K. (2008). *From Plato to Derrida.* Upper Saddle River, NJ: Pearson Prentice Hall.
3. Dewey, J. (2010). *Democracy and education: An introduction to the philosophy of education.* Cedar Lake, MI: ReadaClassic.com.
4. Greene, M. (2009). In search of a critical pedagogy. In A. Darder, M. P. Baltodna, & R. D. Torres, *The critical pedagogy reader* (2nd ed.). New York: Routledge.

5. Freire, P. (2000). *Pedagogy of the oppressed.* New York: Continuum.

6. Sleeter, C. E. (2005). *Un-standardizing curriculum: Multicultural teaching in the standards-based classroom.* Routledge: New York.

7. West, C. (2005). *Democracy matters: Winning the fight against imperialism.* New York: Penguin.

8. Chomsky, N. (2010). *Hopes and prospects.* Chicago: Haymarket Books.

9. Fanon, F. (2004). *The wretched of the earth.* New York: Grove Press; Alexander, M. (2010). *The new Jim Crow: Mass incarceration in the age of colorblindness.* New York: New Press.

10. Myrdal, G. (1944). *An American dilemma: The Negro problem and modern democracy.* New York: Harper & Brothers; de Tocqueville, A., & Grant, S. (2000). *Democracy in America.* Indianapolis: Hackett.

11. Grande, S. (2004). *Red pedagogy: Native American social and political thought.* Lanham, MD: Rowman & Littlefield.

12. Williams, E. (1993). History of the people of Trinidad and Tobago. Brooklyn, NY: A&b Publishers.

CHAPTER 8

Critical Pedagogy in Stark Opposition to Western Neoliberalism and the Corporatization of Schools

A CONVERSATION WITH PETER MCLAREN

In this dialogue, Professor McLaren draws on a critical pedagogy theoretical framework to critically analyze the harmful effects of capitalism on poor working-class people, including factory workers in countries such as Argentina. He points out the resilience with which these workers resisted the arbitrary decision of CEOs who closed the factory where they were working. These CEOs closed the factories when they realized they could no longer maximize their profits. As McLaren eloquently points out, these factory workers, inspired by a strong sense of collectiveness and work ethic, combined with their unshakable determination to take their destiny in their own hands, organized and ran the factory for the equal benefit of each worker. Professor McLaren goes on to talk about the negative influence of U.S. neoliberal policy on third world countries. Along the same line, he provides a sharp critique of universities in the United States that have followed a corporate model of education to fit the logic of the capitalist system. Professor McLaren invites concerned citizens, particularly students, to use their agency to counter the corporatization and militarization of schools. Finally, in linking capitalism to other forms of oppression, such as racism, Professor McLaren maintains, "Racism often keeps White workers from recognizing that it is in their interests to unite with their Black and Brown brothers and sisters and fight their capitalist bosses."

The Dialogue

OrELUS: What should be the main concern of progressive educators about capitalism, including the transnationalization of goods? Further, what role do you think critical pedagogues should play in the fight against capitalism and neoliberalism?

McLAREN: My main concern has been problematizing the state power. In recent decades, the capitalist production process itself has become increasingly transnationalized. We have moved from a world economy to a new epoch known as the global economy. Formerly, the world economy was composed of the development of national economies and national circuits of accumulation that were linked to each other through commodity trade and capital flows in an integrated international market. While nation-states mediated the boundaries between differently articulated modes of production, today national production systems are reorganized and functionally integrated into global circuits, creating a single and increasingly undifferentiated field for world capitalism. We are talking here about what Bill Robinson calls the transnationalization of the production of goods and services (globalization), not just the extension of trade and financial flows across national borders (internationalization).

The new global financial system disperses profits worldwide as the world becomes unified into a single mode of production and a single global system that brings about the organic integration of different countries and regions into a global economy. The consequences of the restructuring of the world productive apparatus are staggering. I agree with Robinson that technological changes are the result of class struggle—in this case, the restraints on accumulation imposed by popular classes worldwide. Global class formation is occurring, with supranational integration of national classes accompanying the transnational integration of national productive structures. This has accelerated the division of the world into a global bourgeoisie (the hegemonic global class fraction) and a global proletariat. That is, dominant groups fuse into a class or class fraction within transnational space. There is an emergent capitalist historic bloc sustained by a transnational capitalist class and represented by a transnational bourgeoisie.

The United States is playing a leadership role on behalf of the emerging transnational elite; that is, the U.S. is taking the lead in developing policies and strategies on behalf of the global capitalist agenda of the transnational elite—and it certainly is an imperialist agenda. It follows from this that revolutionary social struggle must become transnationalized as power from below in order to counter transnationalized capitalist power from above. What we are seeing today in the marketplace is really a continuation of the core ideology of Reaganism: free markets, unregulated corporations, an aggressive militarization abroad, and the suppression of civil liberties and civil rights at home. In a sense, the United States is now closer to the Reagan ideal of the national security state.

One of the major mechanisms used by the ideological state apparatus to prevent a legitimation crisis over the necessity of global capitalism is the school. Students are taught to believe that if capitalism falters, democracy is doomed. But, as Marx argues, capital is a historically produced social relation that can be challenged (most forcefully by those exploited by it). A renewed engagement with and challenge to capital by means of critical revolutionary pedagogy fibrillates our social imagination which largely has been flatlined since the ascendancy of Ronald Reagan and Margaret Thatcher and their successful assault on Keynesian welfare state capitalism.

Meszaros has argued that capitalism's functional division of labor is horizontal and is potentially liberating because it partakes of a socially viable universality—the harmonization of the universal development of the productive forces with the all-around abilities and potentialities of freely associated individuals. However, it is the vertical dimension of capitalism and its hierarchical division of labor that constitutes capital's reproductive horizon and command structure, ensuring that living labor is subsumed by dead labor and that capital's productive developments remain containable by the imperative of surplus labor accumulation. This results in the structural-hierarchical subordination of labor to capital. In other words, this creates a permanent structural crisis within capitalism in contrast to what some believe are only periodic, conjunctural crises. When we talk about the transnational capitalist class, new forms of imperialism, and the like, we need to see this in terms of the theory of the state that educators work with.

There is, for lack of better terms, left-liberal critical pedagogy, liberal critical pedagogy, conservative critical pedagogy, and variants of each of these. And in opposition to these, you have revolutionary critical pedagogy that some of us, myself included, have been trying to develop. These are very rough terms, of course, and there are probably better terms. But the main point I have been making is that we need to be guided by a larger social vision that does not assume that the state and civil society are autonomous.

Let's face it: civil society is part and parcel of state apparatuses. We fool ourselves if we think there is a strong autonomy in civil society. So the larger vision takes into consideration the social totality, the way capitalism has permeated all spheres of social life, including civil society or the public sphere. This mandates that we need to create a social universe outside of capital's value form. Anything short of this will not bring about emancipation. Revolutionary critical pedagogy strives for the abolition of capital as a social relation. This is the major difference between my position and that of many other critical educators.

Critical revolutionary educators are interested in the movements of the world's totality and how this totality is uncovered by human beings, and how, in our uncovering this totality, we develop a particular ontological openness toward being. How can we discover ourselves as historical beings? The results of our actions in and on and through the world do not coincide with our intentions. Why is this? What accounts for the disharmony between the necessity and the freedom of our actions as human beings creating and being created by historical forces? These are questions that animate the work of revolutionary critical educators. Do we make history or are we agents of history?

But inasmuch as critical pedagogy is the topic of many books and articles in North America, it is not something you actually see very often in the public schools. Sometimes you see it in alternative schools. Many educators here in the United States claim that there are not enough industrial workers in the U.S. to claim that we have a working class here, and so there is no need for a socialist revolution. There might not be as many industrial workers as there once were in the United States, but there are many who still produce value the way industrial workers produce value.

There are capitalist workers here—workers who are told what to do by their bosses, who serve the capitalist class. We have high-paid workers, and low-paid workers. Those with good salaries disguise the fact that they are workers. Ninety percent of the people in the United States are workers. Of course, many members of the ruling elite in the United States were never at the mercy of an employer who could terminate his or her job; there are many in this privileged sector who have never been humiliated by a boss, who never came home stooped in pain after a hard day of manual labor. They never were in a situation where they could not feed themselves or their families. But what about the working class and their struggles? The Cold War basically frightened the American public from even uttering the word socialism in public, except to condemn it.

ORELUS: *Can you define critical pedagogy for the reader, explaining what it entails? Also, how have you applied critical pedagogy in both your scholarly and activist work?*

MCLAREN: When I use the term "critical pedagogy," I am referring to more than classroom teaching or popular education that takes place in community settings. I define it as the working out of a systematic dialectic of pedagogy that is organized around a philosophy of praxis. The first aspect of this praxis consists of an imminent critique of conventional pedagogies in order to see if their assumptions and claims are adequate to the type of praxis needed to both understand and challenge and eventually overcome capitalism's expansionistic dynamic. So we need to develop a philosophy of praxis that is able to identify and transcend the dominant contradictions in society, and forms of organization—horizontal and democratic—that best reflect our praxis. It is a praxis of being and becoming, of mental and manual labor, of thinking and doing, of reading and writing the word and the world in the Freirean sense.

Critical pedagogy is both a reading practice where we read the word in the context of the world, and a practical activity where we write ourselves as subjective forces into the text of history—but this does not mean that making history is only an effect of discourse, a form of metonymy, the performative dimension of language, a rhetorical operation, a tropological system. No, reality is more than textual self-difference. Praxis, as I am using the term, is directed at understanding the world dialectically as an effect of class contradictions. So critical pedagogy is a way of challenging the popular imaginary (which has no outside to the text) that normalizes the core cultural foundations of capitalism and the normative force of the state.

In other words, this popular imaginary tells us that there is no alternative to capitalist social relations. So critical pedagogy is a reading and an acting upon the social totality by turning abstract things into a material force, by linking abstract thought to praxis, to revolutionary praxis, to bringing about a social universe that is not based on the value form of labor but is a socialist alternative to capitalism. So here I am looking to critical pedagogy as a social process, a social product, and a social movement that is grounded in both a philosophy of praxis and democratic forms of organization.

Revolutionary critical pedagogy is a praxis, but it also operates within ways of knowing the world, conceptual systems, and the like. As with any system of intelligibility, it needs to be open to the strengths and limitations of different logics, rationalities, systems of classification, and structures of power. We can't fall prey to grandiose illusions and must always be open to criticism.

And finally, revolutionary critical pedagogy is not about the struggle for information (matter in its lowest common denominator) so much as it is about the struggle for knowledge, a place where consciousness can discover itself, a place where knowledge gives way to a creative purposiveness—to a protagonistic agency. But it is even more than this—it is about the struggle to transform such knowledge into wisdom by means of a dialectical reading of the word and the world, that is, in the reciprocally revealed relationship between consciousness and the world, and that which lies beyond the world, and in the unity of diversities in the individual and in the world that unites both the large and the small, the powerful and the powerless, in the dinergic unity of social life. Critical pedagogy is not only about creating the pedagogical context for teaching ourselves the stories of others, but it is about a new way of hearing what we say that enables us to listen in new ways, and hopefully learn to speak in ways that are open to others.

ORELUS: *What is your position about universities that have been following a corporate model of education? How should we, as critical public intellectuals, fight against this corporate form of education?*

McLaren: Well, the university should be about providing free education to the poor. And that is regardless of the qualifications of the students. That is essential. The university should be designed to serve the transformation of the society. Currently the university is under the heel of corporate control and management models of education that stress narrow-minded forms of instrumental knowledge and efficiency, accountability, and the like. The university has lost sight of what is best for the social good, what is best for the people, and especially the poor. It serves the interest of the ruling class, not the interests of creating an inclusive, participatory democracy struggling to create a socialism for the twenty-first century.

There is increasing militarism in the universities, much stronger links to military projects and programs, with officers' training programs, with the Pentagon providing funds for research; we can all agree that public funding for universities is drying up, that the quality of our universities is suffering in its overall academic programs, especially the liberal arts sector, that, in effect, the universities are abandoning the public sphere and embracing the market-based neoliberal rationality that powers the private sphere. The public sphere itself is but a shadow of what it once was, but on the surface it is more dynamic and shimmering, as it now is all spectacle; the culture of consumption has colonized everyday life, and we can, of course, trace this to neoliberalism, to Reagan, Thatcher, and the perilous trajectory we have been part of since that time.

The university should, of course, be the one steady bulwark against the abuse of civic, public, and institutionalized power—the power of the state—but while it does have a small number of professors who speak truth to power, these professors do not have much power to get their message into the corporate media. The corporate media will support the corporate leaders who are now in control of the universities and whose overall mission is to turn the university into a profit-oriented organization.

Instead of dedicating themselves to overcoming necessity, to finding ways of feeding the hungry, providing medical services to the public, challenging the dominant legal system that protects the property interests of the rich, the university is interested in capital accumulation that serves the interests of the ruling class. This is the educational industrial complex, and it is entangled now more than ever with the military industrial complex, the medical industrial complex, the legal industrial complex—what we could call the power complex. Critical systems of intelligibility are not developed in the modern university because universities are interested in the production of certain kinds of instrumental and technical knowledges, knowledges that best assist in the accumulation of capital. We can see this in the way that we educate teachers in the universities.

There is a mania for testing and standardization among the public at large, with politicians serving as the most enthusiastic cheerleaders. Teacher education faces a Faustian predicament: knowledge of the education system and even how schools are situated within the larger social totality of transnational capitalism so as to reproduce labor-power quality cannot spare you, the educator, in this complicity. Moral critiques of schooling in capitalist society are in themselves gravely insufficient, although they can galvanize support for change.

Of course, universities in many ways serve to control knowledge production in the interests of capital. Control over knowledge has always served as an arm of the colonization process, and we are seeing now more and more U.S. companies setting up schools in other countries and creating curriculum packages, testing programs, and trying to market them in poor communities. Such ethnocentric initiatives help to destroy indigenous knowledge systems. Universities should be about dialoguing across communities and negotiating multiple social universes, not participating in epistemic imperialism. This is epistemicide.

Universities should be about helping people to gain access to the culture of power and to challenge the vested interests and limitations of that culture—and simultaneously to transform that culture in the interests of the most exploited members of our society. Universities need to respectfully engage knowledge and conception systems that have been historically marginalized or subjugated in a given society and to reimagine the world in ways that would benefit historically oppressed communities and support the larger struggle for social justice and a socialist alternative to capitalism.

Orelus: *How should students contribute to the construction of a democratic school system and society?*

McLaren: In my view, every student is endowed with the capacity for reasoning critically about his or her life and should be apprised of the opportunity for understanding the complex and multilayered context in which that life is lived; every student is capable and deserving of developing a moral conscience that respects others as active, uniquely creative, and dignified subjects of history. Every student has a right to ask, what has my history, my experiences as an individual living in capitalist society, made of me that I no longer want to be? How can I change my present in order to live in the future with courage, commitment, and a critical disposition that can make the world a better place for all those who suffer and are oppressed?

Those who run the educational system in the United States care nothing about the rights and capacities of students; the system works to keep students good patriots and capitalist workers, who believe their country supports and defends the cause of freedom and prosperity for all around the world. It is an education, in other words, in mystification.

Orelus: *You have eloquently and critically talked about capitalism. As you know, all forms of oppression are intertwined. How do you understand, then, the relationship between classism and racism?*

McLaren: I don't like to use the words "classism" or "socioeconomic status" because, for one thing, socioeconomic status is a term that naturalizes the division of labor—some classes are more advantaged in our society, and others are less so; furthermore, class is not, and cannot be, an "ism." Capitalism relies on the exploitation of human labor. It relies on free labor. It is the grounds of exploitation in capitalist society. For example, while exploitation and oppression are often racialized, and vehemently so, that does not mean racism can be reduced to class exploitation; the two are very much inextricably related. Capital and labor, I believe, represent the most fundamental antagonism in capitalist societies. Racism helps keep capitalism's reproductive juggernaut advancing in its various modalities and incarnations of power. Because of labor market competition, capitalists consciously and unconsciously put different ethnic groups against each other in order to create racial divisions.

White workers fall into the racist trap of feeling they belong to a superior race, and this blinds them to their real interests, which should be working-class solidarity. Racism often keeps White workers from recognizing that it is in their interests to unite with their Black and Brown brothers and sisters and fight their capitalist bosses. Eric Williams has written that slavery was not a result of racism, but racism was a result of slavery; that is, it resulted from one of the most monstrous crimes of capitalism: the systemic slavery within the plantocracies of North America and the West Indies. The idea that Africans were naturally inferior to Europeans justified denying them the rights of Englishmen and systematically enslaving them. Racist ideology became a weapon of class wealth. Capitalism needed a justification for slavery because capitalism relied on the exploitation of free wage labor, formally free, that is (but not in reality). So slavery required racist ideology to justify the exploitation of free wage labor.

Of course the plantocracy would have loved to enslave English indentured servants too, but the enslavement of already arrived immigrants would have created a context that would have prevented future immigration to the so-called New World and provoked widespread armed conflict. The landowners had limited power over the indentured White servants, but that did not prevent them from loathing them just the same. The racist ideology that survived abolition could be seen, for instance, in the brutal colonization of Latin America and Africa by a handful of European and Western powers. Today, racist ideology persists in the corporate media, in popular culture, and even in the social sciences, as well as in the very languages and theories of knowledge that we take for granted, creating epistemologies of empire, epistemologies of ignorance, and forms of epistemological genocide, or epistemicide, where, as a result of the coloniality of power, indigenous knowledges continue to be thrown into the dustbin of history.

ORELUS: *I know you have been traveling in Latin America and other parts of the world, talking about the negative effect of capitalism and neoliberalism on poor working-class people, including factory workers, using critical pedagogy and Marxism as your primary conceptual framework. Please, would you share this experience with us?*

MCLAREN: Professor Nathalia Jaramillo and I were in Argentina for only a week, giving talks at a sociology conference. When we were there, we were invited to speak at one of the occupied factories called IMPA (Industria Metalúrgica y Plástica de Argentina), an aluminum plant that was once privately owned and was now the property of the state. But during the worst economic crisis in the country's history, the workers themselves became the factory's stockholders and managers. When the economy collapsed in 1997 and the factory owners fell deeper and deeper into debt as a result of a severely depressed economy that registered greater than 21 percent unemployment, the owners of many factories simply shut their doors and walked away. What happened was that the owners of these factories stopped paying wages to the workers for several months before declaring bankruptcy or suddenly leaving the country without paying their debts. It was in December of 1997 that the owners of IMPA finally declared bankruptcy.

Rather than watching helplessly as factories closed and their machinery was auctioned off, some workers came together and decided to *recuperate* the factories, begin production again, and reclaim their source of livelihood. The workers taking part in this new phenomenon of self-management demanded that the state guarantee them access to the working capital needed to get their factories back into production. Backed up by neighborhood associations and left-wing groups, the workers have been able to persuade bankruptcy courts to let them take over the company's assets. Founded as a German company in 1910, nationalized in 1945, and transformed into a work cooperative in 1961, IMPA was taken over by its own workers in 1998 and turned into an entirely new space for social and cultural production, as well as a working factory.

At the start, the forty members of the cooperative scraped by on five pesos a day (equivalent to $1.40 at the current exchange rate). Gradually wages went up. Today, the factory's workers are earning $271 a month. They all earn the same wage, except for the overtime that each person puts in.

With workers making aluminum cans, foil, and wrappers, IMPA is the largest of the occupied factories in Argentina. The IMPA recovery proved to be a very pivotal event in the recuperated enterprises movement, and it led to the creation of an umbrella organization, Movimiento Nacional de Empresas Recuperadas (MNER), which continues to help with the occupation of other factories. By 2005, there were more than 180 recuperated factories employing more than 10,000 workers.

The IMPA workers have used a large space in the factory as a neighborhood cultural and arts center, and this is the site where we gave our talk. The contribution to the arts by this factory has gained it favorable publicity and financial support from the city government. There are about 150 students attending adult secondary education lessons in IMPA, and there exists in this facility a free health-care clinic for the people of the Almagro neighborhood.

The Cultural City is a crucial part of IMPA's success story, and in fact IMPA has redefined the entire neighborhood community, if not cultural life throughout Buenos Aires. IMPA has over thirty-five workshops, ranging from poetry to trapeze art, and also hosts weekly concerts and fund-raisers for other occupied factories and neighborhood assemblies, and every Friday and Saturday night large crowds gather in an improvised theater space inside the factory to see Public Works, a highly acclaimed dance-theater troupe. In the evenings, IMPA becomes a space for wonderful artistic creation and free expression.

The municipality rents the premises to the workers' cooperatives on concessionary terms for two years and supports them in their efforts to negotiate with creditors. However, the original owners of some plants have now resurfaced, with hopes of reclaiming their proprietorship, and powerful struggles have ensued as a result.

Recently, the workers at IMPA were faced with an eviction threat issued by Judge Hector Vitale. The judge alleged the unconstitutionality of the law enacted by the Buenos Aires parliament, which in January 2009 decreed the expropriation of this metal industry by the workers. It turned out that Judge Hector Vitale had direct economic interests in the sale of the site where the factory is located. The threat of immediate eviction of the IMPA-occupied factory in Argentina has at least temporarily been lifted. The main creditor of the factory, the state-owned Banco Nación, has given its support to IMPA's workers' cooperative, thus removing the main rationale of the judge for the expropriation of the factory. It is important to note that there are at least two distinct approaches within any given sector or organization of the occupied factories, a reformist co-op wing that does not call for immediate rejection of capitalist ownership (and is backed by the Catholic Church's Pastoral Social and the CTA federation of Argentine workers), and those who are struggling for alternatives to capitalism, for replacing bourgeois state power with an administration of working people. I was told that critical pedagogy—including some of my work—was being used to create the groundwork for some of the high schools that are being created in the factories. I believe that the development of a pedagogy of recuperation, where workers can occupy factories and plants and within them develop schools that can foster anticapitalist, prosocialist values and struggles, is an important project.

Nathalia Jaramillo, Fernando Lazaro, and I have written about some directions we envision for a critical pedagogy of recuperation, and I can summarize some of these here, because they deal with the issue of rethinking race, class, and ethnicity. When we are talking about class in relation to race, it will take tremendous effort to rescue the term "class," which has been so demonized in the United States due to its Cold War association with Marxism and communism. And in this age of Tea Partiers, you can't even mention socialism without someone mentioning Nazi Germany. I agree with E. San Juan that the terms "race," "racial formation," and "racial discourse," and many versions of the intersectionality thesis, do not have enough conceptual reach or depth to get at an understanding of the Marxist conception of class and class struggle.[1] When we are talking about individual experience, or "lived experiences," we need, as San Juan notes, to read these experiences as a material-historical process and as a totality, and in doing so we can't leave out how social relations of production inform social consciousness. We need to develop forms of political agency—what I call a "philosophy of praxis"—to transform social life in the interests of social justice. We make a serious mistake when we reject "class" and "class analysis" as reductive, economistic, and insufficient in explaining much of what accounts for racism in the United States or in other contexts within the social universe of neoliberal capitalism. Class is not something relegated to the sphere of market exchange but needs to be seen as production relations. We need to be much more critical of the Weberian concept of class, which deals mainly with social status and life chances. This is because, as E. San Juan is correct in noting, class has to be understood within the domain of economic, political, and ideological forces. We can't let racial politics displace the political economy of class struggle because we end up with philosophical idealism. Class analysis does not rule out political agency. Far from it.

If we are going to understand and contest structural racism, we need to pay attention to the endemic crisis of global capitalism, geopolitical resource wars, and imperialist military interventions by the U.S. state, as well as national and regional conflicts and so on. I agree with San Juan here. Therefore we need a historical-materialist critical framework, attentive to the social relations of production and the political class conflicts taking place within it. We need to examine the political and social contradictions of different societies in different historical periods and conjuncture, and we need to examine the production of race and racism within an international or global framework of political economy that subtends this ongoing crisis of capitalism. In my more recent writings on the intersection of race and class, I do stress the explanatory primacy of class for analyzing the structural determinants of race, gender, and class oppression—not for analyzing their psychological aspects, or their phenomenological or cultural dimensions, but, and I will repeat this again, for analyzing their structural determinants.

To reduce identity to the experience that people have of their race, class, and gender location is to fail to acknowledge the objective structures of inequality produced by specific historical forces (such as capitalist production relations) that mediate the subjective understandings of both individuals and groups. While relations of oppression on the basis of race, class, and gender invariably intersect, their causes and determinations in capitalist societies can be effectively traced to the social relations of production (but not reduced to them). Most social relations constitutive of difference are considerably shaped by the relations of production and the fact that there exists a racialized and gendered division of labor whose severity and function vary depending upon where one is located in the capitalist global economy. Contemporary capitalist formations (neocolonialist, fascist, imperialist, subimperialist) are functional for various incarnations of racism, sexism, and patriarchy. It is also true that capitalism can survive in relations of relative racial and gender equality—capitalism has become multiculturalized, after all.

Now, having said that, let me also say this: race-based or feminist traditions of struggle are no less important or urgent than class-based ones. What my work attempts to highlight is how class operates as a universal form of exploitation whose abolition is central to the abolition of all manifestations of oppression. Class includes a state apparatus whose conquests and regulations create races and shape gender relations. You have to abolish a class-defending state if you want to make real headway in eliminating racism and patriarchy. Clearly, constructions of race and ethnicity are implicated in the circulation and process of variable capital. My work takes the position that forms of oppression based on categories of difference do not possess relative autonomy from class relations but rather constitute the ways in which oppression is lived and experienced within a class-based system. My work attempts to specify how all forms of social oppression function within an overarching capitalist system. Class denotes exploitative relations between people mediated by their relations to the means of production. This does not mean we reduce race to class, or gender to class. We need to see this relation dialectically. Racism and class exploitation are co-constitutive.

So my approach to social struggle is multipronged: I choose to organize against racism, sexism, class oppression, and White supremacy simultaneously as part of a larger anti-imperialist project directed toward the struggle for socialism. My work on the topic of how race and racism are linked to capitalist social relations argues that forms of nonclass domination such as racism must often be fought in advance of the class struggle. Certainly we cannot make headway in fighting class oppression without fighting racism and sexism. And clearly, racism and sexism must be fought against, and tirelessly so, despite whether or not we have traced their existence to capitalist relations of exploitation. Now, I also believe that race and class have to be looked at together. This stipulates that we begin a dialectical shift in the geopolitics of knowing, understanding, and reasoning. Here I believe we need to take seriously the contributions of indigenous knowledges as a way of intervening in the colonial horizon ensepulchured in structures of domination—economic, political, social, cultural, and epistemic. This is something that Nathalia Jaramillo, Fernando Lazaro, and I have noted in our work in Argentina developing a politics of recuperation.

There needs to be an epistemological revolution that can enable us to move away from the undialectical paradigms, or what Catherine Walsh calls "paradogmas,"[2] of Western concepts of identity, which have for over five centuries participated in acts of epistemological genocide (epistemicide). So we are paying attention to work that has come out of the constituent assemblies both in Ecuador and Bolivia in 2007–2008, and the contributions of the National Confederation of Indigenous Nationalities of Ecuador (CONAIE). And we believe that some important work on delinking from the coloniality of power is being undertaken by writers such as Catherine Walsh, Walter Mignolo, Nelson Maldonaldo-Torres, Lewis Gordon, Ramon Grosfoguel, Joel Spring, Anibal Quijano, Enrique Dussel, Sandy Grande, Linda Tuhiwai Smith, and Graham Smith.

We have reached a point where we need to be very cognizant of the limitations of multiculturalism and instead advance the transversal axioms of interculturality and plurinationality. These concepts have provoked us into reconfiguring and rethinking concepts of nature, justice, and coexistence, as well as the state, society, and social life, through multiple logics, cosmologies, and life systems in their pluriversal forms. The outcome of such a rethinking has the potential to help us initiate a new social contract outside of the neoliberal model that is currently destroying the planetary biosphere. I am not talking about rejecting all of Western modernity in favor of the logics and civilizatory frames of indigenous communities—which would be an essentialist quest for authenticity—although I am suggesting that we begin to utilize epistemological frames that do not originate with the uninational structure of the modern nation-state. We need to reconsider concepts such as "community" and "communalism" from the perspective of *interculturality* (cothinking, coexisting, and coliving grounded in principles of codependence, complementarity, and relationality) rather than from the perspective of multiculturalism (*a recognition of and respect for* different cultural logics, rather than a *thinking with them*, and an adding of different cultures into a mix that is already dominated by liberal, modernist conceptions of the state, the dominating power of the Anglosphere, and neoliberal capitalist relations of production).

So I would argue that we need to work from a position of *interculturalidad*. Interculturalidad is a "model constructed from below and is based on territorial and educational control, self-sustainable development, care of the environment, reciprocity and solidarity, and the strengthening of communal organizations, languages, and cultures."[3] This term reminds us that "our activism must be embedded within, and never separate itself from, the multivoiced hemispheric conversation on resistance, hope, and renewal."[4] We need to place more emphasis on ancestral knowledges (such as Pachamama and "buen vivir," or sumak kawsay) as well as technological and scientific knowledges.

So, when I talk about critical pedagogy as a social movement for the twenty-first century, I am not talking about an unlinear socialism but a pluriversal approach to socialism that takes seriously the epistemic perspective/cosmologies/insights of subalternized peoples. This requires paying attention to the views of those who continue to suffer under the expansion of Western civilization while recognizing that their perspectives in response to colonization may not fully overlap with communist/Marxist responses to capitalism. An inclusion of indigenous perspectives within revolutionary critical pedagogy should recognize that the European genealogy of thought should not dictate what a noncapitalist future should look like. This is important. It is important to stress here, then, a struggle at the level of epistemology while at the same time engaging in class struggle for a postcapitalist future. I call this future socialism, but you may choose another name for it.

Notes

1. San Juan, E. (2009b). Re-visiting race and class in post-9/11 United States of America. Retrieved from http://rizalarchive.blogspot.com/2009_04_01_archive.html.
2. Walsh, C. (in press). Interculturality and the coloniality of power: An "other" thinking and positioning from the colonial difference. In R. Grosfoguel, J. D. Saldivar, & N. Maldonado (Eds.), *Unsettling postcoloniality: Coloniality, transmodernity and border thinking.* Durham, NC: Duke University Press.
3. Meyer, L., Kirwin, J., & Toober, E. (2010). An open-ended closing. In L. Meyer & B. M. Alvarado, *New world of indigenous resistance: Noam Chomsky and voices from North, South, and Central America* (pp. 383–389). San Francisco: City Lights Books.
4. Meyer, Kerwin, & Toober. (2010). p. 397.

CHAPTER 9

Democracy, Schooling, and Neoliberalism

A CONVERSATION WITH NOAM CHOMSKY

This dialogue revolves around schooling, democracy, and U.S. foreign policy. Professor Chomsky critically analyzes the notion of democracy, arguing that it only works for the rich and big corporations and that people, especially ordinary people, are only given the illusion that they are living in a democratic society. He goes further to denounce the hypocrisy of the United States imposing its form of democracy on other countries when in fact there is no participatory democracy here. Professor Chomsky refers to countries such as Bolivia that have organized democratic elections and suggests that the United States should learn from this country instead of trying to export a prefabricated form of democracy to other countries. Professor Chomsky also talks about the language issue, pointing out how it plays a role in the unequal power relations between those who speak languages historically constructed as dominant languages and those who speak the so-called subjugated languages. After critically analyzing the ways that many forms of oppression manifest themselves, Chomsky contends that people need to organize so that they can challenge those in power and fight for their human rights. Likewise, Professor Chomsky encourages concerned citizens to use their agency to counter the corporatization of schools.

The Dialogue

Orelus: *The United States has been trying for decades to impose its Western form of democracy on other countries, particularly on the so-called third world countries. What is your take on the U.S. definition of democracy, and how do you think this country has sold its form of democracy to other countries?*

CHOMSKY: That's mostly mythology. It's ideology. It's just not a fact. In fact, this has been well studied by scholars here. So there are good studies of this so-called democracy promotion movement. The best studies are done by an interesting person, a man named Thomas Carothers, who is a well-known political figure and scholar. He was head of the law and democracy program at the Carnegie Endowment. And he is a neo-Reaganite. He was in the Reagan administration in the State Department in its democracy promotion programs. He wrote several books[1] in which he studied programs that have been successful or have failed. And he thought it was a wonderful idea to promote democracy. But he finally concludes, after having reviewed it from the Reagan years until today, that every U.S. leader is in fact a secret schizophrenic.

We support democracy if and only if it conforms to strategic and economic objectives. Which is another way of saying we don't support democracy at all. We support strategic and economic objectives if it happens that they can go along with formal democracy. Carothers does not seem to understand that; he thinks it's a paradox.

Democracy becomes now a great slogan. He said that during the Reagan administration, U.S. involvement in countries was inversely related to their progress toward democracy. So in South America, there was real progress to democracy, which, he points out, the Reagan administration tried to block but had to tolerate. But in regions where the U.S. had more influence, like the Caribbean and Central America, there was the least progress toward democracy. He's pretty frank about it. He said the U.S. would only tolerate forms of democracy that keep traditional structures in power, that is, dominance by elites that cooperated with U.S. interest. This goes right to the Bush years and everything else. So this is just an ideological trap; it's like when Stalin said he was in favor of democracy.

ORELUS: *Should we then say that democracy does not exist in this country?*

CHOMSKY: That's a different question. With regard to supporting democracy abroad, there is no such thing. We should not even talk about it; the U.S. uses that word to pursue its strategic and economic interests. If it can be covered by formal democracy, that's fine. It looks better if you don't have to apologize for it. You can congratulate yourself for it; that's the objective. In fact, that's obvious, right? There's a lot of talk about promoting democracy in the Middle East, right? The closest U.S. ally in the Arab Muslim world is Saudi Arabia, which is the most extreme fundamentalist dictatorship in the region, if not in the world. There was one free election in the Arab world, in January 2006, a real free election well monitored in Palestine. But it came out the wrong way. So the U.S. and Israel instantly turned to punishing the population for voting the wrong way in a free election.

Commentators, journalists, scholars, and others look at this, and they can't see what's obvious; that is, the U.S. cares nothing about democracy. What it cares about is domination and control. If you can have democracy too, fine. Also, what is a U.S. model of democracy? We are what we call in Iran a guided democracy. In Iran, the candidates for election are vetted by the ruling clerics. How do the candidates run for election here? They are vetted by the business community. Elections are largely bought. Unless you have a huge amount of funding, you can't participate. Obama defeated McCain mainly because the financial industries poured much more money into the Obama campaign than the McCain campaign.

ORELUS: *Can you say more about the notion of a "guided democracy"?*

CHOMSKY: It's a guided democracy because public opinion almost doesn't matter at all. Take the big issue right now: health care. When you read the polls, a large majority of the public continues to want a national health care system. This is not on the agenda. About 80 to 85 percent of the population is in favor of permitting the government to negotiate drug prices, using its purchasing power to negotiate drug prices, which is allowed in every other country but blocked here by law; that's 85 percent, the latest polls reveal. A front-page story in the *New York Times* just a couple days ago said that Obama made a private deal with the drug companies to block it. Where's the democracy?

ORELUS: *Professor Chomsky, how do you see the link between the U.S. contested form of democracy and schooling?*

CHOMSKY: Well, for one thing, what's taught in the classroom is that the U.S. is a leading democracy and supports democracy everywhere. In fact, that's not just in the classroom; that's also taught in graduate school. And it's just not true. So one way in which it impacts the classroom is just by inculcating doctrinal fabrications, but also the structure of schooling tends to be pretty undemocratic. Let's take the No Child Left Behind legislation. That's just training children to be in the Marine Corps, that is to say, not to be creative and independent people. That's its nature.

ORELUS: *You are referring to the No Child Left Behind Act, which is basically all about testing. Many teachers feel that they have to teach to the test; otherwise they might run the danger of losing their jobs. Would you agree with this assertion?*

CHOMSKY: That's right. The teachers are disciplined. They in turn have to discipline the students in order to regurgitate materials that they are supposed to memorize. That's not teaching. In places where there is a real effort to educate, like, say, a graduate education in a science program, you don't do that. Students are supposed to participate; they are supposed to challenge themselves and teachers; they are supposed to inquire. They don't repeat the lectures and tests. That should be true in some form for elementary school.

ORELUS: *So in that case, what role do you think citizens should play in building a democratic society?*

CHOMSKY: It's up to citizens whether they want to accept the system and whether their opinions amount to essentially nothing while policies are determined by concentrations of private capital. They don't have to accept that. Just take what I mentioned earlier about the health-care system; citizens could mobilize, act, and insist that their own wishes be followed and legislated. This is a very atomized and depoliticized society, and people don't do anything. There are functioning democracies in the world. But we can't talk about them.

In the Western Hemisphere, for example, probably the most advanced democracy is the poorest country in South America, Bolivia. There are real elections in which people participate. They know what the issues are; they elected someone from their own ranks, a poor farmer, who is in part at least pursuing policies that come from popular organizations. Voting isn't just a matter of showing up and pushing a button one day; it's a constant ongoing struggle for rights and justice. That's real democracy. Who in the United States could say, "We have to look to Bolivia as a model of democracy because we don't meet that standard"? People, including scholars and academics, would look at you with a blank face.

ORELUS: *How would you imagine citizens being active participants in decisions that affect their lives?*

CHOMSKY: It's not magic. Take electoral primaries. In the United States, what happens is that a candidate announces that he is going to be in your town on a May 15 or something. His advance team tries to organize people to come to a meeting, and then the candidate comes in and tells the crowd, "I'm a wonderful guy, I love you all, here are all the wonderful things I'm going to do," and he goes home. Now, suppose it was a functioning democracy. Well, what would happen is that the citizens of that town would have gotten together and decided what kind of policies they want. And if some candidate says, "I'm coming to your town," the citizens could say, "Well, you can come if you like. But if you come, you're going to sit there and we're going to tell you what we think. What'll be our programs, and if you don't accept them, then go home. If you do accept them, we may vote for you, but only as long as you do what we tell you to do." It's almost the opposite of what happens here; but it's not a pie in the sky. These are not utopian ideas.

ORELUS: *What role do you think the media play in all of this?*

CHOMSKY: The media basically play the role of instilling the faith. For example, when the *New York Times* published the front-page article about Obama making a secret deal with the drug companies, they didn't point out that he's undercutting the wishes of 85 percent of the population. This is a crucial issue, because the problem with his health reform program that his opponents throw up is that it's going to cost too much. In cases like these, it's not the job of the newspapers to tell the truth. They instill systems of doctrine and the ideology of power; not entirely, you hear a criticism here and there, but overwhelmingly that's how it is. But it's not that they're misleading people; it doesn't ever occur to them.

In the case of Bush, the second Bush, when he invaded Iraq, if you look back at his rhetoric, he was very straightforward. As he, Colin Powell, and others kept saying, there was a single question: "Will Saddam Hussein give up his weapons of mass destruction?" That was the single question. They invaded, they looked very hard, and they couldn't find any weapons of mass destruction, so they needed another reason. Eight months later, along came democracy promotion. Bush gave a very well publicized speech at the National Endowment for Democracy in which he talked about our love for democracy and explained that our invasion of Iraq was an effort to bring democracy to the world, and so on. Well, instead of laughing, which is what they should have done, the newspapers just climbed on the bandwagon: "Oh yeah, we're wonderful. We're promoting democracy."

ORELUS: *Do you foresee U.S. imperialism taking a different form or direction in the next decade or so?*

CHOMSKY: It all depends on what the population is willing to do. It's not going to happen by itself. The government will continue to respond pretty much to the needs of those who concentrate power inside society. I don't mean to say that it's mechanical, but it's certainly an overwhelming tendency and a perfectly understandable one. And now, unless citizens organize for different interests, that's what the government will do.

ORELUS: *So the question becomes, why is it that citizens are not organized so that they can collectively demand what they want from the government?*

CHOMSKY: Well, that's a long story. This is very much a business-run society. And throughout its whole history, there has been a struggle, sometimes successful, by sectors of the general population who try to influence a policy and determine the shape of what takes place. But business is constantly fighting a bitter class war and trying to undermine it, and in the last six years it has succeeded pretty well.

This is a depoliticized society; the organizations that constitute forces for democratic change, such as unions, have been attacked and severely weakened. There are no political parties; you can't be a member of a party here participating in policy formation. If you are a Democrat, that just means you follow orders. The case of what the press calls "Obama's army" is revealing. Obama's army is supposed to be very exciting. After the election took place, the press asked people in the Obama administration, "Okay, what are you going to do now that you've mobilized these people?" They say, "Well, we'll work out programs." It's the job of the army to push what they call "Brand Obama." That's more like a dictatorship, not a democracy.

It's a very depoliticized society. It's hard to get people together. It's a very rich country, so people have the right to expect a decent standard of living. Instead, they live difficult lives. The working hours are very high, far higher than Europe; you don't have much time; there are very limited benefits; there's a lot of insecurity—that is very high now. People are just driven to try to maintain their private lives.

ORELUS: *During the presidential campaign, there were a lot of people who thought that under Obama's administration, U.S. domestic and foreign policies would be different. Do you foresee any change in U.S. foreign and domestic policies under his administration?*

CHOMSKY: First off, there wasn't ever any reason to expect any change. I'm not saying that in retrospect. I was writing before the primaries, using his programs on his Web site. He's a centrist Democrat and really never pretended to be anything else. There's a little change because Bush was so far off the spectrum, especially in the first term. There is a spectrum of politics here. It's not monolithic. It's a pretty narrow spectrum, but there is a spectrum. Bush was way off at the extreme. That's why he came under such harsh criticism even within the establishment. So, yes, there's a change back toward the center. But it's mostly a modification of Bush-style extremism of rhetoric and sometimes actions, which have gotten the country in a lot of trouble. There's a reason why the financial institutions, which are the most dominant element in the economy, supported Obama and not McCain. The Bush administration was really driving the country to disaster. The financial institutions own the place, and they don't want it to be destroyed.

ORELUS: *I want to change the subject a little bit. I am going to move from what we have been talking about for the last twenty minutes to language issues. Do you see any link between language and Western imperialism?*

CHOMSKY: Anything we do involves language. Of course, the terminology and the rhetoric is in language. It does reflect the ideology, power, and so on. For example, the last interview I had, about an hour ago, was a long interview on what are the right measures to use in responding and protecting the country from terrorism and combating terrorism. I spent probably the whole interview trying to explain that's just the wrong question.

If you want to stop terrorism, the first step is to stop participating in it. That's a simple way to reduce terrorism. Secondly, if it's the terrorism of others that you're worried about, then find out what the reasons for it are and deal with them. But if you just ask how to stop terrorism, it's as if the doctor said, "I'm going to inoculate you with poisons. Now how should I treat you after that?" That's not the right question. As the language is used, the word "terror" refers to what they do to us, not what we do to them, which is often much worse. And they don't ask about the sources of their terror; they just combat it with force, either domestically or internationally. That's a way of saying we don't care about the problem. And it's the same for everything else, like democracy. It's nothing profound. Language is used in ways that reflect power interests.

ORELUS: *Where does culture fit in? You were referring to how language has been used to lie to or oppress people. What role does culture play in that?*

CHOMSKY: Generally, there are aspects of the dominant culture that are largely sustained on the base of power interests, although there are other factors that shape the way people think, the way they respond, the way they react, the way policies are made, and so on. How could it fail to be true? We could say more about it, but there is nothing profound to say about these topics. Intellectuals do produce complicated texts and polysyllabic words and so on, but basically what we understand is pretty straightforward. It can be said simply in ways that should be clear to everyone.

ORELUS: *Let me ask you a question about the dominant aspect of the English language. As you know, there are some languages that are more valued than others. For example, American and British English have been perceived as Standard English, whereas other Englishes spoken in other countries are seen as inferior. So, as a linguist, where do you stand on this issue?*

CHOMSKY: First of all, that's true now; it wasn't true a century ago. A century ago, British English was the standard, and American English was regarded as a kind of dialect. Well, what changed? Who was the most powerful country in the world a century ago? Who's the most powerful country in the world today? Then it was Britain; now it's the U.S. Like I said, there's nothing profound about these things. They're on the surface. English is the most dominant language because the United States is the richest and by far the most powerful country in the world. So, sure, English is the dominant language, not Swahili.

Orelus: *So, clearly there is a link between language and power. So whichever country has more power tends to use its language to dominate others.*

Chomsky: Well, that's the way national languages are formed. Today people in Italy speak something like what was once a dialect of Florence, not the dozens of other Italian languages that are around. It's because of the process of state formation and the formation of the dominant culture and so on. You hear people talk a lot about endangered languages. Languages are dying all over the world, which is a serious problem. They talk mostly about indigenous languages dying, which is true; they are dying off very fast. But the same is true for languages in Europe. They are dying off very quickly just because of the establishment of a more powerful central state.

Orelus: *You were the one who coined the phrase "universal grammar," which I found fascinating. Would you add anything to that concept? Or do you think there is no need to add anything to it?*

Chomsky: Well, frankly, if I were starting over fifty years ago, I never would have used the phrase. I had assumed that people would be rational enough to use the phrase as it was defined and to pay attention to the fact that it does not have the same meaning as the traditional phrase, although it's related to it. So it's like when a physicist uses the word "work" in a physics text, but they don't expect people to look up the employment statistics. They assume people are rational enough to know that this is an invented term, which has a loose relationship to the informal term "work" but has a technical meaning. The same with "energy," "force," and everything else. So when you talk about force in a physics class, you are not talking about the number of military bases you have. You can easily get people to understand that in physics, but it's hard for them to grasp that in the human sciences.

The term "universal grammar" is radically misunderstood. I was just looking at the current issue of the journal *Language*, the journal of the Linguistic Society, where there are a lot of tantrums about universal grammar based on a failure to comprehend these simple points. So I wouldn't have used the term "universal grammar" if I had recognized the irrationality of the likely reaction. The term "universal grammar," in the modern sense, my sense at least, is used to refer to whatever the genetic component of the language faculty is. That's universal grammar.

Orelus: *You said that if you were to write about this today, you would have chosen a different word. What word would that be, then?*

CHOMSKY: I would have picked some more technical term, which is less likely to be misunderstood. But there is no overcoming human irrationality. That's happened with other things too. I used to talk about "knowledge" of language, but then I realized that, after years of commentary, philosophers are going to misunderstand it. They have a specific theory of knowledge, which has to do with *true belief* and so on. So yes, they interpret it in terms of warranted true belief and doctrines of philosophy. But it has to do with what we internally have represented in our minds—which actually accords better with informal usage. So I made up a new word and said, "Okay, let's call it 'competence,' not 'knowledge.'" Then that got misinterpreted because some people are more competent than others. It's very hard in an irrational culture to do things that aren't going to be misinterpreted.

ORELUS: *The French philosopher Michel Foucault talked about power and knowledge. How do you see the link between those two concepts?*

CHOMSKY: If you have knowledge, it increases your power. The United States is now in a huge financial crisis. Who does the government turn to in order to fix it up? The people who have what's called "knowledge of economics." It happens to be the very people who created the crisis. It doesn't matter if they have knowledge and know technical things about economics; they are the ones who are called upon to fix it. Again, knowledge is power. I don't really much appreciate his work to tell you the truth. He used fairly simple observations and restated them in complicated ways.

ORELUS: *There are different types of knowledge. Why is it that some knowledge is valued while other types are not? For example, if I were to say something, people might not take it into consideration because I am not a powerful person; my words are not important. However, if it were someone serving under President Obama right now, people would most likely listen to that person just because that person is in a powerful position.*

CHOMSKY: Is that controversial or surprising? We understand it already. People who are powerful are in a position to influence and control what others do. That's power. Let's take this financial crisis that we've been through over the last twenty or thirty years, due in no small part to extreme arrogance and confidence on the part of professional economists. Most of them, if not all, are still talking about the wonders of the markets, how markets are efficient, and the government shouldn't tamper with them. This led to a total disaster. It didn't mean that they knew what they were talking about. They didn't. But their ideas were very influential because they happened to be in the short-term interest of people with real power, like Goldman Sachs. Therefore, they were adopted. If someone came along and said, "Look, this is going to lead to disaster. So you guys had better cut back your risky loans and your bonuses to executives," would anybody pay attention? In fact, some did say that to economists, but they ignored it. It did not contribute to the interest of the powerful. I don't frankly think you're going to find anything in this domain that isn't fairly obvious on the face of it.

Note

1. Carothers, T. (1993). *In the name of democracy: U.S. policy toward Latin America in the Reagan years.* Berkeley: University of California Press; Carothers, T. (1999). *Aiding democracy abroad.* Washington, DC: Carnegie Endowment for International Peace; Carothers, T. (2004). *Critical mission: Essays on democracy promotion.* Washington, DC: Carnegie Endowment for International Peace.

Part IV

THE TRIO OF INEQUITIES

CLASS, GENDER, AND RACE

Race, class, and gender issues have a significant effect on almost every aspect of our socioeconomic, individual, and professional lives, and play a fundamental role in the way people, especially people of color and women, have been perceived and treated in society. However, the most common statements people, particularly privileged people, often make to avoid addressing inequality that is race-, gender-, and class-based, are "I don't see color," or "everything can't be about color, social class, or gender." These statements can lead to the justification of the ill treatment of marginalized groups in society. The general tendency to focus on one form of oppression and pay less attention to, or leave others out, should not be ignored because as Anderson and Collins maintain, "Once we understand that race, class, and gender are simultaneous and intersecting systems of relationship and meaning, we come to see the different ways that other categories of experience intersect in society" (p. 5).[1]

Re-examining Race, Class, and Gender Issues in Schools and Beyond

Despite the attempt of those in power to ignore racial, social class, and gender issues, they continue to greatly shape the way many institutions, such as colleges and universities, run. Specifically, race, social class, and gender influence, for example, how teachers perceive and teach students, as well as how students interact with their teachers and peers.[2] Furthermore, race, social class, and gender often serve as a good indicator of who receives high quality education and who does not, and at what school, what kind of expectations teachers set for privileged students as opposed to students from poor working class background, what treatment female students receive in schools from their male teachers in comparison to male students, and through what lenses teachers look at and treat Black, Latino, Native American, and poor, dark-skinned immigrant students, as opposed to their white, middle-class counterparts.[3] In other words, in schools and beyond, race, class, and gender determine who has access to certain resources and privileges; who hold key positions and the subaltern ones; whose voice is being tongue-tied, that is, who is allowed to speak on behalf of whom; who is visible or invisible; who gets promoted or does not; and who is genuinely trusted or not.

Moreover, race, class, and gender impact the interaction among colleagues and often determine who is in powerful positions to make decisions that impact one's life and career. For example, historically, white males, particularly Christian, heterosexual, and able-bodied white males, have been the ones running institutions, such as universities and colleges.[4] They are still the ones who predominantly hold key positions ranging from being presidents, provosts, vice provosts to being deans and chairs of departments at universities. Needless to say, they have the highest salary and influence important decisions as to who should be hired as faculty, and who should be granted tenure and promotion, or full professorship. When professors, particularly female professors and professors of color, seeking assistant, associate, or full professorship positions at universities, they usually find themselves at the mercy of these privileged white males.

Faculty of color and female faculty, particularly female faculty of color, are the minority, let alone queer faculty and faculty with physical and/or mental challenges. Ironically at these institutions, the word diversity is used in their website as a way to attract students and faculty of color and other underrepresented groups.[5] Nonetheless, usually the few faculty and students of color these institutions attempt to attract and recruit do not receive the support they need to succeed. Many eventually leave. The few who choose to stay sometimes fail. When they fail, the institutions often blame them for their failure, refusing to admit they have actually failed them by not giving them the support they need to succeed. For example, tenure track female faculty, particularly single mothers, often do not receive the support they need from their institutions to succeed.[6] Because of sexism and patriarchy, usually these female professors assume most of the responsibility to raise their children, therefore have very limited time to focus on their scholarship and teaching. As a result of these family obligations, which prevent many from meeting the tenure requirements of their department and the university, they are often denied tenure. Female graduate students, including single mothers, face similar challenges.[7]

As a prime example, some of my graduate students have to raise their children and take care of domestic chores, sometimes with limited support from their partners or husbands, while coping with the pressure of fulfilling courses requirements and completing their thesis. In other words, they have to balance their busy schedule between raising their children and fulfilling courses requirements. These are some of the crucial factors that many departments or programs sometimes fail to take into account when reviewing the portfolio of tenure track female faculty members and that of female graduate students. These professors and students of color are often blamed for their own victimization.

Female professors are not alone in facing institutional oppression. Many male professors of color also have to fight against both institutional and individual racism.[8] Despite their male privileges, black/brown male professors face challenges in their classrooms with white students, particularly with privileged white students who sometimes question their competence and intelligence.[9] This form of racial prejudice is rooted in the historical misrepresentation of black and brown people. As Pedro Noguera (2008) notes:

> Throughout much of American history and film, they have been depicted as villains, con men, and feebleminded buffoons. Indeed, the image of the Black man has sometimes been used to symbolize the very embodiment of violence. Most often, black men have been regarded as individuals who should be feared because of their uncontrolled and unrefined masculinity. And their very presence, particularly when they are encountered in groups, has been regarded as a menace to innocents (particularly white women) and a potential danger to the social order. They are the threat that must be policed, controlled, and contained (p. xi).

Black and brown men have been mostly portrayed through the mainstream media as football and basketball players, runners, coaches, singers, house keepers, custodians, bus drivers, or, worse yet, as thugs and drug dealers. Consequently, many male professors of color have been mistaken on university campuses for basketball and football players, coaches, custodians, or for suspected thieves. What happened to Professor Antwi Akom is a prime example of racial stigmatization of male professors of color. Noguera states, "My friend and colleague Antwi Akom, a professor at San Francisco State University, was beaten and arrested by campus police when he entered his office at night (with his key) to retrieve a book while his two young daughters waited for him in their car" (p. xiv).

What happened to distinguished Professor Henry Louis Gate, Jr., also illuminates the high degree in which male professors of color are subject to racial profiling. Professor Gates was racially profiled by a police officer named James Crowley, who was looking for two suspected burglars. According to the

Cambridge Massachusetts police report, a woman called and reported that she saw two males trying to break into a house that happened to be Professor Gates' house. A police officer was sent to the location indicated by a woman to look for the possible suspects. He stepped on the porch of Professor Gates, knocked on his door, and asked him to step out and identify himself. Professor Gates showed the officer his Harvard University identification card, which indicated that he is a professor at this University. Apparently, this identification was insufficient to convince the officer that Professor Gates could not possibly be the burglar. Seemingly, professor gates and the officer exchanged words, and Professor gates was accused of and arrested for "disorderly conduct."[10] Analyzing this high case of racial profiling, Orelus states,

> Being arrested for "disorderly conduct" sounds very familiar to me, and many blacks, Latinos, Native Americans, and other marginalized and racially targeted groups in this country must be familiar with this form of accusation as well. When such groups attempt to challenge officers who are racially profiling them, violating their civil and human rights, they are often accused of being violent, which is usually, if not always, used as a pretext by these police officers to arrest and brutalize them. Many black/brown men and women have been physically and mentally brutalized by police officers, particularly white police officers, who usually claim that they feel threatened by these black/brown men and women. Rodney King, who was savagely beaten by several police officers in Los Angeles in 1992 for supposedly resisting police arrest and being violent to those officers, is a classic example. Of course, countless similar examples can be given (pp. 203–204).[11]

As this highly politicized racial profiling case and others noted above demonstrate race and gender are determining factors that affect men of color, shape the society we all live in, and the school system, which is part of the fabric of this society, that parents rely on and trust would educate their children. As Anderson and Collins eloquently put it, "Understanding race, class, and gender means coming to see the systematic exclusion and exploitation of different groups. This is more than just adding in different group experiences to already established frameworks of thought. It means constructing new analyses that are forced on the centrality of race, class, and gender in the experiences of us all" (p. 4).

We're All Victims of Racial, Class, and Gender Discriminations: To What Degree?

Analyzing the intersectionality of race, social class, and gender is crucial in that it can help people to be aware of both their advantageous and disadvantageous positions in society, regardless of their race, gender, and social class privileges (or lack thereof). For instance, a man of color is disadvantageous in many ways because of institutional racism, but at the same time he is privileged because of his maleness. Some of his male privileges include: (1) not having to worry about being raped and a victim of domestic violence as often as women; (2) not having to worry about being sexually harassed at work and in school as often as women; (3) not having to worry about being underpaid because of his gender; (4) not being told he should not major in physics, chemical engineering, or biochemistry because of his gender; and (5) not having to constantly fight so that his voice can be heard because his colleagues do not take him seriously because of his gender.

On the other hand, the disadvantages for being a man of color include: (1) being denied employment, housing, and a home loan because of his race; (2) being targeted and racially profiled; (3) being convicted for a minor offense and sent to jail; (4) being more likely to receive the death penalty than Caucasian men; and (5) attending underfunded schools located in poor neighborhoods.[12]

Similarly, white women can be both advantaged and disadvantaged. Because of her white privilege, a white woman does not have to worry about racial discrimination that a man or a woman of color has to constantly worry about on a daily basis. Moreover, as many scholars argue, the life expectancy of white people, including white women, is generally higher than that of people of color, who have a higher chance to be poor and suffer of illnesses, such as strokes and heart attacks caused by institutional racism.[13] However, it is important to emphasize that because of sexism, a white woman, regardless of her white privileges, is subject to gender- and sex- based oppressions mentioned above.

Likewise, both poor whites and people of color experience classism though at varying degrees. They usually do not have access to resources to which privileged whites and people of color have access in society. For example, privileged whites and people of color have more resources to attend schools that have high-qualified teachers; they also have access to a much higher quality education and health care than those who are poor.[14]

Though institutional racism impacts all people of color regardless of their social class, the wealthy ones may have a higher chance to be less directly impacted by it. For example, many poor men of color have been sentenced to jail for minor offenses because they could not afford a good lawyer to defend them.[15] However, most likely this would not have happened to wealthy and famous people of color who have benefited from what Pierre Bourdieu called symbolic capital (i.e., the fame and high social status and connections that go along with it), in addition to having the economic capital to hire a good lawyer.[16] Furthermore, wealthy people of color may be less affected in terms of receiving a quality education because they have the economic and social capital to attend elite schools. They also have the economic resources to live in safe or safer neighborhoods than those who are poor.

As a prime example, the two daughters of Barack and Michelle Obama may experience racial discrimination for being black. But they have a much higher chance to attend Harvard or Princeton because of their parents' social status, fame, and legacy than the sons or daughters of poor African American, Native American, Latino/a, Asian, or white working class families. Moreover, they do not have to worry being sick and not have access to high quality health care. Nor do they have to worry about their medical bills like struggling middle class and poor working class people.

Along the same lines, it is worth pointing out that whites, regardless of their gender and social class status, have unearned white privileges, which have protected them from being subject to racial discrimination of which people of color daily suffer. However, if they are poor, they most likely will not have health insurance and most likely will attend schools that are underfunded. Moreover, like poor people of color, they most likely will live in neighborhoods that are neglected and unsafe. As Noguera points out,

> There are poor Whites in rural Maine, Arkansas, and West Virginia whose chances of going to college are no better than that of Blacks in the inner city. Unlike the visibility and attention frequently directed toward poor black Blacks (a mixed blessing at best), poor Whites are almost invisible in America, and few policy initiatives are aimed at addressing their plight. For poor White students, the pursuit of equity in education could also serve as a means to counter the pernicious effects of poverty (p. xxvi).[17]

As demonstrated above, race, class, and gender inequalities are complex issues that require deep analysis. The authors featuring in this section, Antonia Darder, Eduardo Bonilla-Silva, Pedro Noguera, and Dave Stovall, analyze the intersection of race, social class, and gender inequalities and demonstrate how these forms of inequalities affect the subjectivity and the material conditions of people, particularly those who have often been pushed to the margins. Specifically, they examine how many people, including female and students of color, have been perceived and treated because of the socio-historical construction of their gender and race and social class background.

Notes

1. Andersen, M., and Collins, H. P. (1995). *Race, class, and gender: An anthology.* Lanham, MD: Rowman & Littlefield.
2. Weis, L., and Fine, M. (2005). *Beyond silenced voices: Class, race, and gender in United State schools.* New York: State University of New York Press; Fine, M.

(1993). *Disruptive voices: The possibilities of feminist research: Critical perspectives on women and gender.* Michigan: University of Michigan Press; Kozol, J. (2006). *The shame of the nation: The restoration of apartheid schooling in America.* New York: Broadway; Tatum, B. D. (2007). *Can we talk about race? And other conversations in an era of school resegregation.* Boston, MA: Beacon Press.

3. Leonardo, Z. (2009). *Race, whiteness, and education.* New York: Routledge; Nieto, S. (2004). *Affirming diversity: The socio-cultural context of multicultural education.* Boston: Pearson Education, Inc; Gillborn, D. (2008). *Racism and education: Coincidence or conspiracy?* New York, NY: Routledge; Anyon, J. (2005). *Radical possibilities: Public policy, urban education, and a new social movement.* New York: Routledge; Wolff, R. (2009). *Capitalism hits the fan: The global economic meltdown and what to do about it.* New York: Olive Branch Pr; Apple, M. (2009). *Global crisis, social justice, and education.* New York: Routledge; Noguera, P. (2003). *City schools and the American dream.* New York: Teachers College Press.

4. Jensen, B. (2004). *The heart of whiteness: Confronting race, racism, and white privilege.* San Francisco: City Light Books; Blumenfeld, W.J. (2006). Christian privilege and the promotion of "secular" and not so-"secular" mainline Christianity in public schooling and in the larger society. *Equity & Excellence in Education* (3), 195–210.

5. Greene, M. (1993). Diversity and inclusion: Toward a curriculum for human beings. *Teachers College Record 95*(2), 211–221; Cochran-Smith, M. (2004). *Walking the road: Race, diversity and social justice in teacher education.* New York: Teachers College; Yosso, T. (2006). *Critical race counterstories along the Chicana/Chicano educational pipeline.* New York: Routledge.

6. Beverly, J. (2005). Testimonio, subalternity and narrative authority. In Denzin, N., and Lincoln, Y. (2005). (Eds). *The Sage handbook of qualitative research, third edition.* California: Sage; Bartlett, A. (2006). Theory, desire, and maternity: At work in academia. *Hecate 32*(3), 321–333.

7. Wolf-Wendel, L., & Ward, K. (2003) Future prospects for women faculty: Negotiating work and family. In B. Ropers-Huilman (Ed.). *Gendered futures in higher education: critical perspectives for change* (Albany, State University of New York Press), 111–134; Williams, J. (2000). *Unbending gender: Why work and family conflict and what to do about it.* New York: Oxford University Press; Williams, J. C., and Segal, N. (2003). Beyond the maternal wall: relief for family caregivers who are discriminated against on the job. *Harvard Women's Law Journal, 26*(77); Williams, J. (2000) How the tenure track discriminates against women. *Chronicle of Higher Education,* B10; Hewlett, S. A. (2002). *Creating a life: Professional women and the quest for children.* New York: Talk Miramax Books; Ward, K., and Wolf-Wendel, L. (2004). Academic motherhood: Managing complex roles in research universities. *The Review of Higher Education* 27(2), 233–257.

8. Stovall, D. (2006). Forging community in race and class: Critical race theory and the quest for social justice in education. *Race Ethnicity & Education, 9*(3), 243–259.

9. Orelus, P. (forthcoming). Facing with courage racial and linguistic discrimination: The narrative of a Black Caribbean immigrant in the U.S. diaspora. *Diaspora, Indigenous and Minority Education Journal.*

10. Henry Louis Gates, Jr., Police Report Retrieved on December 17, 2010, from www.thesmokinggun.com/file/henry-louis-gates-jr-police-report.

11. Orelus, P. (2009). *The agony of masculinity: Race, gender, and education in the age of "new" racism and patriarchy.* New York: Peter Lang.

12. Noguera, P. (2008). *The trouble with black boys: And other reflections of race, equity, and the future of public education.* New Jersey: John Wiley.

13. Bonilla-Silva, E. (2003). *Racism without racists: Color-blind racism and the persistence of racial inequality in the United States.* Lanham, MD: Rowman & Littlefield; Dyson, M. (2006). *Is Bill Cosby right? Has the middle class lost its mind?* New York: Perseus Books Group; Alexander, M. (2010). *The new Jim Crow: Mass incarceration in the age of colorblindness.* New York: New Press; Haley, A. (2007). *Roots: The saga of an American family. New York: Vanguard Press.*

14. Kozol, J. (2006). *The shame of the nation: The restoration of apartheid schooling in America.* New York: Broadway; Anyon, J. (2005). *Radical possibilities: Public policy, urban education, and new social movement.* New York: Routledge.

15. Alexander, M. (2010). *The new Jim Crow: Mass incarceration in the age of colorblindness.* New York: New Press; Haley, A. (2007). *Roots: The saga of an American family. New York: Vanguard Press.*

16. Bourdieu, P. (1986). The forms of capital. In J. Richardson (Ed.), *Handbook of theory and research for the sociology of education.* New York: Greenwood Press.

17. Noguera, P. (2008). *The trouble with black boys: And other reflections of race, equity, and the future of public education.* New Jersey: John Wiley.

CHAPTER 10

Reexamining Class and Racial Dominations in the *New* Era of Western Capitalism

A CONVERSATION WITH ANTONIA DARDER

The following dialogue took place on November 12, 2009. Throughout this dialogue, Professors Darder and Orelus critically analyze pertinent issues such as classism, capitalism, and institutional racism that have impacted the subjective and material conditions of many people, both academics and non-academics. Professor Darder begins by talking about her experience growing up in abject poverty as a Puerto Rican girl who moved to the United States and struggled as a teenage mother to raise her three children while going to school. She draws on both her lived and professional experiences to tackle issues of class, community engagement, and gender and racial oppressions in schools and beyond. Specifically, she talks about the challenges that professors of color, especially those coming from historically marginalized backgrounds, have faced in academia, which is White-male dominated. Professor Darder provides a sharp critique of scholars who often silence the voice of professors of color, arguing that these scholars have a tendency to speak on behalf of the "other" even though they have never experienced what the "other" has experienced. Professor Darder goes further to demonstrate how the capitalist system has been oppressive to marginalized groups in society. She links this form of oppression to other forms of oppression such as neocolonialism, racism, and U.S. imperialism.

The Dialogue

ORELUS: *Please, would you say a little bit about yourself?*

DARDER: I was born in Puerto Rico. My mother moved to the United States in 1955 when I was almost three years old. I grew up very impoverished. My mother was either on welfare or worked in the garment industry under very harsh conditions. She had some very difficult and untreated emotional problems, which complicated an already very stressful life. We lived with very meager resources and lots of uncertainty. As a child, it was my job to take care of everybody, including my mother. And although I was only a year and half older than my sister, I was responsible for her when my mother went to work or went out. All this made for a tough life growing up. It is probably for this reason that school was often a welcome break from the enormous stress at home. School was a place where I could learn and be free of all the anxieties and tensions constantly brewing at home. I realize that the conditions I experienced as a child were greatly complicated by the fact that my mother had mental health issues—which I attribute today to the very harsh circumstances under which she was trying to survive and raise two daughters. My effort to make sense of my life when I first arrived in the States was also a challenging feat. All of a sudden, the familiar culture, language, way of being, way of feeling, and even the scents of life, which had all been mine, were gone. It was quite a psychic burden to contend with as a very young child. In fact, I often think that the consequences of the enormous cultural clash I experienced have haunted my life until today.

I grew up in East Los Angeles within a low-income Mexicano community. We ended up there because that's where Spanish was commonly used within the neighborhood. There was a small influx of Puerto Ricans that came to California during the 1950s, but the majority of Spanish-speaking folks in Southern California at the time were of Mexican descent. So, although most Puerto Ricans from the island generally moved to New York or Chicago, we ended up in Los Angeles. This is why I tend to feel very at home within a Chicano context. The culture and the language were more familiar to us than that of the White Americanos. The issue of class was also very much at work, so living in a low-income, Spanish-speaking community felt more like home. As you know, migrants and immigrants tend to gravitate to where there is a greater sense of familiarity with their own culture, wherever they settle.

My life initially took a very traditional trajectory. I got married when I was sixteen years old and had three children before I was twenty. Perhaps this was a bit early, but not really that unusual within poor Latino communities. Nevertheless, I always carried the dream that I would someday go to school in order to better my lot in life, which was easy for me, since I enjoyed the academic environment and had been successful in school. When I was twenty-one, I finally enrolled in community college. I got through college pretty much alone while raising my children. I aspired to be a medical doctor, but I was discouraged from going into medicine by a college counselor who felt that, as a single mother with three children, this was far too ambitious of a goal for me. Instead, I was tracked into the nursing program. However, while at Pasadena City College, I found instructors and a female counselor who was very supportive of my efforts. I also had an opportunity there to work as a peer counselor and participate in my first research project, interviewing peers about their experiences at the college.

When I got out of nursing school, I worked in hospitals as a pediatric nurse. However, I must confess that I hated working in hospitals because of the way I was treated. It was a very intense environment. Racism was prevalent in many forms, including the way that Spanish-speaking workers and parents were treated, as well as the nursing staff of color. Moreover, at the time, there were few Latina RNs, and we were often treated like second-class citizens, overscrutinized, and given the worst assignments. Feeling demoralized, I decided to leave hospital nursing and find a way to work with Spanish-speaking children and their families within the community. So I applied for a school nurse job with the Head Start program. I conducted educational health programs with preschool children and their parents. It was actually at Head Start that my interest in cultural difference, inequalities, and education truly began. From Head Start, I moved into mental health work within the Latino community, focusing on issues of child abuse and child sexual assault. I eventually returned to school and earned my license as a psychotherapist, which enabled me to focus on mental health programs and treatment work in low-income schools and community contexts.

My advocacy work in both mental health and education all took place in low-income communities—the same communities where I lived and worked. For five years, I worked for a Latino organization involved in community organizing, cultural arts programs, and popular education. We developed a variety of programs for Latino children and their families and carried out political advocacy work related to education, health, and housing needs. In addition, we were very involved in working to transform educational and land use policies in the city, as well as contending with issues directly tied to multicultural and bilingual education in the public schools. It was during this time that I learned how contentious and very complicated advocacy work can be within poor communities, and the manner in which competing interests often attempt to control community development agendas according to particular philosophical motivations and individual perceptions, generally linked to both class and racialized differences. Nevertheless, working on the ground level with Latino students and community members was an incredible moment in my life, which pushed me to better understand the importance of possessing a well-defined political foundation, especially when working toward social justice, community change, and policy transformation.

When I finally was able to get myself back into graduate school, I left the organization and began teaching at a small private college, which at the time espoused very progressive principles and primarily enrolled female students. Because of my community development knowledge, mental health background, and experience with educational issues, I was hired to teach courses that focused on bicultural development. These courses examined what to me continues to be a central question when thinking about the education of children of color in the United States. What are the conditions that children from different cultural and linguistic communities face when they are forced to navigate an English-speaking cultural milieu while simultaneously contending with the tensions of subordinate-dominant power relations? I worked to explore this question in my courses from a variety of perspectives, including pedagogical, political, cultural, social, and of course economic. I suppose it can be said that it was at this time that my academic work as a critical theorist and Marxist scholar began to take off.

Orelus: *So would you say that your past experience has shaped your class consciousness?*

Darder: Yes, quite right. My personal history is rooted in the experience of growing up as a Puerto Rican child living in poverty. My life was very different even from folks of color who came from more affluent families. Some of these differences were evident in the ways we thought about education and what students in poor communities required in order to work toward empowerment and self-determination. Often more affluent educators still tended to fall into the trap of thinking that they had to make things happen *for* the oppressed, rather than truly participate *with* disenfranchised communities in paving their own path toward more emancipatory possibilities and better material conditions. Here I want to emphasize that class inequalities and racism have both occupied a central preoccupation in my work, along with other forms of injustice that I associate with the manner in which capitalist relations structure fundamental inequalities in order to preserve wealth among the few.

So, to simply talk about race or even issues of racism without looking at the political economy and deeper questions of class struggle is highly distorting and problematic toward building a political direction that can truly support democratic life. In very simple terms, what I had to do to survive was very different from what my more affluent counterparts, even in the Latino community, had to do to survive. The way I used language was very different from the way they spoke. The manner in which I expressed my personality and feelings was hugely different from the manner in which they had been taught to express themselves. That is to say, they knew the codes of power that come from growing up within a particular class context—codes that are generally unexamined and thus unengaged, even among the well-meaning folks. I've seen these dynamics at work in a variety of settings and across low-income communities, whether we're talking about Latino, Black, Native American, Asian, or other racialized populations. I think this is why White working-class kids often seemed more like us than their affluent counterparts. Class distinctions locate populations in very different ways.

This is one of the reasons why I insist that we can't just focus on racism without taking into account the manner in which capitalism, as an ideology, clearly serves to maintain those with money in control over the lives of the majority of the world's population. It is important to understand that this process of class formation occurs in concert with a complex network of social and material conditions, fabricated and sustained by ruling-class interests across all ethnic communities. I am from the civil rights and social movement generation of the 1960s and 1970s. During that era, there still existed a strong class consciousness among many political activists in our communities. That changed dramatically in the 1980s and 1990s when we began to witness a major decline in class analysis and concerns with class struggle. Instead, the discourse of identity politics, affirmative action, and multiculturalism prevailed.

In contrast, I entered political consciousness at a time when questions of class were still considered central to political struggle, policy transformation, and community self-development. As a consequence, many studied Marxist principles and texts, and it made sense to us in very real terms; it provided a powerful lens of analysis from which to better explain our actual life experiences and to better understand the larger social mechanisms that shaped our material conditions. These spoke to the oppression that we saw in our families and our communities, and the struggles in our working conditions and even in our personal lives. So the issue of class could never be off the table. Class issues were integral to understanding the material differences at work all around us. The kids who studied in well-funded schools were far more affluent and had more opportunities than we did. They got to go on vacation with their parents and had access to resources that we could only dream about. Yet they had been taught, whether subtlety or openly, to naturalize their many opportunities and to consider themselves more deserving of these things than those of us who lived in abject poverty and who were often blamed for our own lack of opportunity.

ORELUS: *As you know, all forms of oppression are linked to one another. However, there are some orthodox Marxists who have privileged class issues over race issues, arguing that inequality stemming from capitalism affects Black, Brown, and White people. Where do you stand on this issue?*

DARDER: As I hope my earlier response demonstrates, it is impossible to separate and set up a hierarchy of oppressions, per se. Oppression is oppression. Fundamentally, oppressive attitudes, policies, and conditions all function to reduce access to opportunities for particular groups; to inferiorize, control, exploit, and dominate their participation in society; and to create their fundamental exclusion from political life. Hence, if all oppression ultimately impacts political life, and politics is inextricably linked to the economy, how can we possibly come to understand any form of oppression or inequalities outside the political economy? This is not a matter of privileging class over race, which I see as simply a rhetorical device for competing academic discourses. Instead, I understand this view as one that recognizes the fundamental relationship of capital upon the formation of class relations in U.S. society and around the globe.

In the book *After Race*,[1] Rodolfo Torres and I made a concerted effort to examine the manner in which both theoretical and popular views speak to different forms of oppression, as if somehow they were not indelibly linked to material conditions. In doing so, such views perpetuate a particular political economy, one that conserves and protects capitalism, despite the destructive manner in which neoliberal policies today, for example, harden class relations and function to erode class struggle. Moreover, we can't deny that, for example, gender oppression in our patriarchal society is intimately linked to the political economy. Hence, when women are ambitious and seek to attain power within an institution, whether public or private, these women must, willingly or reluctantly, embrace the prevailing patriarchal logic, which through its unexamined hegemonic structure and design firmly perpetuates gender inequalities, in the same manner that the logic of racism perpetuates racialized capitalist interests.

OrELUS: *It has been argued that racial issues are not talked about often enough in most mainstream U.S. classrooms. If so, how would you explain the silence about racial issues in the school setting?*

DARDER: I think that racial issues are frequently discussed in schools, but in abbreviated, superficial, and often disturbing ways. If you ask some teachers, "Do you discuss racial issues?" they may often say, "Yes, we try to help all children to feel good about themselves, no matter what their race." Or they may tell us that, "We talk about slavery. We do a unit on Martin Luther King or the civil rights era." But these discussions are generally fractured and loosely discussed, which intentionally or not shrouds the larger mechanisms of power at work and the insidious manner in which class inequalities are experienced by racialized populations. This happens because there is such an effort to contain discussions that expose class-based, racialized conflict within the U.S. This fear is hugely associated with an unacknowledged history of violence that has been perpetrated particularly upon the poor and communities of color. Moreover, this violence has been consistently connected with racialized attitudes and behaviors that have been falsely projected onto racialized populations.

What is being silenced or covered up through perfunctory or cursory notions of racism taught in public schools are wide-scale racialized crimes against humanity perpetrated through the impunity of the wealthy and powerful. These crimes have included the genocide of indigenous populations, the incarceration of poor people of color, the sterilization of women of color who have been deemed inferior and unworthy, and the *stupidification*, as Donaldo Macedo often says, of the masses. Unfortunately, ignorance of the relationship between class and racism is also perpetuated by those who experience discomfort and anxiety when they must contend with conflict or dissent. In an effort to squelch dissent, public schools teach a truncated form of democracy that pretends that the impact of racialized crimes against humanity can be dispelled if they are not discussed. It's as if all that has to happen is to not talk about them, and somehow magically they will disappear. But history clearly shows us the folly of such a perspective—rather, that which is ignored persists and putrefies into unrecognizably grotesque conditions.

This racialized silencing mechanism is also at work in contemporary educational institutions, when progressive students or educators attempt to expose the presence of racism still at work in their midst. This is particularly so when they passionately point to the concrete existence of racism. "Racism is at work right here, in this room, in this school, in this classroom." In these instances, it seems that there is so much fear over the passion that fuels efforts to expose the suffering of the oppressed. Those who are invested in preserving the status quo (because they believe the system works for them) try to contain the passion—a passion that I firmly believe is necessary for revolutionary change. In the process, those who experience fear create myths and false notions, whether consciously or not, in the service of conserving asymmetrical power relations that protect their authority and provide them with a sense of control and security. Partly they do this by privileging a dispassionate style of communication. Of course, it is a lot easier to be dispassionate if you are comfortable and things are working in your favor. But what I have consistently argued is that the revolutionary passion of the oppressed has its roots in their suffering. For this reason, many efforts have been made throughout history to contain their passion, because it can potentially fuel social upheaval and transformation. One of the best ways to contain and prevent dissent, then, is to teach students to be afraid of or to always be suspicious of transformational passion, including their own.

Yet there is no way to speak about racism without demanding both institutional and moral change, and thus a deeper engagement with attitudes, policies, practices, and structures that perpetuate racialized processes in schools and society in the first place. So the fear of social change and critical engagement further perpetuates mechanisms of oppression, which can result in brutalizing forces that both colonize and dehumanize every aspect of our daily existence.

These are the mechanisms that criminalize and demonize poor youth of color, setting them up to fail in schools or to be gunned down by police officers who have been sworn to protect them.

ORELUS: *So what has been your experience teaching courses that address issues of democracy, equality, social equality, and citizenship? What have been your students' reactions or responses?*

DARDER: Well, as you can imagine, there has always been a variety of responses. Working-class students, particularly working-class students of color (but even White students), tend to respond very positively. They welcome the opportunity to think about class issues, and they dig deeper in their research to understand how these apply to their work. Partly what I see is that they welcome a language to help them articulate the experiences of oppression that they have had to contend with throughout their lives. Suddenly they find a voice within them with which to discuss issues that are important to them, and they find a place where their voices and their passion are supported. They have a place to articulate and engage these issues in critically thoughtful ways. But just as there are those students that are very happy for this newfound opportunity, there are also those who immediately go on the defense. Then there are others who become very confused with the presentation of new paradigms for interpreting their realities.

I think the reason for these responses is that most of the students have not been in an environment that consistently challenges them to be more critical about the social and material conditions that shape their lives. So when one brings another paradigm into play, one with which to engage these difficult and complex issues, it can confuse them and cause them anxiety, frustration, and even rage. In many ways, this work is asking them to learn to both read and critique their commonsensical world—the world they have known to be truth—so they can also experience feelings of guilt and shame as they discover the consequences of some of their own unexamined assumptions or notions of the other. However, I recognize that these types of responses or reactions are not really helpful. We don't need these students to feel ashamed or guilty for what they didn't know. What we need from them is to be willing to sit and stay at the table, to engage honestly with the socioeconomic, political, and racialized conditions that have historically shaped their own families and communities, as well as the broader social context. The goal is to move toward a more grounded place of understanding so that we might discover *together* the commonalities and differences from which we can grow and develop understanding and solidarity.

Of course, there are students who won't even take my courses. There are also those who at times stumble into my class and then become very aggressive with me, particularly if they are solidly grounded in the logic of capitalism.

They come into my class and become very angry and agitated, and I have to deal thoughtfully with their issues. I say this because I realize that I am fully involved in a pedagogical process with the class as a whole, beyond simply the students as individuals. How I contend with students who struggle provides material for critical reflection and practice for us all. At times these students claim to feel like they are the minority in my class. Suddenly their experience of power is totally turned on its head. So, as an educator, I have to be prepared to deal with these responses as a matter of course. All this is to say that some students respond in a very positive and uplifting way, while others are very aggressive and sometimes even violent toward me. Now that I am older and with many years of experience, I deal with all of this with greater patience and humility. But it used to be tough for me, because I felt I was simply seen as this working-class woman of color, whom they still did not perceive as deserving or having a truly legitimate teaching role. Some students, whether directly or indirectly, seemed to have been taught that a person who looks like me (in terms of gender, ethnicity, or class) could not be trusted to be adequately competent to teach them, because I was below them in social stature. This would cause me great frustration given that such unexamined attitudes or assumptions of inferiority can often intimidate or cause us to doubt ourselves, despite how prepared we might be. This is tied with the matter in which class privilege and entitlement were not part of our paradigm as children growing up in the barrio. On the contrary, there was often a sign of surprise or even disbelief when poor barrio children excelled in school. It is worth noting that such problematic responses by teachers seldom escape the awareness of the children they teach, nor their parents and community.

ORELUS: *I was going to ask you what your experience has been as a female professor of color in a White-dominated institution like academia. Please, would you say more about this experience?*

DARDER: Truthfully, for the most part, it has been a nightmare! It has been extremely difficult because, as I came to realize, I entered academia with very different cultural, class, gendered, and political sensibilities. More importantly, I had no real preparation with respect to the professional culture of academia. I didn't come from a family of people who were formally educated. The way people construct popular discourse in the barrio in comparison to the culture of higher education is very different. Even now, I seem to possess a very different ideological position than most of my colleagues, including many on the Left. Moreover, I have a very clear commitment to a larger political project that requires connection with communities. My work isn't about a career, so all of this is very disconcerting for those who benefit from the system, irrespective of their espoused political leanings. In a lot of ways, I have felt like I am seen a bit like a traitor, a disenfranchised person who was *allowed* entry into the ivory halls, but who can't be trusted to protect the privilege or conserve allegiance to the institution. There has been an unspoken expectation that I should abandon my collective political commitment in favor of an individual focus on my scholarship, primarily as an extension and resource for the university. But since I have been simply unwilling to do so, I have known much isolation and marginalization as a consequence. Moreover, I realize that, as a working-class woman of color, I was never expected to enter into academia and be successful.

On another note, I realize that I can't be naive. I must acknowledge that I have refused to enter the culture of academia, solely as an individual. I firmly believe that to have done so would have stripped me of my passion and my very soul. Instead, I continue to see myself, dialectically, as both an individual and a member of a larger community of struggle. I believe that, most of all, my collective sensibilities have made it difficult for me to acclimate to a world that is furiously competitive and individualistic.

Similarly, in a world where the culture expects one to posture oneself as being always knowledgeable (even when one doesn't really know much about what the hell is being said!), my class insecurities, tied to the racialized process of inferiorization referred to earlier, have probably made the experience far more brutal. What is so sad here is that seldom is this issue ever discussed openly when speaking about retaining faculty of color. Yet this silence prevents us from naming this form of class oppression and thus from developing a more humane system of interaction within the university that would allow us to critically engage attitudes, policies, and practices that ultimately debilitate us all, robbing us of important contributions and wisdom about the other.

Another thing here, as most people know only too well, in the academy the egos fly wild. Because it is so furiously individualistic and competitive, everyone thinks they are the authority on everything, even if they have never lived or experienced certain questions at any level. So a lot of what goes on is purely abstract—even with respect to progressive politics. You have scholars who claim to know so much about poverty or diversity but who have not lived it beyond the research they have done and the books they have read or written. Then you have people who have not only studied the field of diversity but have actually lived with the impact of racism and other forms of oppression and have known it directly through their daily lives. These people can articulate these experiences in ways that many researchers and colleagues in the academy can never do.

The marginalization of such knowledge is very disconcerting, and more so when abstract intellectuals attempt to delegitimize those who are grounded in experiences of social oppression. So it is frustrating when one has intimate knowledge of particular conditions of social injustice and can still be rendered invisible or marginalized by those in power. Often this marginalization includes being excluded from university work where one's expertise should logically be welcomed.

Such traditional practices of exclusion function effectively to silence particular knowledge, while aggrandizing those views that are more in tune with the politics or agenda of the institution. In the process, snippy little personal remarks are made about a person to make it seem as if it is not about political or ideological difference, but rather that a marginalized scholar's exclusion is about some personality problem the person possesses. Hence, one can be deemed the "angry Latina" or "not a good team player," and so forth.

For someone like me—who came into academia with a grounded political commitment, a real love for what I do, and believing that progressive work could make a fundamental difference, that it mattered—trying to be part of a system that is truly antidemocratic is stressful and a horrendous challenge. This leaves folks like me always feeling like maybe we don't deserve to be here or that what we have to offer doesn't matter. Then, when you see far less accomplished folks, including people of color, elevated because they are considered to be a team player, that is, they fit better into the traditional mode of the university, it makes the experience even more disconcerting. I say this because, so often, accommodating faculty and administrators of color are well utilized to undermine and diminish the efforts of more radical scholars of color who are struggling to critique the social injustices within the institution and who call for change.

As I mentioned earlier, many of us who grew up very poor and ended up in the academy struggle internally with the subtle and not-so-subtle messages of deficit that we have received. There is a part of us that remains hypervigilant, feeling always somewhat anxious and insecure on some level. We often wonder whether we are in over our head. It is weird because we are just as intelligent and capable as our privileged counterparts. But the impact of racism still enacts itself and creates in us self-doubt about our competencies. It doesn't matter how many books we publish. I see this personal dynamic at work in attitudes and practices of folks of color and working-class people across disciplines.

This aspect of the experience makes it tough to remain in the academy unscathed emotionally or psychologically. What helped me was coming into the environment with some knowledge of what it was like to be a working-class woman of color in an unwelcoming environment trying to get through graduate school. So, from the beginning of my tenure as a faculty member, I committed myself to working with students who came out of very similar social contexts as mine—that is, to work with very poor working-class students of color. By working with them, I came to realize that the knowledge I carried about my own experiences could enable me to support students in effective ways, especially when they were having doubts about the legitimacy of their research or the credibility of their own thinking and theories. This became a very tangible way in which I could support students to think out and transcend their academic anxieties so that they could develop confidence in their own judgment.

Sometimes, all this is a matter of gaining confidence in oneself as a valuable, thinking human being. Unfortunately, one of the primary messages tied to racism is that people of color are innately intellectually inferior. What I try to do with students is support and nourish their sense of self-confidence, their abilities to connect with each other as colleagues and comrades, and through this process support the development of political courage and grace.

I often tell them that developing their scholarship and academic practice for social change will at times be very difficult work, and it is not going to be easy to stay true to their political principles. There are times when they are going to have to stand alone; and as such, they are going to have to find strength and courage in themselves; otherwise, living duplicity (speaking one thing and doing another) will disable and disempower their efforts. For these reasons, I consider this type of support and engagement with students as just part of our daily work as progressive faculty. It is not just about students' intellectual development. It entails a holistic, integral approach to teaching, understanding that students will need all of their human faculties, not just their intellect, to be effective agents of change in the world. Moreover, they will need all the physical, emotional, spiritual, and intellectual resources they can cultivate within themselves in order to survive the stresses of radical politics and to remain true to an agenda of activist scholarship and a commitment to very real and ongoing community concerns.

ORELUS: *In your work, you also talk about the link that should exist between democracy and schooling. Could you say a little bit more about that?*

DARDER: There are so many places to go with this kind of question. For me, the issue is about how we create culturally and linguistically democratic contexts within classrooms and schools. By that I mean, how do we create truly emancipatory contexts where students, from the get-go, feel that they come in with knowledge that is valuable and can be integrated into the process of their learning so that they can feel that they are respected in the classroom, irrespective of whether they are studying history, science, or language arts. I would like poor and working-class students to be acknowledged as capable human beings with worthy knowledge and personal experiences, and for them to know that their understanding of the world has a place for expression and interrogation within the classroom. Moreover, I strongly believe that classroom pedagogy must function to support students in developing a clear sense of schools as public spaces where the construction, perpetuation, and evolution of democratic life takes place. This has to do with the right of students to voice their views, to participate openly, and to influence the conditions that impact classroom life.

Pedagogically, all this has a lot to do with understanding what goes on in the classroom and beyond. This entails a sense of civic involvement, stimulated by the manner in which we, as educators, enact democratic life within the schools.

Such an approach creates opportunities for students to be involved in the civic life of the classroom, by cultivating democratic principles of life. This is precisely where critical principles come into play in our teaching. Unless we are willing to create an environment where ideologies can be unveiled and contested and students can grapple with the particularities of the historical, cultural, and economic foundations that shape how they think about themselves, one another, and the world, we cannot seriously claim to be committed to democratic schooling. Such a vision requires, for example, a classroom context in which working-class students of color can think and question why certain opportunities are not open to them and can start thinking about ways to contend with the inequalities they face.

I believe our role as educators is to create an environment where students, particularly those from disenfranchised communities, can experience themselves as legitimate members of society. This can support students from these communities in developing a greater sense of confidence, both as individuals and as collective subjects of history. I consider this a pedagogical imperative in thwarting the dehumanizing impact of neoliberal policies and practices within education, such as high-stakes testing, as well as the rampant bureaucratic corporatization of educational institutions, which further intensifies the myth of meritocracy.

ORELUS: *But how can it be possible to create democratic life within the classroom when we have universities that have been following a corporate model of education?*

DARDER: There are multiple issues at work here. First of all, it is only possible to create more democratic relations within the classroom when educators acknowledge and take responsibility for the power they wield with their students. This is one important reason that I and many other critical education theorists believe that schooling is such an important political project, because in almost any classroom setting, teachers always have some power, albeit not absolutely, through their authority to decide the nature of the classroom discourse and the manner in which the curriculum will be taught and students will participate. For example, although teachers may indeed have to utilize state-mandated curriculum and state-mandated textbooks, they still have some power to determine how those materials are engaged, how they are discussed and deconstructed, and how the power relationships that inform the construction of classroom materials are unveiled. Educators have the opportunity to create a context that surfaces important questions or that shrouds their discussion. As critical educators, we also have the responsibility to struggle within our institutions and do what we can to remain connected to larger community struggles and needs. Teachers, as parents, are workers, and often the camouflaging of this relationship through notions of teacher professionalism obscures opportunities for teachers to work with parents in changing oppressive conditions that impact the lives of students. This is to say that the professionalizing of teacher practice can function to obstruct the development of solidarity between teachers and parents.

I also recognize that there seldom exists a completely closed culture of oppression within most schools. The rhetoric of democratic ideals, however, is often ensconced within the contradictory power relations of a school. So although there may be some liberal aspects operating, there is also this horrendous bureaucratization and corporatization of the curriculum and of teaching practice at work.

Teaching is reduced to an instrumental practice of, for example, teaching to the test, which deskills teachers and objectifies them and their students. Hence, a major challenge for most teachers is to not fall prey to debilitating despair or to paralytic fatalism. I think this can happen to most of us when we begin to feel that our teaching doesn't matter or when we are expected to function in prescriptive ways that strip us of our creativity and social agency. Yet I want to insist that we always have some power within our lives and within our classrooms. So the question is, are we going to turn over our power to others, or are we going to own the power that is rightly ours and move collectively, rather than individualistically, so that the power of our collective social agency can function to create new democratic spaces?

Another important aspect of creating democratic life within the classroom is that of being psychologically and emotionally present. The reason I say this is that the most powerful leaning I've seen happen is in the context of relationships that feel that they matter. We, as educators, must then be fully present—that is, bring our focus and passion to the moment of teaching, despite the millions of things that are happening in our lives and in the world. If I were sitting here trying to talk to you and lost in ten million other things, the quality of our interaction would be very different, as would be yours. It's the same in the classroom. We have a tremendous responsibility, as critical educators, to be present to our students and to exercise our power in emancipatory ways that allow them to experience democratic life in vivo. There is clearly a liberating process at work in such a pedagogical context. What I am also pointing to here is the importance of not falling into a dynamic where we might be politically correct in our content, but pedagogically oppressive in our practice.

Hence, I firmly believe that it is our willingness to be present that allows us to function with greater social consciousness in our classrooms, which also provides us with greater opportunities to respond in ways that nourish democratic relationships. And, if students experience this in their daily life, they will expand their understanding of what a democratic context feels like within their bodies and across their relationships. So even if they go on and end up in a more authoritarian classroom context later on, they will not forget what they experienced previously, the expansiveness in their learning that they felt within their bodies, minds, and hearts. This is the faith that I hold on to, since we cannot control the future of our students once they leave our classrooms. I sincerely believe that once a human being tastes a sense of freedom and the power of consciousness that emerges from participation within an egalitarian and emancipatory context, the memory remains with them; and, more importantly, they will struggle to reengage and reconnect with this liberatory power, sooner or later, once it has been known.

ORELUS: *Before I moved here, I was never called Black because Blackness wasn't then so much an issue for me like class was. I knew I was poor; I knew my parents were poor. But since I moved here, I have been called different names. So how has your experience been, moving from your colonized land of Puerto Rico to the imperialist land, the United States?*

DARDER: I was very young when I arrived in the States, whereas you were older. That is an important difference because, although we were both inserted into a very unfamiliar cultural context—which included how people move, speak, engage, and so on—you entered with a better formed sense of yourself as a cultural subject. Nevertheless, I would argue that the experiences provoked confusion and anxieties for us both. All the differences we experienced, within our own developmental moment, left us trying to figure out what was going on around us. Life felt familiar and somewhat more secure in our country of origin. At our own stage, we felt a greater understanding of what was expected of us within our cultural milieu. Once in the States, everything changed. It was visceral. In addition to all this, we had to contend with the sense of being treated as inferior.

Beyond the familiar class issues that we might have felt, the sense of being racialized was learned and intensified in the U.S. So although we may have experienced disenfranchisement in relationship to poverty in our own countries, there were many more forces at work here, and they suddenly seemed more obvious when we had to interact with the world. This is not to say that in Puerto Rico or Haiti there isn't racism, because we know there is. But racism, as it is enacted in the United States, has a far more brutalizing impact on the lives of immigrants or those of us who come from U.S. colonies. Often we are treated as if we are stupid, just simply in the way we are talked to by those with authority or those who feel more entitled and privileged. Despite all my education and accomplishments, it still happens to me, and I know it still happens to you as well. One can be in a store, and a clerk will watch you as if you were a thief. It's so frustrating. It has to do with the manner in which racism is at work in U.S. society and how people of color are perceived. Yet, paradoxically, there is also an element of invisibility at the same time. It is easy to be rendered invisible in this context or to be marginalized by simply being deemed "troublesome" or "angry" or "unfit."

But another aspect of this is that we receive a subtle message that things would go well for us if we were simply willing to pledge our allegiance to the status quo—despite its oppressive policies and practices to our communities. The consequence here is that when we raise issues tied to inequalities or social injustice, we are perceived as traitors who are trying to dismantle their pristine notions of the American dream, rather than as people who are deeply committed to the struggle for social justice, human rights, and economic democracy for all. When such a dynamic surfaces, we are either marginalized or rendered invisible within the institution. These are some of the ways in which I feel these forms of oppression have been at work in my life.

Another issue that, of course, we have had to contend with is that of culture and language. The culture and the language that a person is born into is a significant aspect of how one defines the self and how one understands differences in this country. English is the language of power in the U.S. and, for the most part, within the hegemonic process of globalization. The culture and language of colonized people are deemed inferior, and the people themselves are rendered suspect with respect to intellect and moral capacities.

In a million different ways, teachers enact attitudes that, subtlety or not so subtlety, cause us to doubt our capacities and our legitimacy. I think it is important to distinguish here that this generally is not the same experience as when individuals enter into a totally different cultural and linguistic context by choice and as empowered and entitled subjects. For those of us who must grapple with processes of racialization that inferiorize our existence, we are often left with an intense sense of separateness and of not fully belonging anywhere. At least this was my experience and that of many students of color I have known, especially immigrant students who have had to struggle to make their way within the U.S. academic system.

ORELUS: *The U.S. political system has been dominated by heterosexual, Christian, and able-bodied White males for centuries. Now we have the first Black president, Barack Obama. Do you think Obama's presidency has the potential to improve race relations in this country?*

DARDER: In all honesty, I am not so optimistic. I think that Barack Obama's presidency has had an impact on how people contend with racism, in that some feel freer to express their racism again, while others feel more hopeful that a Black president might mean real positive changes in attitudes about race that are now at work. Some may see this moment as an opportunity to address more openly those injustices related to racism and to challenge policies and practices that racialize students.

However, I am not convinced that one person, even if he is president, can ultimately change the conditions of ruling-class oppression and the economics that sustain class, racialized, gendered, and sexual inequalities. Moreover, we can't pretend that Obama isn't now a part of that elite class. What I am saying here is that his professed sensibilities, motivations, and ambitions for change are not enough. He must contend with the aristocratic elites of the corporate and political world that ultimately paid for his presidency and that can make or break his presidency, and with it a second term. This has already been made evident in his contradictory engagement with the Wall Street crisis and even the BP fiasco in the Gulf Coast.

We are also seeing, even now, that there are those who are using this opportunity to declare that racism is over and that the United States has truly evolved into a democratic nation. After all, we elected a Black man who has a Muslim name. Unfortunately, such naive thinking belies the manner in which the ideology and practices tied to racism function and creates false notions that can disrupt the efforts and legitimacy of those whose work continues to expose racism in this country. Consequently, a new dynamic of oppression is exercised, one in which critical educators are, for example, now deemed out of step with the times and obstructive to progress, or our efforts are belittled as unnecessary in this new "post-racial" era. In some cases, criticism is personalized. Or we are seen as simply disgruntled people who should go back where we came from!

This goes back to what we were talking about earlier. When you question the status quo, suddenly it's about your troubled personality, not about ideology, inequalities, and social injustice. It's like we are criminals because we continue to question the gross economic and social inequalities at work with schooling and the larger society. Why do we continue to push? Aren't we satisfied? We finally got a Black president. Why aren't we satisfied? To me, the electoral system as it currently exists functions to support and sustain the interests of the ruling class. That is to say that a class struggle is still being waged, and any and all efforts, whether politically, economically, or academically, to obscure gross inequalities simply cannot change the evidence of unemployment, the absence of health care, poor schooling, mortgage fallout, incarceration, infant mortality, and increasing poverty in the United States.

So, in a lot of ways it doesn't matter who the hell is president in the United States. Sad to say, there are a whole lot of folks who are going to be poor under any capitalist regime, and blamed for their poverty! Perhaps this is now more so than ever. Whatever the case, what we cannot ignore is that under capitalism, and the current neoliberal era is no exception, abject poverty is absolutely necessary. How can we have a capitalist system without high levels of inequality and social injustice?

Capitalist values are inextricably tied to profit-making corporatization, which is inherently exploitative. Unfortunately, most of the safety net, including the majority of the social welfare programs of another era—when the state still saw itself as having some social responsibility to the people—has been dismantled, accelerating the disenfranchisement and impoverishment of a larger sector of the population.

Most of us know people who formerly thought of themselves as middle class, but who have lost their jobs to downsizing and their homes to the mortgage schemes of the last decade. The cost of food is astronomical. Health-care costs are outrageous. Yet the wealthy do not have to contend with these basic survival questions. Instead, as Naomi Klein so aptly writes, the elite, guided by the shock doctrine, fully benefit from the economic downturn being faced by the majority.[2]

So, when I examine the dire impact of neoliberal policies across sectors of the population in this country and abroad today, I cannot but conclude that the main problem in the U.S. is economic and not solely the color line. Yes, racism is a major issue, but I firmly believe that the main problem in this society is one of increasing economic apartheid and the manner in which racism, along with other forms of oppression, continue to be utilized to perpetuate the acceleration of inequalities that are necessary for capitalism to prevail, not only in this country but internationally. So, the question for me remains, what is President Barack Obama going to do with his great power and influence to transform the current financial crisis that is at the root of gross economic inequalities, the betrayal of human rights, and the severance of our national commitment to social justice and democratic life in the United States?

Notes

1. Darder, A., & Torres, R. (2004). *After race: Racism after multiculturalism*. New York: New York University Press.
2. Klein, N. (2007). *The shock doctrine: The rise of disaster capitalism*. New York: Metropolitan Books.

CHAPTER 11

Beyond Obama's Historical Symbolism: The Heavy Weight of Being Black/ Brown in a Racist Society

A CONVERSATION WITH EDUARDO BONILLA-SILVA

This phone interview between Professors Eduardo Bonilla-Silva and Pierre Orelus took place on September 18, 2008, two months before Barack Obama was elected president. In this dialogue, Professors Bonilla-Silva and Pierre Orelus critically examine the ways in which institutional racism has impacted the subjective and material conditions of people of color, particularly men of color. They further analyze the extent to which Black masculinity has been historically misrepresented. They then point out how the misrepresentation of men of color has led to their stigmatization and ill treatment in society. Professor Bonilla-Silva particularly questions Obama's domestic and foreign policies and stance on race, arguing that his presidency will not lead to the betterment of socioeconomic conditions for poor Black/Brown people. Professor Bonilla-Silva goes on to say that Obama, a Black man, will be "a symbol for White people." Throughout this dialogue, Professor Bonilla-Silva critically examines the harmful effects of the intersectional oppressions of race, racism, sexuality, gender, and social class on poor Black, White, and Latino/a women, men, and queer people.

The Dialogue

ORELUS: *What does it mean to be a Black man in this country, or for that matter, in the world?*

Bonilla-Silva: Blackness changes depending on your location. You are from the Caribbean, so, as you know, in many Caribbean nations, and actually in many countries in the world, Blackness is contested (everyone who can avoids the label) because our identity as Black people is sort of sanctioned within a nationalistic discourse. In such places, making a game of Blackness is a common thing, because in a way you are viewed as ruining the nation; talking about race is dividing the nation, dividing the people who are presumably united in a happy family. Now what this does is hide the history of racial oppression. It's just a different form of organizing the racial structures of these countries. We know that our notion of Blackness changes depending on context, so it's not by chance that many Blacks, particularly from the Hispanic Caribbean, become extremely race conscious when they switch racial boats; it's more so for Blacks from Puerto Rico, Cuba, Colombia, the Dominican Republic, Venezuela, and Mexico, in places like the U.S.

Again, this does not mean that we don't have a racial structure in Puerto Rico, Cuba, and so on. It means that Blackness is differently structured; therefore, the space to recognize Blackness and to develop a Black consciousness is much harder in those places. If you allow me to use the concept of Marx in relation to race, in the Americas we are a "race in itself" without being a "race for itself." We recognize here immediately that we are treated differently, that we are regarded differently, and thus there is a space to recognize our Blackness; therefore, here, we become racially conscious and aware.

Orelus: *So let me ask you a follow-up question on this issue. Do you believe that the ongoing effect of slavery and colonialism has something to do with the way people of color, especially Black men, have been treated?*

Bonilla-Silva: Yes, but I also want to add that obviously it is not just because of the history of slavery and colonialism. All modern history produced racial structures that remain in place. These structures are different depending on the country in question, but they exist nonetheless. Let me explain. In many countries, including the U.S., the way of avoiding dealing with the race question is to make the claim that racism was something really bad that they had in the past because of slavery.

In the case of the U.S., we claim that slavery was bad, but after it was abolished, that was the end of racism (Jim Crow has vanished from Whites' imaginary). I want to argue that that's not the case, because in all the Caribbean and the Americas after the abolition of slavery, we were somewhat metamorphosed into a different racial order. Today, a hundred plus years after the abolition of slavery in our countries, we still have a racial order—one differently structured, but a racial order nonetheless. Therefore our continued struggle for the recognition of our identity and equality is not just a struggle based on legacies but a struggle based on the contemporary structure of racism.

ORELUS: *So are you saying that slavery does have an effect on the way we have been treated as Black people, that the way this system is structured does not allow Black people to come to voice? In other words, we continue being a victim of the history of slavery?*

BONILLA-SILVA: I am saying more than that. I am saying that the mere abolition of slavery was not the end of racial order. The abolition of slavery led the world to a new racial order. We don't need to revisit history. The point is that the abolition of slavery did not lead to equality; it led to a different system of racial subordination that lasted in most places over a hundred years. For example, I just came from a trip to the island of Bermuda. Just to share with you an interesting fact, Black folks who represent the majority of the population there were not allowed to have a "one man, one vote" deal until 1968; so this means that even though slavery was abolished in the nineteenth century, they had an official second-class citizenship until 1968. Then, from 1968 onward, they have had an unofficial second-class citizen social status. Even though now they have what the White folks call "Black power" (they are in charge of governing the nation-state), they don't control the economy. Therefore, as you know, if you don't control the economy, controlling politics is nothing.

ORELUS: *Are we experiencing a new form of colonialism?*

BONILLA-SILVA: There is a new form of oppression. We can call it neocolonialism, which is a contemporary version of colonialism. We can call it many ways, or use whatever terms you want to use. Colonial or racial domination did not end with the abolition of slavery; it was just metamorphosed, and that is not only typical of the Caribbean. Black folks in the U.S., for example, are not oppressed today just because of the effects of slavery, but because there are new ways of reproducing White privilege and White supremacy.

ORELUS: *The battle against the misrepresentation of people of color, particularly the dark-skinned ones, through the mass corporate media, schools, and even churches, is a perpetual battle. How would you suggest that we fight in a way that would not lead to the perpetuation of negative stereotypes against us?*

BONILLA-SILVA: I am doing some work on that subject right now. A lot of our struggle is based on the assumption of rationality, that is, on the assumption that if we just convince White folks of the folly of their thinking, we will be able to "overcome," as segments of the civil rights movement tried to do. The problem with that assumption is something that I call in my new work the "racial grammar," a "deep structure" that allows us to see some things as racial and others as not, to call some things racial and others not; this grammar organizes not just our cognitions, but also our emotions.

The racial grammar will never allow the facts of race to be interpreted the way we think they should be interpreted by Whites. For example, we provide them with data on the unemployment of Black people, and White people interpret it as, "You are unemployed because you are lazy." We provide them with data on the overrepresentation of Black people in the penal system, and White people interpret that as, "That's because you are violent." You provide data on Blacks having lesser income and lesser education than Whites, and White people interpret that as, "Of course, that's because you are stupid and lazy."

Therefore, what I am suggesting we do is to follow a lot of the ideas of Caribbean thinkers like Fanon and others. All intellectuals, like Bob Marley said, need to begin a process of "emancipation from mental slavery." For this, although we welcome progressive Whites as our allies, we need not depend on them; we have to begin fighting, no matter what and no matter where, ourselves and with our own ideas; it is a combination of a progressive and nationalist stand. We can't hide our own sense of history, sense of self, of practice, and of logic; we don't have to continue the assumption that we have to use their ideas to free ourselves. In this process, obviously, the central element will always be the same that we have always used—that is, the struggle. We need to continue the long struggle for liberation. By this I mean social movement politics rather than this foolishness of believing that electoral politics will free us from racial domination.

For example, look at the Obama phenomenon; the assumption is that by voting in an election we are going to free ourselves. It's an illusion. Unlike the U.S., where there had never been a Black person in charge, we who are from the Caribbean, because of our history and our struggle, have learned the hard way that leaders should be judged not by the color of their skin, but by the content of their *politics*. Therefore, I don't care to have a Black leader if the position of that leader happens to be reactionary.

If my Black leader claims that he wants to have a thousand more people in the military, I am not happy with that; if my Black leader is for espionage, I don't like that Black leader. If my Black leader tells me that he wants to follow the same politics that the U.S. has followed in Palestine, I don't want that Black leader. Our liberation should come from struggle, from sociopolitical movement and from organization, rather than from hoping to convince (which is what Obama has been trying to do) White folks that he is a soft, nice, smart Negro that they can trust and who will not raise hell on the racial front.

ORELUS: *Obama has been getting both national and international attention perhaps because of his racial hybridity, but certainly because of his charisma and what he represents, or rather because of how he is being represented by the mainstream media. Do you believe Obama will be able to deliver what he has been promising to people in his campaign, or do you think he has just been allowed to perform as part of a show put together by White hegemonic, heterosexual, and Christian men?*

BONILLA-SILVA: Absolutely! The way he has shaped his politics and policies and his persona on every occasion is by reminding his audience that his mother is White and his father is not from the United States but from Africa. In the U.S., his ethnic Blackness is more tolerable for Whites than Blackness from the United States. If his father were a Black man from the south side of Chicago, his hybridity would be a big problem. Furthermore, he has avoided using the term "racism" in his campaign. Actually, the only time he used it was to chastise Reverend Wright, who claimed that racism was endemic. According to Obama, racism has not been endemic in America, which suggests that Reverend Wright is crazy for believing this to be the case. He has obviously made a color-blind appeal, a nationalistic appeal by saying things such as, "I don't see a Black America, or a Latino America, or a White America; I only see the United States of America." He needs to go to an eye doctor and get some new glasses so he can see that we still have a White America, and a Black America, and a Latino America. I don't think he would help us with the so-called "racial divide," because the racial divide is not based on a misunderstanding; our racial divide is based on inequality. What you need to have is policies that address the root causes of inequality among racial groups, as well as a policy of reparation. None of these things is on Obama's agenda. Therefore, what you are going to get is a symbol—Obama, a Black man, will be a symbol for White people that we are finally over race because we have a Black president. For Black people, on the other hand, it would be a short-lived symbol, as he will not deliver on the racial or even the class front.

Black people have put their emotions, their aspirations, in this Black man, but people don't eat emotions or aspirations. After a few years of having Obama as president and living in the same conditions, they will mimic that old commercial and ask, "President Obama, *where's the beef?*"

ORELUS: *Maleness as an identity is fluid. Let's take the example of a Black man who was born and grew up in a White neighborhood, who went to a school predominantly attended by White students, and who mostly interacted with White men and women. This Black man might perform his maleness differently than a Black man who was born and grew up in a predominantly Black community. How do you think Obama has performed his maleness publically and politically?*

BONILLA-SILVA: Obviously, this is a complex matter, so I might not have all the answers. But Blackness is unstable; it is always contested, as well as masculinity. And as you suggested, it is connected to class position and context; based on what I have learned from people who know him, Obama has different performances of masculinity. For example, because he doesn't want to raise hell and upset Whites, in the campaign he has kept a soft masculinity, almost a feminine approach. For example, he is chastised, called names, and he never fights back.

But most Black men from a working-class background would be in the business of kicking ass, in the business of fighting back, in the business of defending, to use a sexist term, their manhood.

Obama, who has performed an almost feminine public persona and performance for mostly White audiences, apparently has a different persona when he is with his people. If you, for example, go to YouTube and see some of his speeches before Black audiences, he really switches from so-called Standard English to an English that is close to the so-called Black English. He is more sort of a *homie* in his style. Although he is always suave (maybe that is part of his persona), he performs a different masculinity with Black audiences.

For all of us, our class and the context we navigate determine how we perform masculinity. Presumably, you and I as professors should perform a softer version of masculinity that is nonthreatening to our colleagues. I play that game somewhat, but I don't give any corners to White folks; I say it as I see it, so I don't give corners; I don't change my performance whether I am with Whites or Black folks. I show White people, using the Black term, "a lot of color."

ORELUS: *Do you see any connection between Blackness and masculinity? In other words, do you think that the way Black men behave is related to their Blackness, their racial identity?*

BONILLA-SILVA: I haven't thought much about this connection between masculinity, gender identity and performance, and racial identity and performance. I do think that for people who have been put down (I am talking about men, so for women the analysis may be somewhat different), for Black men who have been ostracized, literally castrated and so on and so forth, I understand why in some segments of the population the version of masculinity takes the form of a hypermasculinity. When you are put down, you can choose to either die or fight back by being hypermasculine; this approach is somewhat connected to racial oppression. For the middle-class folks (besides Obama) such as Colin Powell, mimicking Whiteness is part of their strategy to achieve mobility—you have another version of masculinity, a softer version acceptable to Whites.

A lot of people that you see in the business world have similar softer personas because that is the ticket to mobility. In addition to the connection between the softer version of masculinity and Blackness, there is the light-skin factor, the phenotypical characteristics that help many middle-class Blacks and wannabe middle-class Blacks achieve mobility.

ORELUS: *Do you think the way Black men nowadays behave has something to do with the history of slavery?*

BONILLA-SILVA: I would never deny the historical impact of slavery. Slavery impacted us, and such an impact will last for generations. But I do want to state that after slavery ended, other forms of oppression continued the pattern of racial subordination; so if one wants to understand contemporary versions of Black masculinity, one has to understand that after slavery, there was a continuation of the violence exercised against Black men, in the labor market, in the streets, and so forth. Therefore, Black men have to perform two jobs: (1) to be obedient in public interactions with Whites or else suffer from indignities and potential death, and (2) as a consequence of this, to be hypermasculine at home. Do you see my point?

Orelus: *Are you saying that racism has something to do with the way Black men behave in society?*

Bonilla-Silva: Absolutely! The whole thing is intrinsically connected. By the way, we are talking about Black people, but what about White males who also have the connection to racism in terms of their performance of masculinity? But the subject is Blackness. Whatever we Black men do today is deeply connected to the racial order. I don't want to get theoretical on this, but we did have patriarchy before slavery was inflicted upon us, so it is not that before slavery we didn't have patriarchal versions of masculinity among the people we call Black today. What I am saying is that after slavery, the way we performed masculinity changed because of the racial order.

Orelus: *Black men are targeted wherever they go because of their skin tone. Obviously we cannot stop living, so what should we do? Should we head back to Africa as Marcus Garvey once proposed, or should we try to integrate into the White world as Martin Luther King once dreamed of?*

Bonilla-Silva: It depends on how you define Blackness. We could say that most of the world is comprised of people of color. If that is the case, we don't need to go back to Africa; we have places and histories. I am, for example, a Black Puerto Rican, so I have the Blackness and then the Latino ethnicity. You took the pessimistic view. I would take the optimistic view. It is true that racism has been with us for five hundred years; we saw the transition from slavery to Jim Crow and from Jim Crow to what I call in my work the "new racism." So yes, we still have racism, but we are moving forward because we have fought, we have resisted racial subordination.

There have been fundamental changes in the racial order. If we have to choose between being a slave and being a person living under Jim Crow, I prefer Jim Crow; between being a person living under Jim Crow and a person enduring the new racism deal we live today, I prefer the racial hell we live today. The struggle will continue.

The hope is ultimately to eliminate race as a category of domination and oppression and to move toward the transformation of race into culture or benign ethnicity. Will that happen? I remain optimistic. I do know that I will never stop fighting, and I will never tell folks out there to stop fighting. One can pick a totally pessimistic standpoint and say, "You know what? There is no point in fighting because you will never win." I feel that had we done that in the past, we would still be enslaved. So our job is to continue the struggle, to continue pushing, pushing, and pushing, but being fully aware that between now and the final liberation, there may be all sorts of stages. We need to fight this monster we are enduring today while recognizing that in fifty years that monster will hopefully be somewhat nicer.

OrELUS: *I wasn't suggesting that we should go back to Africa. That is one of the arguments that have been made in the past.*

BONILLA-SILVA: I know. I do know why, in certain moments in history, we as people have advocated for the separation option. We still have this view in the Nation of Islam. However, although there is a beauty in the argument of "Leave me the hell alone," we are owed for the injuries caused to us by White supremacy. Therefore, our struggle is to get reparations, whether White folks like it or not. We will probably have to impose this on them—that is, to provide reparation for the injuries they caused us. I am not going anywhere, neither to Africa nor to a section in the South of the United States like some folks in the 1930s suggested. NO! I want my money here: in Michigan, Wisconsin, New Mexico, North Carolina, Texas, anywhere that I am; I want my reparation. I want to push for a society in which we truly become a multicultural nation where race is no longer a factor of domination.

ORELUS: *How do you understand the role that the interconnection between racism and capitalism plays in oppressing people of color?*

BONILLA-SILVA: You know very well that we in the Caribbean had Eric Williams who told us way back that capitalism was a racialized system. His work has been followed by other Black scholars. These scholars argue that capitalism is a racialized system; therefore the struggle for liberation against racism also needs to be the struggle for liberation against capitalist oppression. The secret of the future is how to articulate a politics that allows us to put together the racial, class, and gender struggle in one common struggle. Will that ever happen? I don't have a formula, and I don't believe in formulas; but I believe you need to articulate a politics, and I trust movements to develop a fine print of a program to do so. That is the clue: understanding that the racial order is a class order, and it has been so for five hundred years.

ORELUS: *I do recognize that there is a clear link between racism and capitalism. However, I would say that there are countries such as Cuba where supposedly there is a socialist system, but Black folks are oppressed. How would you explain this?*

BONILLA-SILVA: The racial order in Cuba deserves special attention and needs to be critically analyzed. Before Cuba became what it is today, it had a racial order. Bringing in socialist leaders in the racial capitalist traditions of the past did not transform the culture and the practices of racism there. Therefore, racism is still part of Cuba. Now, do we truly want to see Cuba as a socialist order when in reality there is in power an authoritarian regime with a lot of capitalist components to it? But if you push me, I will tell you that ultimately the struggle will continue, whether it is in a capitalist economy, a mixed economy, or an economy that calls itself "socialist."

The struggle that I suggested before about race, class, and gender cannot be one that is limited to one country, because the world has been well interconnected. You cannot have freedom in one corner and none elsewhere; that is the way the world system operates.

ORELUS: *In the U.S., we are living in a system that is capitalist and racist. Are you saying that in order to come to voice and set ourselves free, we need to fight both capitalism and racism at the same time?*

BONILLA-SILVA: Not only in the U.S. We have to develop solidarity worldwide. Think about the struggle that we are having nowadays in the United States. We will never be free until we understand that our struggle is the struggle of Mexican workers; it is the struggle of workers everywhere. To put it simply, how can the U.S. free itself from the capitalist racist order when Lou Dobbs tells American workers in his CNN show every night, "I am for you; therefore, like you, I hate Mexicans." This will never allow us to develop a politics, a morality of class and race solidarity. You cannot realize class and racial solidarity and unite workers of America without having a clear view of the world system. If you don't, your struggle will be limited, and you will collapse.

If White workers go for a White populist struggle that says, "We White 'workers of the world' in America want to be free and must get rid of all the minority workers so that we can have *our* socialist system," such an approach would never work and would never lead them to freedom. The struggle has to be anticapitalist and antiracist at the global level. I am not being an idealist. I understand that people have to start the struggle where they are, so as American workers, we need to start making the demands at home. But it is the job of those engaged in the larger politics to make the connections so as to avoid a nationalistic view, which can impede the much needed global solidarity.

ORELUS: *Many scholars who are from the so-called third world, when they talk about racism—I am referring to those who are living in the United States—usually focus on racism taking place in the United States, but not on racism that is alive and well in their native countries. What is your stance on this issue?*

BONILLA-SILVA: It's everywhere.

Orelus: *You are from Puerto Rico, but in your book* Racism without Racists, *I didn't see any analysis of the racism that has been happening in Puerto Rico. I have friends who are from there, especially Afro-Puerto Ricans. They always talk about the racism they experienced when they were living there, but you don't really talk about that in your book. Was it a conscious choice?*

Bonilla-Silva: The data for the book were obviously collected in the United States. But I gave a talk on the book in Puerto Rico, and I began and concluded by saying that I had learned about color-blind racism not in the U.S. but in Puerto Rico. So I do make a claim that racism is not an American problem; it is not a South African problem; it is a world systemic problem. Puerto Rico is an older nation-state than the United States, albeit a colonial one. Puerto Rico has a hundred-years-longer racial history than the U.S. Now the question becomes, why don't we talk about race in Puerto Rico, Cuba, Colombia, and so forth? It is because of the way the racial order was structured. We have been playing the color-blind drama longer than the United States, which means that our racial order is ultimately more effective in maintaining domination than the American order is.

In my recent work, I claim that the American racial order is becoming like the racial order in Latin America. If this happens, then racial inequality and White supremacy will be deeper, because it is easier to dominate when you have no space to see, talk about, or process race as a legitimate category. In Puerto Rico, we claim that "we are all Americans," that we no longer see race; we follow Obama's logic, if you will. If we follow the nonsense that we don't see any race in this country, that we are all Americans, then we would be moving in the direction of Latin America. Down the road, we would be like Puerto Ricans, Cubans, or Venezuelans. We don't have racism in this country; the only racism in the world would be that of South Africa.

So the issue for us in the Americas, in the larger sense of the word "America," is how do we develop a politics of race in places where there is no discursive space to talk about race? That is a hard issue. Those of us who are interested in changing our countries have been talking about it for some time. I am working on projects that address the race question in Puerto Rico; but when I was working on this particular book (*Racism without Racists*), I was getting my feet into academia just like you. Now I am sort of a free man of color, so I can do whatever I damn well please.

This Friday, I am bringing this colleague, sociologist Tukufu Zuberi, from the University of Pennsylvania. He and I are now working on projects to make connections, Pan-African connections. He has deep connections in several African countries and in Colombia, Venezuela, and so on. We are working to generate discussions about racial stratification in the U.S. and in other places so as to learn about how race is structured in places like Cuba, Colombia, Puerto

Rico, and elsewhere. Obviously, as a Puerto Rican, my ultimate goal (it is sort of a personal goal) is to produce work, as well as a politics, that addresses the race question in Puerto Rico. I did not start with this concern in my career, even though all my work with regard to race is always connected to other countries, because I was based in the U.S. and had to work for tenure. You, as someone who is from the Caribbean, can see the connections between all I have written and race issues in the Americas.

Now I am a free man. Now I don't have to be kissing anyone's back; I can do what I want to do, which is ultimately to do work and politics about race in Puerto Rico and the larger Caribbean.

Orelus: *You know that all forms of oppression are related; so if we have to fight against racism, we should also fight against other forms of oppression, such as homophobia. We know that in the Caribbean there is a lot of homophobia. What is your political and personal position on this issue?*

Bonilla-Silva: I do believe that ultimately it is the task of progressive politicians to fight against all sorts of oppression. If anyone is oppressed, then no one is truly free. With that said, I want to make an appeal for us to be clear that I will struggle fundamentally for my rights. I am not expecting White people to liberate me. Women should not expect men to liberate them; gays and lesbians should not be silly enough to expect heterosexuals to liberate them. This means that one first organizes with your logical allies—people who are in the same position, suffering from the same oppression—and then from there you expand the coalition.

But I am not in the business of believing—you probably can relate to this; those of us who are of a certain age remember the socialist appeal—the old Marxist line of "Don't bring your race concerns, your gender concerns, or your concerns about homophobia, because we struggle for class solidarity and socialism." I will engage in a race-based struggle that is sensitive to all other forms of oppression, but I will not allow anyone to tell me that my suffering is "secondary" to the real and fundamental issue, which is class. That is bullshit!

Therefore, although I am in solidarity with everyone who suffers from any form of oppression, my fundamental task is to explore the race-class interaction. From there I would express solidarity with other folks, and hopefully they will also express solidarity with our movement. Then we may develop a larger political movement for human emancipation.

Orelus: *We cannot expect women or Black people to fight against racism and sexism alone, because, as you know, we as men have contributed to maintaining the patriarchal system.*

Bonilla-Silva: Of course. Again, because we have benefited from patriarchy, they (women) need to organize. Their struggle is to organize first with their logical allies—all women. From there they should push us, and the hope is that progressive men like you and I will join them in that struggle for liberation from patriarchy and sexism as an ideology and as a practice. It would be silly for them to expect us to lead their movement. Where do you begin? Do you begin organizing men? Or do you begin organizing women? You and I as Black men, do we begin organizing Black people? Or do we begin organizing White people? The logic of the politics has to be, we organize first with people who are experiencing a similar oppression. From there we make a larger appeal.

Orelus: *Throughout your work, you have addressed racial issues. How did you get interested in this issue?*

Bonilla-Silva: As a Black Puerto Rican, I never had a 100 percent consciousness of racial matters because that is what Puerto Rico, Cuba, Mexico, and Brazil give you: a sort of divided identity, no space to talk and think about race. Consequently, one suffers indignities that are translated and read as examples of individual prejudice, but not as expressions of systemic racism. I came to the U.S. with the sense that racial matters in Puerto Rico were different from those in the U.S. And I came to the U.S. as a vulgar Marxist to do class analysis and class politics. I then joined movements in Wisconsin dealing with racial matters, and that was sort of the beginning of my transition.

Like many Caribbean folks, it was the contact with the U.S. reality that allowed me to rethink my own history back home and to get serious about racial issues in the U.S. But I am always sort of going back home and thinking about prejudice in Puerto Rico. Before I started dealing with race in the U.S., I started reliving my own history and began to be extremely concerned about understanding the racial and historical past of the country. Initially, my dissertation had nothing to do with race; it was on squatting in Puerto Rico, specifically the political economy of squatters in my country. As soon as I became a professor in Michigan, I had already made an emotional, political, and theoretical move into the race terrain, and I have been in that terrain for the last fifteen years.

Orelus: *Some orthodox Marxists tend to focus more on the class issue than on the race issue. In other words, for them it doesn't matter if you are Black, White, or Brown, because we are all oppressed by capitalism. How do you understand such a position?*

Bonilla-Silva: I was like that for some time. I believed that racism and sexism were ideologies developed by the bourgeoisie to divide workers. But if you are a Black Marxist and someone calls you "Nigger," it is hard to make an argument that this is simply an ideological phenomenon. You read and understand that White workers get better rights in this society than minority workers, and that this is not a mere ideology but a practice. I obviously no longer take that position, but I have to tell you that I did, and this is part of the growth, the intellectual and political growth for many of us. We make our politics and our conscience based on our material life. There are spaces, political and cultural, that you could not have ever thought about. In a country like Puerto Rico, even calling someone Black is still an issue; there is no space for that; it is viewed as an insult. Therefore, no one wants to be called Black.

In the Dominican Republic, there are a lot of dark-skinned folks. But Dominican folks don't want to call themselves Black. For them, being Black is being Haitian. They say things like, "I am not Haitian; I am Mulatto; I am Indian; I am White; I am Dominican; I am anything but Black." Again, like many Caribbean folks, I have developed a political and cultural outlook drawn fundamentally on my experiences and on my milieu. I can give you hundreds of examples of how race mattered in my own life, but there was no space for developing a clear consciousness about racial politics and about how to interpret them as expressions of institutional racism.

ORELUS: *In your work, you also made the distinction between light-skinned Black and dark-skinned Black. Has the whole issue of light skin versus dark skin influenced your work?*

BONILLA-SILVA: In the sociological tradition, we do a lot of empirical research that clearly shows that light-skinned Blacks as well as light-skinned Latinos do significantly better in life than dark-skinned ones. There is no mystery of why that is the case. Historically, White folks have exhibited a preference to light-skinned children because the assumption is that if you have light skin, it is because you are mixed. Malcolm X talked about the "field Negroes" and the "house Negroes." The house Negroes were usually the product of interracial rape. Historically, the system has rewarded lightness, as it makes folks closer to the European look and more acceptable to Whites (Obama is a case in point), and penalized those of us who are darker. With regard to this issue, I did not develop anything new. We have had it for a long time.

What is new in my work is this argument about the U.S. now moving into a Latin American type of racial order, which I claim is going to be comprised of three different groups: Whites on top, a middle group that I call "honorary Whites," and a large group at the bottom, an amorphous group that I call the "collective Black."

If you look at the entire spectrum of Black people, it is true that some dark-skinned Black folks do well (e.g., Oprah, Michael Jordan). But if you have data for all Blacks or all Latinos, you will find that the best predictor of mobility is skin tone—those with light skin are more likely to attain mobility than those who are dark. So if you come from a poor family and you are darker, you are less likely to achieve mobility than a lighter member in your own family. Similarly, in an upper-class family, the darker ones are less likely to achieve mobility than the lighter ones. People always say, "What about Oprah?" Our sociological response is that the individual case does not challenge the pattern. For every Oprah, there are hundreds of thousands of dark-skinned Black folks who never achieve much. So we need to look at the collective life chances of Black people.

CHAPTER 12

Confront Racial and Gender Oppressions in Schools

A CONVERSATION WITH PEDRO NOGUERA

In this dialogue, Professor Noguera discusses interwoven issues such as institutional racism, poverty, the incarceration of Latino and Black youth, and student academic achievement. Professor Noguera begins by sharing his experience as a professor of color in academia, which he states has been positive overall despite some racist and racial incidents he faced when he was invited by some students of color at Berkeley to be the commencement speaker. Though Professor Noguera recognizes that White people have benefited from institutional racism, he argues that both White and Black people have been victims of poverty and capitalism. He therefore makes an appeal to collectively fight against wealth inequality. As for the incarceration of Black and Latino males, he states that racism has a lot to do with it and that it is a new form of slavery; these inmates are being exploited in their cells by selling their labor for pennies. While Professor Noguera feels that having a Black president is a good sign, he states that people should not have the illusion that racism is over and that we are living in a post-racial era.

The Dialogue

Orelus: *Please, would you begin by talking about your experience as a professor of color in the U.S. academy?*

Noguera: I enjoy what I do. I feel very fortunate to do the things I do. I have had a great time in academia, and I feel very privileged. I really enjoy teaching. I taught undergraduates, often in large lecture halls. Sometimes I had over 350 students. Now I am teaching mostly doctoral students, and my experience has been very positive. I find that students are very receptive to learning about complex issues. I have learned how to be good at creating an environment where we can talk about difficult and often controversial issues in a respectful manner. Students appreciate that. So I would say generally it has been a very good experience for me.

ORELUS: *I was watching a video about you on YouTube where you stated that the good thing about going to the Caribbean is that when you are there, you don't have to worry about being Black because everybody looks like you. What exactly did you mean by that?*

NOGUERA: It is such a good feeling. When you are a minority, particularly in a country like the U.S. with a history of slavery, racism, and discrimination, you often feel a heightened sense of stress due to distrust and scrutiny in both overt and subtle forms. This takes a toll on a person, and a lot of times you only realize that once you are not in that situation. The fact that we get accustomed to it is a real problem. I found that when I am in a setting where there are people of color, you no longer have to be aware of your identity. This can actually reduce stress. You are just free to be yourself, rather than having this heightened sense of awareness about your racial identity, or the fact that people may be judging you based upon your identity.

ORELUS: *As you know, it is really a challenge for faculty of color working at institutions that are predominantly White. Can you briefly trace your journey being a professor of color at institutions such as Harvard University, where I met you about eight years ago, and Berkeley?*

NOGUERA: In both places, I felt that I had a great experience. As you know, there are always drawbacks in any job. I would say one drawback is that when you are one of a few faculty of color, you get a lot of demands made on you from students who are looking for advice and for the kind of unique perspective that you may bring. I certainly experienced that both at Berkeley and at Harvard, but I didn't mind that, because I enjoy what I do. I don't mind being an adviser and a mentor to students. I see it as part of the job.

At Berkeley, there was one instance where I was asked by the students to be the commencement speaker, which I thought was a great honor. The reason they asked me was because they had approached several celebrities to speak, and they had been turned down. At the last minute, they realized they didn't have a speaker. So their advisers said, "Well, ask a professor on campus. The students said they wanted me, so they came to me." So I thought it was an honor. But the day of the commencement, the local newspaper ran a story in which they said,

"Well, in the past there were dignitaries who spoke at the commencement. This year, it's just a lowly assistant professor." They didn't say "lowly," but that was the implication of what they were saying.

The students learned that an alumnus said how outrageous it was that I was a commencement speaker. When that alumnus person had graduated, John F. Kennedy was the speaker. Then the paper ran a cartoon of someone speaking for the graduates with a broom in his hand. This was absolutely highly insulting. But what was interesting was that the students got outraged and wrote letters to the tribune explaining why they chose me, reacting to the racist implication of the comments.

Orelus: *How did this unpleasant experience affect both your professional and your personal life?*

Noguera: I would say not a lot. I'm a realist. I know that we are the minority, and in a certain way a token, right? By that, I mean that until I came to Berkeley, there was no one with a focus on urban education. There was no one focused on race. So I occupied a certain kind of niche within the university that often made it seem as though you are there only for that purpose. That can stigmatize you. At the same time, I have never allowed it to stigmatize me. I have always used it as a strength and as an opportunity, and it has always worked to my advantage.

Orelus: *What has been your students' reaction when you discuss racial issues in an urban context in your courses?*

Noguera: Well, they are predominantly Whites because these are elite institutions that mostly serve White students. I engage them first by referring to history. I always think history is an important starting point because people need to understand the kind of historical bases of race, racism, and racial inequality in America. So I always start with history before I get to theory, and I always try to do it in a way that allows all students, regardless of their background, to feel like they are a part of the conversation and not simply being talked about or being attacked even. What is important is that, as a person of color, I create an environment where White students can learn and not feel as if they are being made guilty for crimes that they didn't commit.

Orelus: *How has your work on urban education, race, and gender issues been received by your colleagues?*

Noguera: I have to say it has not been a problem. I have gotten a lot of support from my colleagues. When I was up for tenure, I was unanimously supported. I can't say there is a real downside regarding the way my colleagues have treated me over the years.

Orelus: *There has been a lot of talk about a post-racial era. Do you think that because we have Obama as the first Black president, the race relations between Blacks and Whites and people of color will improve? Do you think we are better off now than we were, say, fifty years ago?*

Noguera: I don't think we are in a kind of post-racial period. Racism is certainly alive. The president himself is experiencing that right now in terms of the attacks that have been launched against him. At the same time, there is a quantitative change now. When you have a Black president, it also suggests that there is a much greater number of people in this country that accept the idea of having a Black person in a leadership position. It's not only that we have a Black governor in Massachusetts and a Black governor in New York. We have several icons, from Oprah Winfrey to Michael Jackson, who have crossed borders. There has been a change in racial attitudes, but that doesn't mean we are in a post-racial era.

We also have surplus examples of racial profiling by the police and discrimination in the workplace. So I don't think we are by any means in a post-racial period, but I do think it's going to change, and it is important to acknowledge the change; it's a change for greater tolerance, much greater tolerance. For example, people who hold openly racist views feel as though they have to keep those views to themselves. It doesn't mean the views have gone away. So there has been a change in racial attitudes. You see that in other ways as well, in terms of a growing presence of people of color in leadership roles and in professional positions across the country. But we always have to be attentive to the ways that different classes interact, because the needs of the poor, particularly the needs of the poor Black and Latino people in this country, are increasingly not addressed. That's a sign that it is not simply about a question of race. It is also a question of class.

Orelus: *Let's say that Obama doesn't get reelected, or let's say he gets elected for four more years; what is going to happen after those eight years are over as far race relations in this country are concerned?*

Noguera: Well, we don't know. But I know we are living in a dynamic and changing time. If you would have asked me three years ago if a Black man would or could ever get elected, I would have said no. But one did. So it's these things that are hard to predict. We can't predict the ways things will change; but we do see certain trends, and these trends are toward greater tolerance. You see that right now just in terms of the number of people in interracial marriages. The number of children who are the products of those relationships is growing. It grows every year. All those are signs of change; it doesn't mean that racism or discrimination is gone by any means. But it does mean that it's not a static situation. The other thing we need to think about is that sometimes you will have Black police committing racial profiling, such as the case with Sean Bell. This young man was killed by five police officers, including officers of color. So these issues are a lot of times more complicated than they were perhaps in the 1950s.

Orelus: *From your experience as a professor, how do you see social class stratification play itself out among people of color?*

Noguera: This to me is a big issue, because it is very clear that those with education are able to experience class mobility, like you and me, who are professors at universities. Clearly, we are benefiting from this system. There are many people who are not, and they are in many cases stuck and have very dim prospects because of institutional racism, and because of the way in which inequality grows and widens over time. These issues of those who have been forgotten and abandoned by the system are really the kinds of issues that we have to pay much more attention to. That is why those are the content and focus of my work in education.

Orelus: *There are many orthodox Marxists who have privileged class issues over race issues. What is your opinion about this?*

Noguera: You always have to look at them together. It's not one or the other; it's dynamic. You also have to look at gender. We have a crisis right now facing Black men, but it's not all Black men. It's mostly poor, working-class Black men. So you have to look at those intersections of race, class, and gender. In my own work, I have been focusing a lot on trying to understand why so many Black and Latino men are in crisis, are not graduating from school, are not employed, and are overrepresented in the nation's prisons. That is where you see issues related to race, class, and culture matter, that some people who are concentrated in ghettos and barrios don't have access to education. They are in a much more difficult situation. They don't have access to the opportunities that exist in this country that others have access to. It is because of the political economy of this country.

We don't have an industrial base anymore. So the kinds of jobs available to people who are unskilled are very limited right now and in some cases are nonexistent. If you look at the cities that were once industrial centers, like Detroit, Buffalo, or Cleveland, they are the places with the highest unemployment rate right now. The steel industry is not there. So you basically have a large segment of the population, particularly the Black population, that has been affected and marginalized by these changes in the economy.

Orelus: *Do you think Obama should find ways to make sure those companies stay here in the U.S. so people with limited skills can actually work and earn a living?*

Noguera: Yes, it is related to globalization. The fact is that manufacturers can get the same goods produced in Mexico or in Taiwan for much cheaper rates than they can here. So the capital has left, and some cities are left behind, and lots of people who are dependent on those jobs are now jobless. But that's a process that you can't say is racist. It is more than that because there are White workers who have been left behind as well.

ORELUS: *It has a lot to do with capitalism. Would you agree? What should be done about that?*

NOGUERA: That's right. Absolutely. And there is no easy answer to that one. To a large degree it's about opportunity. I am actually working in New Jersey trying to look at ways in which we can create stronger links between schools and job opportunities, because if we don't do that, we will never break the cycle of poverty; but it's not easy. I am hoping there are opportunities in renewable energy and the medical fields, but it's as much a hope as anything.

ORELUS: *Many immigrants of color have been labeled many names, like "illegal aliens" and "dirty immigrants." As someone with immigrant parents, what is your opinion about the labels that have been imposed on these immigrants?*

NOGUERA: Well, racial categories and the dynamics of race in America are very American. They are not universal. That's why it is very important to know our students, to understand that these categories and the way people think about race is very much a product of American history. As soon as you travel abroad, you start to realize there is a very different sense and notion of race. Sometimes there are some other reasons as well. That's why when you study these issues you have to understand the history behind them.

ORELUS: *Slavery, colonization, and racism are interconnected. How do you see that connection?*

NOGUERA: Yes, they are interconnected. Although we call globalization something new, it is really just a continuation of imperialism, of mercantilism, of colonization, and of the dynamics of world trade. So it's just a modern form of the same kinds of economic processes. Racism also evolves the same way. We don't have slavery anymore, but we have prisons that are predominantly comprised of Black people in this country, wherein they work for little pay; so there is slave labor in prisons. It is important to understand the way certain patterns of stratification reproduce. Obviously it's better than earning nothing or sitting around doing nothing. However, this becomes another way to rationalize what has been happening in order to exploit their labor in prisons. That's the official reason. The visual reason is that it's profitable; it's more cost effective than simply having people sit there. In fact, it has become another way to exploit and take advantage of oppressed groups.

ORELUS: *If they maximize their profit by having those prisoners working for almost nothing, then what would be the incentive to dismantle that system?*

NOGUERA: That's the problem. The only way you make change in this context is to organize. Unless there is a social boom in this country to challenge these systems of oppression, there will be no change at all. It took the civil rights movement to challenge the system in this country. It took a women's movement to give women the right to vote and to ensure a woman equal pay and gender equity in the workforce. So there is social movement that has historically brought about reforms, from Social Security to the end of racially segregated schools. Part of the reason why President Obama is having so much trouble with getting the health-care bill passed is that there is no movement for health-care reform. The president can't do it all by himself, which is what he is trying to do.

ORELUS: *Speaking of Obama, I would like to ask what you think of his secretary of education, Arne Duncan. As you know, he is in favor of charter schools. What is your take on that?*

NOGUERA: I have not been impressed so far. I don't see much vision there. I don't think they are even clear about what needs to change, so I have been disappointed. Charter schools are sometimes necessary; there are some schools that are so sick and dysfunctional that they have to be shut down. But that should also be the last resort, not the first one. There are too many schools that are not performing for that to be the only approach to take. You have to have a variety of strategies. The first thing you need to do is ask why those schools are failing in the first place and address those issues. You have to be more creative.

ORELUS: *Instead of closing down the schools, what about providing resources to the schools so that they can be functional?*

NOGUERA: Sometimes that's an issue. Are resources the problem? To be fair, there are schools that have gotten lots of resources that also haven't improved. The issues are more complex because a lot of times you have people working in the schools who really don't value or care about the kids. So the problem is not simply the resources; it's the personnel.

ORELUS: *In that case, the need would be to train people who want to become teachers.*

NOGUERA: Well, that's true. To recruit people who want to work with the students in our schools is another big challenge because it's not like we just have an ample supply of those people waiting. We have to educate and prepare them. It's a lot of work to be done. So much of the problem with the failure of schools is about the connection between education and poverty. Schools can't solve the problems of poverty by themselves. That's why the federal government approaches them to narrow the focus on achievement and focus on how to address some of the other issues that face poor children.

ORELUS: *I know you have been working with boys who are incarcerated. Is there anything you would like to share with me about your work?*

NOGUERA: The main thing I am working on now is a project that tries to transform New York schools by building partnerships between the schools and community organizations. That can address some of the nonacademic needs of students. But we have also been looking at studying what is happening to Black and Latino boys in New York City and trying to develop interventions so that we lose fewer students. We have also been looking at whether or not separating boys into single-sex schools is a factor. So that's another big project I have been working on.

ORELUS: *I went to a high school that was only attended by males, and there was a lot of competition between the male students. But I wonder if separating boys from girls would make a difference in their academic achievement.*

NOGUERA: Well, the thing is that you still have to focus on the quality of education. It's not simply separation that would make a difference in their achievement. But I do see that some schools, which have found ways to separate the boys and girls, are getting better. That's something we have to continue to study.

CHAPTER 13

I Say It How It Is: Exposing Racial Issues in the Classroom and Beyond

A CONVERSATION WITH DAVID STOVALL

In this phone interview, Professor David Stovall discusses community engagement, institutional racism, wealth disparity, and social inequality in schools and beyond. Professor Stovall draws on critical race theory, along with his lived and professional experiences working with marginalized groups in diverse communities, to analyze and unveil the gross and brutal forms of oppression these groups have experienced. He goes further to link these oppressions to the larger socioeconomic and political context. Specifically, Professor Stovall illuminates the extent to which asymmetrical power relations have led many historically marginalized groups, including female students and professors of color, to the margins. He explains how a few men and women of color have been appointed in key positions and used by those who control the White power structure to fake racial diversity, thereby perpetuating the status quo. Professor Stovall encourages us to actively engage with the community, assume our civic responsibility, and develop a language of possibility and critique to counter hegemonic dominations in schools and beyond.

The Dialogue

ORELUS: *Please, would you begin by telling me a little bit about yourself in terms of where you were born and grew up and your academic journey?*

Stovall: I was born and raised in Chicago. I went to undergraduate and graduate schools at the University of Illinois at Urbana-Champaign. While I was an undergraduate student, I was introduced to community organizing. When I made the decision to go to graduate school, it was largely with the idea of using what I would learn in graduate school as a researcher to bring it back to communities like the ones that I actually came from here in Chicago. Throughout graduate school, I tried to figure out what were available resources to bring back to my communities. One of the things that I actually discovered while working with community organizers was that there was the need to interpret data collected for research purposes. So what I have been doing for almost twenty years is to help people in the community make sense of and properly use the resources they have. It has been a long journey in terms of trying to put that work together.

Orelus: *Have your experiences working with people in your community informed your decision to become a teacher working with historically marginalized groups?*

Stovall: Absolutely. These experiences inform 85 to 90 percent of what I do now. I am currently teaching a social studies class at a local high school. That came out of a larger community initiative aimed to actually develop a school in a neighborhood that was promised a school previously but this promise was never fulfilled. So people in that community went on nineteen hunger strikes to make sure that they got that school. They contacted me after the hunger strikes to work with them on developing a curriculum for the school. A colleague of mine and I who were on the design team of the curriculum wrote a proposal. We promised the people in the community that we would teach a course at that high school as part of our commitment to the community. So I am just continuing to fulfill that promise that I made seven years ago.

Orelus: *How has race informed decisions that you may have made in your classrooms?*

Stovall: In the United States, we have done a very poor job in dealing with race in terms of understanding and processing it and even recognizing its resilience. In my classes, I start off with this disclaimer. We don't even say more about it other than saying it is a social construct. So, how do we actually begin to engage racial realities that we are often rewarded for shying away from? Nothing bad happens to us if we don't talk about race. You are granted a better position if you don't talk about race, people's suffering, and resisting and confronting oppression. I start off my classes saying to my students, "Look, this is what you are going to be hearing; this is what we are going to be talking about. Now, if this is not to your liking, I take no offense if folks decide to drop my class; that is not a problem, but I want to be clear in terms of what it is that I talk about in my classes."

ORELUS: *Some White people have often refused to talk about race. How do you explain that?*

STOVALL: There are many reasons. But the primary one is discomfort. In some cases, you are going to have to confront a very sordid history, and a lot of it is rooted even in people's families. The unwillingness to confront and address certain racial issues has to do with people's lack of courage to say, "It's okay to confront these issues." People need to confront these ideas, but if they are racist or insensitive, it will cause them some level of discomfort. In many ways, we want to push race aside as if racism never happened. It's this notion around denial and discomfort. Those are the two main culprits as to why some White folks don't want to talk about race.

ORELUS: *Can you share with me some of the forms of resistance you may have faced in your classrooms from students, particularly from White privileged students, when you attempt to address racial issues?*

STOVALL: When I start with the disclaimer that I mentioned before, I don't get as much resistance because I am transparent about racial issues. I say to my students, "I'll say things in my class you might not like or don't want to hear, but that doesn't dismiss it from the historical record." With this disclaimer, I have gotten very little resistance. Let me give you an example. Some students actually came into my office and said they overheard another student saying that the history I was talking about in class was all my history and not American history. The next day, I brought this up in class, asking the class, when we talk about history, or when we talk about something being a person's history, or, for that matter, when we talk about American history, what is American history? How do we qualify that? What do we understand about American history? Why are some groups included and others excluded? These questions really kind of cut out any type of active resistance. There might be some passive resistance in terms of writing a paper, refuting what has been said in class, but there has been very little active resistance in my classrooms.

ORELUS: *Many professors of color, myself included, have expressed great concerns about the way they have been treated in some institutions because of their racial, ethnic, and linguistic backgrounds and sometimes country of origin. What has been your experience as a professor of color in the U.S. academy and beyond?*

STOVALL: In some institutions, race is positioned as something external to the life of the university. I challenge this tendency and say, "Look, you talk about recruiting faculty of color, but what tangible efforts have you made to recruit them? More importantly, what have you done to protect faculty of color? If you have placed folks in a hostile environment, how could you expect them to stay?" I have been asking folks over time how they can expect faculty of color to adhere to these hostile environments. Who in their right mind would stay in a hostile environment? So that has really been big on my own radar in terms of paying attention to how these environments can in many ways be very hostile and unwelcoming to faculty of color. And I have noticed quite a bit of that here at my own institution and at universities across the country.

ORELUS: *So how does one navigate through a system or an institution that is really racist?*

STOVALL: One of the most important things is to find community outside the university context. There are other people in the world who can reaffirm your sanity, and it is not always within the university context, because sometimes the university can be a very toxic environment. Because of that toxicity, we can develop this sense of hopelessness. You never want to get into a space where you feel powerless or hopeless. So in order to address that, you need to find a community outside of the university space. Anything as simple as having dinner with like-minded friends or being engaged with community work outside of the university context is actually healthy and can save your sanity. Those spaces external to the university are critical in navigating the university space. The second piece is minimizing the context as much as humanly possible with those toxic elements of the university and letting folks know where you stand so they won't try to steer you in a different way, or push you into things that are not in tune with what you are trying to do. Be explicit and say, "This isn't what I am trying to do, and here is what I am doing to make those things happen." You can talk about your research and your community engagements that way. They can't really refute those claims. So those are the ways in which I navigate the university space currently.

ORELUS: *Many scholars, particularly orthodox Marxists, have privileged class issues over race issues, arguing that socioeconomic inequality stemming from capitalism affects both Blacks and Whites. Where do you stand on this issue?*

STOVALL: For me that argument is outdated and really doesn't take into account the real ways in which race has permeated even class relationships. So to say that one caused the other is the wrong argument. You can't separate the two because they inform each other. Some Marxists talk about the notion of a market economy and scientific materialism. My response is that you can't always dismiss social constructs that actually dictate how those things deviate so that Blacks' suffering can be equated to Whites' suffering. It is done on the assumption that all things are equal, but that is not the case. So it is really important to understand that depolarization in terms of looking at the dynamics of race and class, and definitely how they inform each other. To say that we got one over the other is the wrong argument.

ORELUS: *So how do you think capitalism contributes to the perpetuation of racism?*

STOVALL: First, we need to ask, who gets what and who controls human resources and the means of production? Who is controlling access to the production of goods and services, and how are those goods and services distributed across race, class, and gender lines? We also need to take into account how capitalism and free market economies work. In addition, we have to take into account who controls the market. If there is a person of color in a privileged position, we actually need to investigate whether or not this person is actually given the real power that his or her position holds. Clarence Thomas is a Supreme Court justice, but does he actually have influence on that committee of nine powerful people? I would argue no. In fact, he is much more a puppet than an active contributor. Michael Steele is the chairman of the Republican National Committee. Does he have any say or influence in that party? I would argue no. He has been used to oppose the Obama administration without the Republican Party being called racist. So, looking at this system and its relationships with capitalism is definitely crucial. That is what we really have to pay attention to.

ORELUS: *You have used some examples to illustrate how men and women of color have been used to cover up institutional racism. Now we have Barack Obama as president, who is surrounded mostly by conservative White males. How much do you think Obama can effect fundamental socioeconomic changes in this country?*

STOVALL: It is important to really understand how power and large-scale corporate electoral politics work. Those in power are only going to select a person that will keep their interests at the center, and that is a classic case with Obama. Obama's policies are moderate at best. So he was a safe choice. This whole notion about Obama representing any type of radical change is a joke. Does he have some influence? Yes. But is that influence greatly relegated by the power and the population of White males that surround him? Yes. That's really what we need to pay attention to.

ORELUS: *So do you think Obama's presidency will contribute to improved race relations between people of color and Whites?*

STOVALL: No, because the idea of his administration is that the less we can say about race, the less we have to worry about it, and they have kind of taken that role. Let's take health care for example. This goes back to your earlier question around capitalism. If you noticed, the Obama administration has said nothing about poor people. We have never heard that term coming out of his administration. So when you don't say things like "poor" or "race," it's a way to actually exclude these terms from American middle-class discourse. Who are we talking about when we use the concept of middle class? This is kind of the language of aspiration. Middle class is something that you could become a part of, but the reality is that we have poor people, and those poor people are by and large people of color. We have to pay attention to that when we talk about suffering and the elimination of programs aimed at social uplift. We know who the elimination of these programs is affecting, and we are also clear about the very salient language around race and class. His administration has leaned much more toward class-based language, and even in that class-based language, he has eliminated the term "poor people," and that's just an injustice. With the recent health-care debate, that was when we first started to hear about poor people. But before then, it just wasn't part of the lexicon. That's an issue his administration is going to have to address, especially if you are talking about programs designed to solve socioeconomic problems facing us poor people.

Orelus: *In talking about class and race, what roles do you think those two forms of oppression play in the decision that the secretary of education made to close many public schools that he claimed are not performing? Right in Chicago where you are now, there are many public schools that are about to be closed and will be transformed into charter schools. What is your position on that?*

Stovall: This whole notion around charter schools is linked to the marketization of education. This is commodifying education. This is turning education into a market that we know doesn't work. And it is also solidifying a group of young people who are being declared disposable. So when you have these charter schools that are operated by private corporations, then there is always going to be an issue of exclusion. So my question is always, who is going to have access to these quality schools? More importantly, are these new schools going to bridge the equity and inequality gap? What we have seen happening here in Chicago over the last ten years is that charter school performance does not exceed traditional public schools.

We also need to ask whether charter schools exclude or include parents around the issue of allowing parents to choose the best schools for their children. Scholars like Pauline Lipman, Janice Smith, Rachael Weber, and myself, through a collective called the Collaborative for Equity and Justice in Education, have created this direct relationship between housing and education. As communities are being gentrified, they are now being offered new schools because schools are the determining factor a family takes into account when choosing a place to live. Now we are having these kinds of boutique schools developed for these new upper-class folks who are moving in. The other questions that we have to ask are: Who is being pushed out? What happens to those folks who are pushed out? And what kind of school do they get? Again the cycle has repeated itself. Those who have been pushed out and removed geographically now have been shuffled into subpar, underperforming, underresourced, underserved schools. So the charter school situation is not about choice by any scope of the word.

ORELUS: *Does the decision that the Obama administration has taken to close those public schools remind you of the Jim Crow era?*

STOVALL: Yes. That is a perfect analogy in terms of who will be excluded and who is actually making it nearly impossible for the people who need the public schools the most.

ORELUS: *Is this also like a counterattack against the decision of* Brown v. Board of Education, *which has somewhat opened some space for minority students, although segregation has been increased since that decision was made in 1954?*

STOVALL: Actually, I would ask a different question: Have we really addressed what the Browns were fighting for? I would say no. The Browns were actually arguing for a quality education. They weren't asking to go to school with White folks. That's what we have made of the *Brown* decision, and that misses the argument. We really haven't looked at the *Brown* decision deeply enough when we are actually talking about quality education for all.

The question the Browns were asking was, why should a student of color in Kansas have to go to school eight miles away from the neighborhood where there is a perfectly good school that is well resourced, well funded, and has quality teachers? Why can't everybody in the city access this school? The idea of separate but equal was unconstitutional because the word "separate" already qualifies some schools as unequal. Actually, if we look deeper into the *Brown* court decision, we realize that when school districts were desegregated, a lot of African Americans who were teachers and principals in segregated African American schools couldn't find jobs in those integrated schools. So, again, we still have to contend that race was central in what the Browns were arguing for in 1954. They were asking for quality education so that those schools they were attending, regardless of where they were located, would be well funded, well resourced, and would have supportive teachers. That's a point often missed around the *Brown* decision.

ORELUS: *We have many schools that are underfunded, especially schools that African Americans, Latinos, Native Americans, poor Whites, and other marginalized groups attend. How do you explain that?*

STOVALL: This is a very explicit question around budget allocations. If you look at states where schools are funded by some property tax equation, then you have to ask a larger question: Why are the richest kids getting the best schools and the poorest kids, who are often students of color, getting the worst schools? We have to ask another question: Isn't the property tax equation in itself inherently unequal in terms of determining who will get what? That is where we have to start looking in terms of appropriation and use of funds for schools. That is why we have continued in this state that we are in.

My concern is always, who will be excluded? In this corporate model, the gatekeeping mechanism becomes more solidified. Who gets admitted to college, especially prestigious institutions, is primarily determined by way of test scores and family lineage, that is, who has a sibling at the university and their family's contribution to the university. If that becomes the primary qualification for admission to colleges and universities, then we will have a certain group of folks who will be completely excluded. The corporate model is essentially about what can be taught, how it can be taught, what perspectives can be presented, and whether or not those perspectives are detrimental or dangerous to the university. So this is a larger question around exclusion and academic freedom. Those two things need to be taken into account when we talk about corporate models of higher education.

Orelus: *So do you think that all professors and students will be affected by the direction that universities are taking? Or do you think this corporate model of education will mostly affect faculty and students of color?*

Stovall: Students of color and faculty of color will be hit the hardest. But first-generation White students from low-income families will also be hit pretty hard. In higher education, female faculty and faculty of color are more isolated than their male counterparts. They are often castigated with the worst evaluations and peer reviews. If we add the issue of sexuality to the equation, you have quadruple oppression. If you look at tenured faculty of color in relationship to their sexual orientation and gender, you will see great discrepancies in terms of who has been granted tenure and selected for positions at elite research institutions. These issues are inextricably linked. It is really important to pay attention to issues of gender and what women, particularly women of color, have been experiencing over the last fifty years.

Orelus: *So how about female graduate students of color?*

Stovall: Same thing. Female graduate students of color have been experiencing isolation and have not been selected for prestigious research fellowships; nor have they been given the opportunity to engage with the research community.

Orelus: *You are one of the scholars who are vested in critical race theory. To what extent do you think critical race theory has contributed to some level of awareness about racial issues?*

STOVALL: Critical race theory has done a couple of things. It needs to do more, and it is important to say that. One of the things it has done is that it has allowed faculty of color to engage in a space where they can name race explicitly in terms of their experiences and how those experiences are critical to understanding how people of color have been treated and positioned from K–12 to college and university levels. I would also say that critical race theory has made an explicit call for people to relinquish this notion of thinking that our solution to racial problems facing society at large will be solved solely in the realm of academia. It is upon us who are engaged in critical race theory to be involved in the community. To me, that is the greatest contribution.

ORELUS: *How much effect do you think the scholarly work of critical race theory has on the life of the masses?*

STOVALL: Very little at the theoretical level. But once we start to address issues like poverty, racism, health care, employment, and the prison industrial complex and start to team up with those entities, people will see the contribution of critical race theory. So that is how it can have a positive effect on people's daily reality. That is the work that I am trying to engage, and that is where we need to push critical race theory. We have to take a different turn in terms of starting to engage the community, because those writings are important for the historical record. They are important reference points, but they may not be addressing suffering or addressing the human condition at large. And that is where we have to push the critical race theory work. Let's say that somebody is writing an article, or distributing a book, though a book may have a little more influence than an article in terms of its accessibility, what impact does that article have on the community? I am not too sure it has a great impact.

ORELUS: *Can you share what it has been like for you as a man of color in academia?*

STOVALL: For me, it is the whole notion around understanding what has happened to folks like myself and the responsibility to work to change our human condition. To me it is extremely important to engage both personally and broadly in this type of work. How can we facilitate and support spaces of resistance and healing when it comes to looking at the conditions of people's color in the United States and throughout the world?

ORELUS: *To what extent do you think imperialism affects people of color, not only those who were born in the U.S. but also in the Caribbean, in Africa, in Asia, and so forth?*

STOVALL: The whole notion of the imperialist state and imperial power trying to maintain a foothold in much of the global south and the developing world is despicable in terms of what they have done over the years, such as robbing folks of resources, turning one ethnic group against the other, and creating warfare. Really understanding the legacy of imperialism and how it has impacted the rest of the world is critically important. This can also create a point of unity for people who have experienced these same types of suffering.

ORELUS: *So what should our role be as university professors to fight against U.S. imperialism?*

STOVALL: Continuing to write in accessible spaces is critical. If we actually start writing in an accessible manner, we will then be able to engage a broader audience. If we can continue to write powerful critiques while engaging with communities on the ground, we will have a greater impact on the world. I always want to come back to the notion of the community because the combination of academic and community work is necessary. Showing that the places where you exist are not only in the written word is key. What we write needs to be put out there and distributed broadly. That's the role that people in academia should play. Those are the things that we can and should do.

Conclusion

You just finished reading most or all of the chapters of this book, except this conclusion. By now you should have a sound understanding of racial, class, gender, sexual, and linguistic oppressions committed against women, gays, people of color, and poor working-class men and women. Furthermore, by now you should have a better understanding of the way this web of oppression affects the subjectivity and material conditions, as well as the learning processes and academic growth, of students, especially poor female students, poor students of color, and poor White students. Moreover, it should be clearer to you that students, teachers, and professors, including female students and professors of color, have been discriminated against and marginalized at many institutions because of their gender, race, social class, language, or country of origin.

In addition, by now you should know that democracy, justice, and freedom are fundamentally empty words for the marginalized in many countries, including capitalist countries like the United States and the UK, and that these words have only worked for those in power. Also, by now you should know that the way language is used in schools and in the media can be oppressive or liberating, that some languages have been subjugated, and consequently those who speak those languages have been pushed to the margins. Finally, by now you should know that many universities have been following a corporate model and have practiced surveillance, thereby leaving a very limited space for progressive professors to do critical social justice types of work.

By now you should not lack key information and knowledge that you have long been deprived of about racial, social class, gender, sexual, and linguistic oppressions, as critically analyzed throughout this book. Hence, what is or should be your responsibility? What do you plan to do next with this information and knowledge you have acquired? To paraphrase one of my colleagues, Dr. Marisol Ruiz, are you going to keep it to yourself and continue to become a knowledge keeper rather than a knowledge disseminator? Are you going to continue being silent about these forms of oppression that affect you, your family, your spouse, your students, your neighbors, your colleagues, your community, and members of society at large? Or are you going to take a stance in your classroom, your community, and at home against any form of oppression occurring there?

Moreover, are you going to join those whose voices have been silenced in your institution, your community, your house, and your workplace to stand up for social justice and equity? Or are you going to remain silent and close your eyes to the social injustice that is rampant in these places because you only care about protecting your job, your own life, and maintaining your unearned White, male, and heterosexual privileges? In other words, are you going along with the status quo refusing to use your heterosexual, male, White, and social class privileges to effect social change? Or are you going to do the right thing for humanity, that is, aligning with those who have been oppressed because of their race, social class, gender, language, and sexuality? I hope you will choose to be a friend of humanity, which entails taking a stance against any form of oppression, be it based on race, gender, class, sex, or language.

As noted in the introduction, this book is not a recipe or a panacea for solving all types of social problems. Instead, it is written in the hope that it will stir in you some level of compassion for humanity so that you can align with the "wretched of the earth," as Frantz Fanon (2004) eloquently put it. This is precisely why I gathered many borderless intellectuals, progressives, and dissident voices and minds in this book in order to provide you with an array of progressive and novel ideas about social justice issues such as race, class, gender, sexuality, and language issues. So I hope that you will use the acquired knowledge that you have learned from this book and put it to work, that is, use this knowledge and information in your daily activities to effect some kind of social change in your classroom, your community, at home, at work, and in society at large.

As a friend of humanity (if you are not one yet, please try to be one), what role would you like to play to better the world where we all live, and what would you like to be remembered for when your final day on this earth comes? A person who was complicit with the capitalist, racist, sexist, and heterosexist system that has exploited, marginalized, and discriminated against those who were not born with "the right skin," who have a different sexual orientation, who were not born into or do not have the "right class," or who do not speak with the "right Western accent"? A passive recipient and consumer of the neoliberal and imperialist propaganda that has been circulated in the media and in schools, or a dissident who challenges this form of propaganda? A passive spectator and consumer of the Western prefabricated form of "democracy," or an active participant and builder of a participatory form of democracy?

I urge you to take a stand for and join those who have been oppressed because of their race, gender, language, sexuality, social class, and lower status in society. They can be your classmates, friends, neighbors, relatives, and colleagues; students who work as graduate assistants with professors who treat them as subalterns; students and professors of color who have been targeted and marginalized at institutions where they are studying, teaching, and doing research; female professors and students who are single mothers and who do not receive adequate support from their professors, their colleagues, and their departments or programs so they can succeed in their careers and studies; or workers who are selling their labor in factories and sweatshops to enrich CEOs of major corporate companies. Please do not wait to do the right thing for humanity, for the time to do so is now!

Afterword

Christine E. Sleeter

When Pierre Orelus invited me to be interviewed for this book, I was intrigued not so much by what I would say, but rather by the conversations that would develop through the book. Having now had the opportunity to read and reflect on them, I find myself energized. At the same time, I am aware that many readers who are new to thinking through issues as they are discussed here may feel overwhelmed. I have had students initially receive such analyses with feelings of frustration, hopelessness, and anger at me for bringing them up. If capitalism now engulfs most of the world's economies, how do you take it on? If racism is endemic to the history and structure of the United States, as well as much of the rest of the world, is meaningful antiracist work even possible? If those who dominate are disproportionately White, wealthy men, does being White and male automatically make one "bad"?

I concur with the book's interviewees that conditions discussed here underscore the need for democratic engagement and action, even while our public understanding of democracy is quite insipid. I also agree that action must begin with a clear analysis not only of what the problems are, but where their roots lie. The interviews in this book place into sharp relief the nature of the political landscape within which schools are situated. As interviewees make clear, considerable "ideological fog," to borrow a phrase from Paulo Freire, continues to obscure powerful ways in which education and democracy are pressed into unjust and often inhumane configurations.

There is a very strong tendency in the U.S. to individualize and psychologize social problems. By this I mean interpreting human behavior solely in terms of the presumed motives, efforts, and abilities of individuals, with little regard for how lives are impacted by social systems and relationships. This tendency is reinforced by how everyday media frame events and issues, particularly the soap opera archetype that now dominates news reporting, with its heroes, villains, and high drama.

Take for example public interpretations of problems in a local school district that serves mainly low-income Latino/a students, a large proportion of whom are immigrants. In the newspaper, one reads of inept and to some extent corrupt administrators and school board members whose ineffectiveness is manifest in budget problems and students' low test scores. One reads that students struggle because they are not fluent in English, and that bilingual education has failed to develop their English, thereby demonstrating its ineffectiveness. When the budget for the district is faced with large cuts, although stories of teachers and parents protesting the cuts are featured, there is little or no mention of the impact on students of the subsequent loss of newer teachers, many of whom are Latino/a; expanded class sizes; and reduced extracurricular activities. Instead, the public is told that because of the district's persistent mismanagement and low achievement, new school reform ideas and new leaders must be brought in from the outside.

This book offers powerful alternative lenses for thinking differently about such a scenario. Situating the district within an analysis of the expansion of global capitalism directs attention to the reduction of public funding for public services across the board, with privatized services (or public-private hybrids) replacing the public. The primary underlying question then becomes, who benefits most from this shift? For example, while the largely Latino school district had an average student-teacher ratio of 23.6, spending an average of $10,700 per pupil, a White wealthy school district nearby maintained an average student-teacher ratio of 15.4 and spent twice as much per pupil. Who, then, has access to preparation for professional work and business ownership, and who is afforded preparation more linked to working in the service economy and agricultural labor? In addition, why does the U.S. continue to channel so much tax revenue into a military budget that is as large as the military budgets of the rest of the world combined, while failing to resource the public good at home? Who is profiting, and how is the public at large being convinced that this is all acceptable?

Situating the Latino district within an analysis of race prompts additional questions. One might ask why racial housing segregation persists, while publicly there is discussion of racism having been relegated to the dustbin of history and school desegregation as being no longer needed. One might probe the relationship between housing segregation and the struggles of immigrant children to become fluently bilingual, as well as disinterest among native English speakers in also becoming bilingual. One might analyze racism in policies requiring that achievement be measured in English regardless of the language that students and their families speak, and the subsequent pressure that failing to meet adequate yearly progress (AYP) year after year places on schools serving large numbers of immigrant students and students of color. In addition, one might analyze the growing prescriptiveness of curricula for such students that edges out consideration of culture, language, and identity as legitimate springboards for learning.

This book takes the position that schooling and pedagogy should be analyzed through the lens of multiple relations and systems of power, including systems of class, race, gender, language, and sexual orientation. I concur with Zeus Leonardo in urging us to learn "how to think from both [or multiple] sides of the aisle." Each relationship of oppression offers a lens or an angle of vision through which problems can be analyzed. If one begins, for example, by asking how patriarchy continues to work despite gains women have made in attending and graduating from higher education, one "sees" different things than if one starts with an analysis of race or class. David Gillborn makes the very important point that we cannot simply toss analyses of race, class, and gender together, but rather we need to become better at analyzing cases "on the ground" in ways that attend to how these relationship work with and through each other. Returning to the Latino school district example, one might ask in what ways White people's gendered understanding of Latino/as impacts on White resistance to housing integration and assumptions about what is "good enough" for children attending school in that district.

I believe that the reframing of pedagogy and schooling that this book offers can act as a powerful antidote to the historical amnesia that is common among educators and the public and that is ultimately disempowering. Historically, people have engaged in organized struggle; one can point to numerous struggles that have mattered. History also teaches us that one cannot stop struggling once a victory has been achieved. As several interviewees emphasized, it would be a mistake to view the election of Barack Obama to the presidency as the culmination of an organized struggle, but rather as a victory, which has spawned a vigorous but anticipated backlash, in an ongoing struggle.

Ultimately, if this book prompts thinking—whether it takes the form of nodding one's head in agreement, taking issue with the points of view of the interviewees, or doing some investigation into problems within one's own community, I believe that invigorating democracy requires that people ask questions and think. We cannot afford to simply allow others—TV commentators, textbook writers, or even teachers and professors—to tell us what to think. We must become better at routinely looking below the surface for ourselves. And then we need to join with others to act, starting at local levels. Making social change is not impossible; it is a collective process that can be learned.

Bibliography

Alexander, M. (2010). *The new Jim Crow: Mass incarceration in the age of colorblindness.* New York: New Press.

Allen, R. L. (2002). The globalization of White supremacy: Toward a critical discourse on the racialization of the world. *Educational Theory, 51*(4), 467–485.

Allen, R. L. (2009). What about poor White people? In W. Ayers, T. Quinn, & D. Stovall (Eds.), *Handbook of social justice in education* (pp. 209–230). New York: Routledge.

Allen, T. (1997). *The invention of the White race: Vol. 2. The origin of racial oppression in Anglo-America.* New York: Verso.

Althusser, L. (1971). *Lenin and philosophy* (B. Brewster, Trans.). New York: Monthly Review Press.

Andersen, M., & Collins, H. P. (1995). *Race, class, and gender: An anthology.* Lanham, MD: Rowman & Littlefield.

Anyon, J. (2005). *Radical possibilities: Public policy, urban education, and a new social movement.* New York: Routledge.

Apple, M. (2009). *Global crisis, social justice, and education.* New York: Routledge.

Baird, F., & Kaufmann, K. (2008). *From Plato to Derrida.* Upper Saddle River, NJ: Pearson Prentice Hall.

Bartlett, A. (2006). Theory, desire, and maternity: At work in academia. *Hecate, 32*(3), 321–333.

Bell, D. (1992). *Faces at the bottom of the well: The permanence of racism.* Chapter 6. New York: Basic Books.

Beverly, J. (2005). Testimonio, subalternity and narrative authority. In N. Denzin & Y. Lincoln (Eds.), *The Sage handbook of qualitative research* (3rd ed.). California: Sage Publications.

Blumenfeld, W. J. (2006). Christian privilege and the promotion of "secular" and not-so-"secular" mainline Christianity in public schooling and in the larger society. *Equity & Excellence in Education, 3*, 195–210.

Bonilla-Silva, E. (2003). *Racism without racists: Color-blind racism and the persistence of racial inequality in the United States*. Lanham, MD: Rowman & Littlefield.

Bonilla-Silva, E. (2005). Introduction—"Racism" and "new racism": The contours of racial dynamics in contemporary America. In Z. Leonardo (Ed.), *Critical pedagogy and race* (pp. 1–36). Malden, MA: Blackwell.

Bonilla-Silva, E. (2010). *Anything but racism: How social scientists limit the significance of race*. New York: Routledge.

Bourdieu, P. (1986). The forms of capital. In J. Richardson (Ed.), *Handbook of theory and research for the sociology of education*. New York: Greenwood Press.

Bourdieu, P. (1999). *Language and symbolic power* (J. Thompson, Trans.; G. Raymond & M. Adamson, Eds.). Cambridge, MA: Harvard University Press.

Brown, M., Carney, M., Currie, E., Duster, T., Oppenheimer, D., Shultz, M., & Wellman, D. (2003). *Whitewashing race: The myth of a color-blind society*. Berkeley: University of California Press.

Buras, K. (2008). *Rightist multiculturalism*. New York: Routledge.

Butler, J. (2006). *Gender trouble: Feminism and the subversion of identity*. New York: Routledge.

Carothers, T. (1993). *In the name of democracy: U.S. policy toward Latin America in the Reagan years*. Berkeley: University of California Press.

Carothers, T. (1999). *Aiding democracy abroad*. Washington, DC: Carnegie Endowment for International Peace.

Carothers, T. (2004). *Critical mission: essays on democracy promotion*. Washington, DC: Carnegie Endowment for International Peace.

Caruso, E. M., Mead, N. L., & Balcetis, E. (2009). Political partisanship influences perception of biracial candidates' skin tone. *Proceedings of the National Academy of Sciences of the United States of America, 106*(48), 20168–20173.

Césaire, A. (2000). *Discourse on colonialism*. New York: Monthly Review Press. First published in 1955.

Chomsky, N. (2010). *Hopes and Prospects*. Chicago: Haymarket Books.

Churchill, W. (2005). *Since predator came*. Oakland, CA: AK Press.

Cochran-Smith, M. (2004). *Walking the road: Race, diversity and social justice in teacher education*. New York: Teachers College.

Crenshaw, K. W. (2002). The first decade. *UCLA Law Review, 49*, 1343–1372.

Darder, A., & Torres, R. (2004). After race: Racism after multiculturalism. New York: New York University Press.

de Beauvoir, S. (1984). In Alice Schwarzer, *After The Second Sex: Conversations with Simone de Beauvoir*. New York: Pantheon.

de Tocqueville, A., & Grant, S. (2000). *Democracy in America*. Indianapolis: Hackett.

Dewey, J. (2010). *Democracy and education: An introduction to the philosophy of education*. Cedar Lake, MI: ReadaClassic.com.

D'Souza, D. (2010, September 27). How Obama thinks. *Forbes*. Retrieved from http://www.forbes.com/forbes/2010/0927/politics-socialism-capitalism-private-enterprises-obama-business-problem_print.html.

Du Bois, W. E. B. (1989). *The souls of Black folk.* New York: Penguin Books. First published in 1904.

Du Bois, W. E. B. (1998). *Black reconstruction in America, 1860–1880.* New York: Free Press. First published in 1935.

Dyer, R. (1997). *White.* London: Routledge.

Dyson, M. (2006). *Is Bill Cosby right? Has the middle class lost its mind?* New York: Perseus Books.

Dyson, M. E. (2009). *Can you hear me now? The inspiration, wisdom, and insight of Michael Eric Dyson.* New York: Basic Civitas Books.

Essed, P., & Goldberg, D. T. (2002). Introduction: From racial demarcations to multiple identifications. In P. Essed & D. T. Goldberg (Eds.), *Race critical theories* (pp. 1–11). Malden, MA: Blackwell.

Fanon, F. (2004). *The wretched of the earth* (R. Philcox, Trans.). New York: Grove Press, 1963.

Fine, M. (1993). *Disruptive voices: The possibilities of feminist research (critical perspectives on women and gender).* Ann Arbor: University of Michigan Press.

Foucault, M., & Gordon, C. (1980). *Power/knowledge: Selected interviews and other writings, 1972–1977.* New York: Knopf Doubleday.

Fraser, N. (1997). *Justice interrupts.* New York: Routledge.

Freire, P. (1994). *Pedagogy of hope* (R. Barr, Trans.). New York: Continuum.

Freire, P. (2000). *Pedagogy of the oppressed.* New York: Continuum.

Freire, P., & Faundez, A. (1989). *Learning to question: A pedagogy of liberation.* New York: Continuum.

Freire, P., & Macedo, D. (1987). *Reading the word and the world.* South Hadley, MA: Bergin & Garvey.

Gillborn, D. (2008). *Racism and education: Coincidence or conspiracy?* New York: Routledge.

Gillborn, D. (2009). Risk-free racism: Whiteness and so-called "free speech." *Wake Forest Law Review, 44*(2), 535–555.

Gillborn, D., & Youdell, D. (2009). Critical perspectives on race and schooling. In James A. Banks (Ed.), *The Routledge international companion to multicultural education* (pp. 173–185). New York: Routledge.

Giroux, H. (2010). Neoliberalism, pedagogy, and cultural politics: Beyond the theatre of cruelty. In Z. Leonardo (Ed.), *Handbook of cultural politics and education* (pp. 49–70). Rotterdam, The Netherlands: Sense Publishers.

Giroux, H., & Giroux, S. (2006). *Take back higher education: Race, youth and the crisis of democracy in the post-civil rights era.* New York: Palgrave Macmillan.

Gramsci, A. (1971). *Selections from the prison notebooks* (Q. H. G. N. Smith, Trans. and Ed.). New York: International Publishers.

Grande, S. (2004). *Red pedagogy: Native American social and political thought.* Lanham, MD: Rowman & Littlefield.

Greene, M. (1993). Diversity and inclusion: Toward a curriculum for human beings. *Teachers College Record,* 95(2), 211–221.

Greene, M. (2009). In search of a critical pedagogy. In A. Darder, M. P. Baltodna, & R. D. Torres, *The Critical Pedagogy Reader* (2nd ed.). New York: Routledge.

Grosfoguel, R. (2007). The epistemic decolonial turn: Beyond political-economy paradigms. *Cultural Studies, 21*(2), 211–223.

Haley, A. (2007). *Roots: The saga of an American family*. New York: Vanguard Press.

Hartsock, N. (1987, Fall). Rethinking modernism: Minority vs. majority theories. *Cultural Critique, 7*, 187–206.

Hewlett, S. A. (2002). *Creating a life: Professional women and the quest for children*. New York: Talk Miramax Books.

hooks, b. (1990). *Race, gender, and cultural politics*. Boston: South End Press.

hooks, b. (2006). *Outlaw culture: Resisting representations*. New York: Routledge.

Ignatiev, N. (1997). The point is not to interpret Whiteness but to abolish it. Talk given at the Conference on the Making and Unmaking of Whiteness, University of California, Berkeley. Available at http://racetraitor.org/albolishthepoint.htm (accessed July 26, 2007).

Jameson, F. (1991). *Postmodernism, or, the cultural logic of late capitalism*. Durham, NC: Duke University Press.

Jensen, B. (2004). *The heart of Whiteness: Confronting race, racism, and White privilege*. San Francisco: City Lights Books.

Klein, N. (2007). *The shock doctrine: The rise of disaster capitalism*. New York: Metropolitan Books.

Klor de Alva, J., Shorris, E., & West, C. (2000). Our next race question: The uneasiness between Blacks and Latinos. In R. Delgado & J. Stefancic (Eds.), *Critical White studies* (pp. 482–492). Philadelphia: Temple University Press.

Kozol, J. (2006). *The shame of the nation: The restoration of apartheid schooling in America*. New York: Broadway.

Ladson-Billings, G. (2005). The evolving role of critical race theory in educational research. *Race Ethnicity & Education, 8*(1), 115–119.

Ladson-Billings, G., & Tate, W. F., IV. (1995). Toward a critical race theory of education. *Teachers College Record, 97*(1), 47–68.

Lawrence, D. (2006). *And still I rise: Seeking justice for Stephen*. London: Faber & Faber.

Lebowitz, M. (2003). *Beyond capital: Marx's political economy of the working class* (Rev. ed.). London: Palgrave Macmillan.

Leonardo, Z. (2009a). *Race, Whiteness, and education*. New York: Routledge.

Leonardo, Z. (2009b). Reading Whiteness: Anti-racist pedagogy against White racial knowledge. In W. Ayers, T. Quinn, & D. Stovall (Eds.), *Handbook of social justice in education* (pp. 231–248). New York: Routledge.

Leonardo, Z. (2010). Whiteness and New Orleans: Racio-economic analysis and the politics of urban space. Afterword to K. Buras, with J. Randels, K. ya Salaam, & Students at the Center (Eds.), *Pedagogy, policy, and the privatized city: Stories of dispossession and defiance from New Orleans* (pp. 159–162). New York: Teachers College Press.

Leonardo, Z. (in press). After the glow: Post-race discourses and other educational prognoses. *Educational Philosophy and Theory*.

Lerner, M., & West, C. (1996). *Jews and Blacks*. New York: Plume/Penguin.

Lipsitz, G. (2006). *The possessive investment in Whiteness: How White people profit from identity politics* (Rev. and expanded ed.). Philadelphia: Temple University Press.

Lopez, I. H. (2006). *White by law*. New York: New York University Press.

Maldonado-Torres, N. (2007). On the coloniality of being: Contributions to the development of a concept. *Cultural Studies, 21*(20–23), 240–270.

Marable, M. (2006a). Empire, racism and resistance. Retrieved from Trumpet America, http://www.trumpetamerica.org/061222ta2116.html.

Marable, M. (2006b). *Living Black history: How reimagining the African-American past can remake America's racial future.* New York: Basic Civitas Books.

Martinot, Steve. (2010). *The duality of class systems in US capitalism.* Manuscript.

Marx, K. (2010). *Capital: A critique of political economy.* Charleston, SC: CreateSpace.

Massey, D., & Denton, N. (1993). *American apartheid: Segregation and the making of the underclass.* Cambridge, MA: Harvard University.

Matsuda, M., Charles, L., Delgado, R., & Crenshaw, K. (1993). *Words that wound: Critical race theory, assaultive speech, and the first amendment.* Boulder, CO: Westview Press.

McLaren, P. (2005). *Capitalists and conquerors: A critical pedagogy against empire.* Lanham, MD: Rowman & Littlefield.

McLaren, P. (in press). Revenge of the Confederacy. Preface to Abul Pitre's *Freedom fighters: African American students and the struggle for Black history in school.* Lanham, MD: Rowman & Littlefield.

Meyer, L., Kirwin, J., & Toober, E. (2010). An open-ended closing. In L. Meyer & B. M. Alvarado, *New world of indigenous resistance: Noam Chomsky and voices from North, South, and Central America* (pp. 383–389). San Francisco: City Lights Books.

Mignolo, W. (2000). *Local histories/global designs: Essays on the coloniality of power, subaltern knowledges and border thinking.* Princeton, NJ: Princeton University Press.

Mills, C. (1997). *The racial contract.* Ithaca, NY: Cornell University Press.

Mills, C. (2003). *From class to race: Essays in White Marxism and Black radicalism.* Lanham, MD: Rowman & Littlefield.

Myrdal, G. (1944). *An American dilemma: The Negro problem and modern democracy.* New York: Harper & Brothers.

Nieto, S. (2002). *Language, culture, and teaching: Critical perspectives for a new century.* New York: Lawrence Erlbaum Associates.

Nieto, S. (2004). *Affirming diversity: The socio-cultural context of multicultural education.* Boston: Pearson Education.

Noguera, P. (2003). *City schools and the American dream.* New York: Teachers College Press.

Noguera, P. (2008). *The trouble with Black boys: . . . and other reflections of race, equity, and the future of public education.* New Jersey: John Wiley.

Omi, M., & Winant, H. (1994). *Racial formation in the United States: From the 1960s to the 1990s* (2nd ed.). New York: Routledge.

Orelus, P. (2009). *The agony of masculinity: Race, gender, and education in the age of "new" racism and patriarchy.* New York: Peter Lang.

Orelus, P. (in press). Facing with courage racial and linguistic discrimination: The narrative of a Black Caribbean immigrant in the U.S. diaspora. *Diaspora, Indigenous and Minority Education Journal.*

Page, S. (2008). *The difference: How the power of diversity creates better groups, firms, schools, and societies.* Princeton, NJ: Princeton University Press.

Plato. (1992). *Republic* (G. A. M. Crube, Trans.). Indianapolis: Hackett.

Pomeroy, A. F. (2004). Why Marx, why now? A recollection of Dunayevskaya's power of negativity. *Cultural Logic, 7.* Retrieved from http://clogic.eserver.org/2004/pomeroy.html.

Prashad, V. (2007). *The darker nations: A people's history of the third world.* New York: New Press.

Provenzo, E. (2002). *Du Bois on education.* Lanham, MD: Alta Mira Press.

Quijano, A. & Ennis, M. (2000). Coloniality of power, Eurocentrism, and Latin America. *Nepantla: Views from South, 1,* 533–580.

Roediger, D. (1991). *The wages of Whiteness.* New York: Verso.

Roediger, D. (1994). *Toward the abolition of Whiteness.* New York: Verso.

Said, E. (2000). *Reflections on exile.* Cambridge, MA: Harvard University Press.

Sandoval, C. (2000). *Methodology of the oppressed.* Minneapolis: University of Minnesota Press.

San Juan, E. (2009a). Forward to *Post-Marxism as compromise formation,* by Gregory Meyerson. *Cultural Logic.* Retrieved from http://clogic.eserver.org/2009/Meyerson.pdf.

San Juan, E. (2009b). Re-visiting race and class in post-9/11 United States of America. Retrieved from http://rizalarchive.blogspot.com/2009_04_01_archive.html.

Shawki, A. (2006). *Black liberation and socialism.* Chicago: Haymarket Books.

Sleeter, C. E. (2005). *Un-standardizing curriculum: Multicultural teaching in the standards-based classroom.* New York: Routledge.

Smith, L. T. (1999). *Decolonizing methodologies: Research and indigenous peoples.* London: Zed Books.

Solorzano, D. G. (1998). Critical race theory, racial and gender microaggressions, and the experiences of Chicana and Chicano scholars. *International Journal of Qualitative Studies in Education, 11,* 121–136.

Spivak, G. C. (1988). Can the subaltern speak? In C. Nelson & L. Grossberg (Eds.), *Marxism and the interpretation of culture* (pp. 271–313). Basingstoke: Macmillan Education.

Stovall, D. (2006). Forging community in race and class: Critical race theory and the quest for social justice in education. *Race Ethnicity & Education, 9*(3), 243–259.

Tatum, B. D. (2007). *Can we talk about race? And other conversations in an era of school resegregation.* Boston, MA: Beacon Press.

Taylor, K.-Y. (2011). Race, class and Marxism. In *socialistworker.org.* Retrieved from http://socialistworker.org/2011/01/04/race-class-and-marxism.

Thomas, P. (1997). *Down these mean streets.* New York: Vintage.

Walsh, C. (in press). Interculturality and the coloniality of power: An "other" thinking and positioning from the colonial difference. In R. Grosfoguel, J. D. Saldivar, & N. Maldonado (Eds.), *Unsettling postcoloniality: Coloniality, transmodernity and border thinking.* Durham, NC: Duke University Press.

Ward, K., & Wolf-Wendel, L. (Winter 2004). Academic motherhood: Managing complex roles in research universities. *Review of Higher Education, 27*(2), pp. 233–257.

Warmington, P. (2009). Taking race out of scare quotes: Race-conscious social analysis in an ostensibly post-racial world. *Race Ethnicity & Education, 12*(3), 281–296.

Wa Thiong'o, N. (2008). *Decolonizing the mind: The politics of language in African literature.* Portsmouth, NH: Heinemann.

Weis, L., & Fine, M. (2005). *Beyond silenced voices: Class, race, and gender in United States schools.* New York: SUNY Press.

West, C. (2001). *Race matters.* Boston, MA: Beacon Press.

West, C. (2005). *Democracy matters: Winning the fight against imperialism.* New York: Penguin Books.

West, C. (2008). *Hope on a tightrope: Words and wisdom.* New York: Smiley Books.

West, C. (2010). *Brother West: Living and loving out loud; A memoir.* New York: Smiley Books.

Williams, E. (1993). *History of the people of Trinidad and Tobago.* Brooklyn, NY: A&b Publishers.

Williams, J. (2000). How the tenure track discriminates against women. *Chronicle of Higher Education*, B10.

Williams, J. (2000). *Unbending gender: Why work and gamily conflict and what to do about it.* New York: Oxford University Press.

Williams, J. C., & Segal, N. (2003). Beyond the maternal wall: Relief for family caregivers who are discriminated against on the job. *Harvard Women's Law Journal, 26,* 77.

Winant, H. (2002). *The world is a ghetto: Race and democracy since World War II.* New York: Basic Books.

Wise, T. (2010). *Colorblind: The rise of post-racial politics and the retreat from racial equity.* San Francisco: City Lights Books.

Wolff, R. (2009). *Capitalism hits the fan: The global economic meltdown and what to do about it.* New York: Olive Branch Press.

Wolf-Wendel, L., & Ward, K. (2003). Future prospects for women faculty: Negotiating work and family. In B. Ropers-Huilman (Ed.), *Gendered futures in higher education: Critical perspectives for change* (pp. 111–134). Albany: SUNY Press.

Woodson, C. (2000). *The mis-education of the Negro.* New York: African American Images.

Yosso, T. (2006). *Critical race counterstories along the Chicana/Chicano educational pipeline.* New York: Routledge.

Zinn, H. (2001). *A people's history of the United States.* New York: HarperCollins.

Žižek, S. (2010). *Living in the ends of time.* UK: Verso.

Index

About the Author

A former high school teacher, **Dr. Pierre Wilbert Orelus** is assistant professor in the Curriculum and Instruction Department at New Mexico State University. He is the past chair of the Post-colonial and Education Special Interest Group (SIG) at the American Educational Research Association. Professor Orelus has received several awards and fellowships, including New Mexico state Dean of Education Award for Excellence in Research, ALANA Minority Fellowship, ACCELA Fellowship, and New Perspectives Fellowship. Professor Orelus's research interests include post-colonial studies; critical race theory; TESOL (teaching English to Speakers of Other Languages) and bilingual education; gender studies, particularly masculinity and maleness; Caribbean studies; and cultural studies. Dr. Orelus is the author of several books, including *Education under Occupation*, *Academic Achievers: Whose Definition?* and *The Agony of Masculinity*. In praising Dr. Orelus' book, *The Agony of Masculinity*, the acclaimed African American scholar Cornel West stated, "Orelus is an intellectual freedom fighter whose deep insights and sharp analyses of institutional racism and black masculinity deserve our attention."

CPSIA information can be obtained at www.ICGtesting.com
265369BV00004B/1/P

9 781442 204553